KU-503-249

CONTENTS

PENGUIN BOOKS

TUDOR ENGLAND

Born at Hove in 1908, S. T. Bindoff was educated at Brighton Grammar School, where he worked under a great history master, A. E. Wilson, and at University College, London. He was on the history staff there from 1935 to 1951, after which he travelled to America as Visiting Professor to Columbia University in New York, Wellesley College and Harvard University. He was made a Fellow of University College in 1958, and of Queen Mary College, London, where he was latterly Professor of History, in 1977.

Professor Bindoff's other writings, apart from many reviews and articles for historical journals, were *The Scheldt Question to 1939* (1945) for which he was elected to membership of the Dutch Historical Society, and *Elizabethan Government and Society* (ed., 1961). He died in 1980.

THE PELICAN HISTORY OF ENGLAND

Edited by J. E. Morpurgo

S. T. BINDOFF

TUDOR ENGLAND

PENGUIN BOOKS

PENGUIN BOOKS

Published by the Penguin Group
Penguin Books Ltd, 27 Wrights Lane, London W8 5TZ, England
Penguin Books USA Inc., 375 Hudson Street, New York, New York 10014, USA
Penguin Books Australia Ltd, Ringwood, Victoria, Australia
Penguin Books Canada Ltd, 10 Alcorn Avenue, Toronto, Ontario, Canada M4V 3B2
Penguin Books (NZ) Ltd, 182–190 Wairau Road, Auckland 10, New Zealand

Penguin Books Ltd, Registered Offices: Harmondsworth, Middlesex, England

First published by Pelican Books 1950
Reprinted in Penguin Books 1991
5 7 9 10 8 6 4

Printed in England by Clays Ltd, St Ives plc
Set in Monophoto Baskerville

PROLOGUE: 1485

THE battle was over. On a stretch of high ground in the midland heart of the kingdom twenty thousand men had met in fierce, clumsy combat, and the day had ended in the decisive defeat of the stronger army. Its leader, the King, had been killed fighting heroically, and men had seen his naked corpse slung across his horse's back and borne away to an obscure grave. His captains were dead, captured, or in flight, his troops broken and demoralized. But in the victor's army all was rejoicing. In following the claimant to the throne his supporters had chosen the winning side, and when they saw the golden circlet which had fallen from the King's head placed upon their leader's, their lingering doubts fled before the conviction that God had blessed his cause, and they hailed him joyously as their sovereign.

The day was 22 August 1485; the battlefield was to be named after the small neighbouring town of Market Bosworth; the fallen King was the third and ablest of English monarchs who bore the name Richard; and the man whom the battle made a king was to be the seventh and perhaps the greatest of those who bore the name Henry. By 1485 Englishmen had grown wearily accustomed to a polity in which rival factions contended for the crown and 'he who lost the day lost the kingdom also'. The middle-aged could remember its happening three times before. In 1461 Henry VI had lost the kingdom at Towton to the Earl of March, who then became Edward IV. In 1470 Edward lost it to his own former henchman Warwick, the 'Kingmaker', who restored the puppet Henry VI. Eight

7

months later Warwick and Henry VI were beaten by the returning Edward, who succeeded in keeping the throne until his death in 1483. And now Richard III, who had murdered, instead of fighting, his way to the throne had lost throne and life to Henry VII. The Wars of the Roses we call them, this thirty-year contest between the White Rose of York and the Red Rose of Lancaster, the two branches of the Plantagenet line, for possession of the English throne. As civil wars go, they were neither protracted nor costly. The fighting was sporadic, the armies small, the material losses inconsiderable. Indeed, the Wars of the Roses, like the politics which gave rise to them, were scarcely more than a sport which great men indulged in while the country as a whole stuck doggedly to the more important business of feeding, warming and clothing itself. But anarchy is a dangerous pastime, and every year saw its crimson stain spread a little further across the fabric of English society. A Crown which had become a football was ceasing to be a referee, and a game which begins by doing without a referee runs a risk of finishing without a ball. Right was beginning to yield to might at all levels and in all relationships of society, and four centuries of heroic effort by kings and statesmen to establish the reign of law seemed in danger of being brought to nought amid a surfeit of kings and a shortage of statesmen.

Was the victor of Bosworth to be just another king, dressed in a little brief authority as captain of a sinking ship with a mutinous crew? Or was he, after all, the Messianic statesman who could deliver both Crown and Kingdom from bondage to a bankrupt political system? Such are the questions which, if they were not indeed in the minds of Englishmen, we may take the liberty of putting there, as Henry VII rode up from Leicestershire to London to take possession of his kingdom.

8

I

ENGLAND AND THE ENGLISH

THE England across whose middle shires Henry VII passed to his throne wore an appearance very different from that which the name now conjures up in our minds. It was not merely that four and a half centuries ago the face of England had scarcely felt the blistering touch of industrial and urbanized man, but that a large part of England had scarcely been touched by man at all. For in 1485 the age-long process by which our forefathers civilized the landscape was still far from complete. We have to picture the countryside as a sort of agrarian archipelago, with innumerable islands of cultivation set in a sea of 'waste'. Only in a few densely-settled regions had these islands, with their fringes of pasture, already been multiplied and enlarged to produce a man-made landscape such as we know today. Elsewhere the proportion of unimproved or semi-improved land remained high, with considerable stretches presenting an appearance hardly changed from prehistoric times. These areas were, for the most part, clothed by the remnants of the deciduous oak forest with which Nature had once covered – and should she ever regain her lost dominion would again cover – the greater part of these islands. Today there survive only the merest fragments of that pristine forest, and the whole woodland area, whether old or new, amounts to but a twentieth of the country's surface. In 1500 the proportion must have been much higher. England was a leafier country then, and the old rhyme found, in varying forms, in many districts:

From Blacon Point to Hillbree
A squirrel may jump from tree to tree

must still have been widely true. Not all of this woodland retained its natural density. There were the great woods – Sherwood, Selwood, Dean, the Weald, Epping, and romantic Arden – which remained virtually untouched. But between them and the improved grounds came the great intermediate category of scrub, brushwood and thicket, where the trees were being thinned out by the combined action of man and beast.

The woodlands of early Tudor England were the refuge of her shrinking population of wild animals. By 1500 the wolf had all but followed the bear, the elk and the lynx into the category of extinct mammals. But wild swine, wild cats, and wild or semi-wild cattle were still fairly common, especially in the North and West, and the native red deer, today represented by a solitary herd on Exmoor, then survived in several parts of the country. They, and the woodlands which sheltered them, owed their preservation in part to the maintenance, for several hundred years, of the Royal Forests, those areas, part woodland, part open country, within whose bounds the needs of the sportsman took precedence over those of the farmer. But England's woodlands served a more valuable purpose than that of providing her kings and nobles with their favourite recreation. They were among the most important of the nation's natural resources. Timber was as indispensable to medieval civilization as coal and metal are to ours. Without it our ancestors could not have fed, warmed, clothed, or armed themselves, have built the carts, bridges and ships by which they transported their wares, or the towns where they exchanged them. For a thousand years and more they were able to satisfy their timber-needs without taking thought for the future. They had long since learned that they could not go on raising food from the soil without putting something back into it. They were slower to grasp that they could not go on destroying trees, and take no steps to replace them, without eventually bankrupting themselves of timber. The greatest contribution of the Middle Ages to timber conservation had been inspired by no worthier motive than the welfare of the chase. But before 1500 there were signs of a more enlightened interest in the matter. The system which, under the name of 'coppice with standards', was to become the norm of English forestry practice, had already been evolved – the word 'coppice' itself dates from about 1470. The original advantage of giving the oak 'standards' enough lateral space to spread their crowns is said to have been the curved timber and 'knee-pieces' thus obtained for shipbuilding, while the hazel coppice which grew beneath their canopy served a great variety of purposes. The system was given statutory sanction in 1544, when the number of standards was fixed at twelve per acre. By then, indeed, woodland wealth was fast giving place to woodland poverty. The leaping demand for timber – for an expanding navy and merchant marine, for more and larger houses, for implements of all kinds, and above all for charcoal for smelting iron – quickly outran the dwindling supply, and before the Tudors had ceased to reign parts of England were facing a timber famine.

Unaided, man could scarcely have wrought such devastation on the natural forest. But man had a most potent ally in his domesticated animals, and above all in his flocks of sheep. The sheep population of England had undergone a remarkable increase during the later Middle Ages. Today England and Wales contain about twenty million sheep, or one sheep to every two human beings. Five centuries ago sheep may have numbered about eight millions, that is, there were about three sheep to every human. Englishmen were soon to complain that 'sheep do eat up men'. Certainly sheep had long been 'eating up' trees. The classic illustration is the influence of the great Northern flocks, especially those of the Cistercian abbeys, upon the vegetation of the English Highland Zone. From the twelfth century to the sixteenth, sheep had been the dominant agents of change in the natural conditions, and through them in the way of life, obtaining north of the Trent. The 'golden hoof' turned mossland into cotton-grass and heather moor into matgrass, and slowly destroyed the oak, the hazel, and the birch. The wolf, the shepherd's worst enemy, was exterminated, and the red deer gradually confined to fewer and smaller fastnesses. By the early sixteenth century it was only on the Borders that there persisted, under the influence of predatory humans, the natural conditions necessary to the survival of the larger predatory animals. The same war of attrition had been going on, although less spectacularly, in other parts of the country, and it was certainly true of the animal kingdom that the meek had inherited the earth. The victory had not been without its cost. In the language of Malthus, the sheep population was continually pressing upon its means of subsistence, and of the resultant checks disease at least was in regular operation. The early years of the sixteenth century, in particular, appear to have seen heavy mortality through outbreaks of 'murrain'. By then it is likely that the increased mobility of flocks, and the use of unsuitable land as sheep-walk, were helping to promote and spread disease. By then, too, the sheep's struggle for living space was being waged not only against the forest but also against the field.

Familiar as we are with a situation in which, however intensively it may be farmed, our land can feed only a fraction of its inhabitants, we find it difficult to conceive of one in which, without any improvement in agricultural efficiency, the same land could have sustained two or three times as many people as dwelt in it. Yet this was the case with early Tudor England, and when in 1497 a Venetian observer expressed the view that the population of the island bore no relation to its fertility he was putting his finger on a cardinal point in the national economy. It is likely enough that when he wrote the contrast between the two was more striking than it would have been a century or more earlier. For everything points to the fact that during that time the area of land under cultivation, instead of continuing to expand, underwent a contraction. Between the Black Death and the close of the fifteenth century there was, Professor Postan tells us, a widespread and continual growth in the number of vacant holdings, of farms for which no tenants could be found. In some parts of the country whole villages were abandoned and their fields allowed to revert to the 'waste'. Even the ease with which the more enterprising tenants enlarged their individual holdings only reflects the lack of competition for the surplus land. In more recent times such conditions would mean that the English farmer was failing to hold his own, and a declining rural population would be offset by a rising urban one. But the fifteenth century had no such compensatory growth to show; on the contrary, its industrial and commercial life exhibits the same tendency towards stagnation. So general and persistent a decline in the nation's economic effort is scarcely explicable save in terms of a shrinkage of its human resources. Fewer mouths to fill, and fewer hands producing the food to fill them, these alone can account for England's failure to maintain, in the fifteenth century, the level of output which she had achieved in the thirteenth.

Down to the middle of the eighteenth century the population of England, like those of all her neighbours, grew at a rate which cannot but appear slow when set against the

astonishing increase since that time. The six centuries
before 1750 raised the figure from perhaps one and a half
millions to upwards of five; the two centuries since 1750
have seen the five millions become forty. But if the earlier
progress was slow, it was also – so far as the scanty evidence
goes – fairly steady. Its single great setback resulted from
one of those pandemics of plague of which only three are
known to recorded history.* These visitations exhibit a
certain uniformity of pattern. The first onset is the most
violent. The plague sweeps across whole continents
engulfing town and country alike, and claiming huge
numbers of victims. Then comes the long aftermath of
recurring outbreaks, at first general and then progressively
localized, with towns as their chief target. Plague is primarily a rodent infection. Its permanent habitat is the wild
rats of prairie and forest, whence diseased animals period-
ically carry it to populated areas, transferring it to human
beings through the medium of the fleas which prey on both.
It is because there are more rats as well as more humans
in towns that plague goes on recurring there after it has
disappeared from the countryside; and the larger the town
the longer the period of recurrence. It was the four hundred
years from the mid fourteenth to the mid eighteenth
century which saw the second of these pandemics run its
course in Europe. In England (where the plague-carrying
black rat had probably been introduced from the East at
the time of the Crusades) it opened with the tremendous
disaster of the Black Death, which may have destroyed a
third or more of the entire population. Twelve years
later the plague returned in what was to prove only the
second of a long series of outbreaks. There seems reason to
believe that until shortly after 1400 these outbreaks continued to affect both town and country, that from then

*The first began in the fourth century A.D., the third (still in progress)
in 1894.

until about 1500 it was London and, to a diminishing extent, the provincial towns which suffered, and that after 1500 London, and towns infected from London, alone were touched. It was a heavy price that the capital had to pay for her size and her pre-eminence as a port. Not until after the Great Plague of 1665 did the extermination of the black rat by the fiercer but less infectious brown rat, and the greater resistance to infestation of the new brick- and stone-built city properties, lift from Londoners the shadow under which they had so long lived and died.

But it was then two centuries since that shadow had been lifted from the country as a whole, and the England of 1485 was an England which was already beginning to feel the quickening effect of an upward trend in its population-curve. How much the success of early Tudor government owed to its coincidence with this demographic change is something which defies calculation. That change certainly underlay more than one of the developments which were to characterize the new age. The fifteenth-century retreat of arable before pasture, of crops before sheep, was a logical readjustment of the rural economy to the needs and capacities of a declining population. It had involved little hardship and provoked no resistance. But a population which was beginning to increase again had either to recover the lost acres for the plough or to work its reduced ploughlands more intensively. There was, as we have seen, no real shortage of land either for crop-raising or sheep-rearing. Nor does the ingenious theory that English farm-land had been exhausted by continuous cropping appear to fit the known facts of the situation. But the balance between land and labour, which for some generations had stood in favour of land, was now beginning to move back, and, temporarily at least, land-surfeit gave place to land-hunger. It was no longer only sheep which competed among themselves, but men who competed with sheep, for the kindly fruits of the earth. Given time, their competition would lead to, and be relieved by, the improvements of more land. But its immediate effect was a sharp struggle between the two forms of land utilization, a struggle which also tended to become a conflict between the two great divisions of rural society, the landlords, who leaned towards sheep-farming, and the tenants, whose livelihood still depended in the first place upon the raising of crops. And what made that struggle even sharper was the fact that English agriculture, beside feeding and clothing a growing population at home, was also called upon to clothe a growing number of foreigners.

Early Tudor England was to a large extent self-sufficient. Practically all the necessities of life, food, clothing, fuel and housing, were produced from native resources by native effort, and it was to satisfy these primary needs that the great mass of the population laboured at its daily tasks. Production was for the most part organized in innumerable small units. In the country the farm, the hamlet and the village lived on what they could grow or make for themselves, and on the sale of any surplus in the local market town; while in the towns craftsmen applied themselves to their one-man businesses, making the boots and shoes, the caps and cloaks, the implements and harness for townsmen and countrymen alike. Once a week town and country met to make the exchange at a market which came near to realizing the medieval ideal of direct contact between producer and consumer. This was the traditional economy, which had hardly altered for some centuries, and which still set the pattern of work and the standard of life of perhaps nine out of every ten English men and women. The work was long and hard, and the standard of life achieved, measured by the 'austerity' of our own day, almost unimaginably low. Most Englishmen lived on a diet which was often meagre and always monotonous, and was little calculated to promote resistance to disease; wore coarse and ill-fitting clothes which harboured dirt and vermin; and lived in hovels whose squalor would affront the modern slum-dweller. Theirs was, indeed, the margin of subsistence, and their hold on life and livelihood a tenuous thread all too easily snapped.

But the nation was not wholly engaged in scratching a living out of its own soil. For England was already a part, and an essential part, of a larger economy, an economy which embraced all Europe and was on the point of expanding to embrace half the world. From ancient times England had been one of Europe's 'primary producers', the source of raw materials for Continental industry. First it had been her metals which were most in demand; Cornish tin and Mendip lead had fed the smithies of the South. Then, in the twelfth century, wool had leapt into first place. Flanders and North Italy, the workshops of the medieval world, had absorbed immense quantities of English wool, the finest that was to be had, and England had multiplied her sheep to meet the demand. Reaching a peak in the mid fourteenth century, the wool trade had since gone into decline, and by 1500 it had shrunk to a tithe of its former volume. The Merchants of the Staple, the state-sponsored mercantile corporation which monopolized the wool trade, had undergone a corresponding decline, and they found growing difficulty in fulfilling their public obligations, which included the upkeep of the garrison of Calais, England's military and economic bridgehead on the Continent. Thus although in Henry VII's day the Staple still ranked as one of the pillars of the kingdom, it was a pillar set upon a sinking foundation. The wool that had once fed Flemish looms was now largely consumed by a native cloth industry. By means of an 'industrial revolution' hardly less momentous than the later and more familiar one, England had transformed herself, between 1350 and 1450, into a large-scale producer and exporter of woollen cloth.

It is a commonplace that foreign trade has always exerted an influence upon economic development out of all proportion to its volume. While at the opening of the sixteenth century England was exporting every year some 80,000 cloths, for every one of these there may have been consumed two or three at home. Yet it was the over-seas cloth trade which was to prove one of the most powerful dissolvents of the traditional economy. The 'pull' of that trade was made all the stronger by the developments which took place in it just about this time. Until the early fifteenth century it had been carried on directly between all the leading English ports and wide stretches of the Continental seaboard. But towards the middle of that century this expansion of English trading connexions had been abruptly checked. The merchants of the East Coast were driven back across the North Sea by the hostile forces of the German Hanse, while those of the South-West had to contend with mounting difficulties in Western and Southern Europe, including the impact of the last phase of the Hundred Years War. Both groups had there-fore tended to turn to the one great channel which remained open, the Netherlands, and the tentacles of English over-seas trade which had stretched out to touch Europe at many points now turned inwards to fasten upon this one débouché. The resulting concentration went far towards making the cloth trade what economists call a 'natural monopoly', and those who set out to exploit it were the merchants of the South-East, especially the Londoners, who had originally opened up the Antwerp trade and who regarded it with a proprietary air. When they found their provincial rivals infiltrating into this trade they reacted strongly. They already disposed of a rudimentary organization. London merchants specializing in overseas trade – Adventurers as they were called – had come to form 'cells' within the City Companies of which they were members, and from soon after 1450 these became the nucleus of a new commercial organization. The process of unification was gradual, but in 1486 the City authorities formally created the Fellowship of the Merchant Adventurers of London. It was this organization which the members now set about converting into a bulwark of their vested interest in the Antwerp trade. Their aim was to make membership of their society, and compliance with its regulations, binding upon all who engaged in that trade. Membership could be secured by apprenticeship, by patrimony, or by redemption. Since the first two avenues were in practice open only to those living in or near London, provincial merchants, who already had their own Fellowships, would be eligible for the London Company only by way of the third, and it was open to that Company to fix the redemption-fee at a discouragingly high figure. That this is what happened is borne out by the complaints of the provincial merchants against the excessive fees and other vexations to which they were subjected. During the early years of Henry VII's reign the Antwerp trade was dislocated by political upheavals. But in 1496 Henry negotiated with the Netherlands the favourable commercial treaty known to posterity as the Intercursus Magnus. The new era of economic intimacy thus inaugurated swelled the stream of English commercial enterprise flowing into the Antwerp trade and brought to a head the struggle between the Londoners and their competitors. The King himself was compelled to intervene and in 1497 an act of parliament imposed a settlement which is a landmark in the history of the Merchant Adventurers. If at first sight this settlement, with its admission to the Netherlands market of any merchant in return for a specified, and much reduced, composition-fee, appears a decided setback to the Company's exclusivist programme, its real significance was quite otherwise. For by fixing this fee parliament had by implication recognized the Company's right to exact payment, and compliance with regulations, from all merchants trading within its area. The act thus marks the first step in the process which would gradually convert an unofficial and loosely organized trading association into a monopolistic corporation upheld by the state and enjoying the most intimate relations with it. The Merchant Adventurers were already on the way to becoming the new Staple.

The growth of the cloth trade, its increasing concentration along the London-Antwerp 'axis', and the nascent monopoly over it of the Merchant Adventurers, these features of the national economy at the opening of the Tudor period were to have important repercussions in various branches of English life, some of which will call for later discussion. Here we must be content to trace the most obvious sequence, through the industry which produced the cloth to the agriculture which supplied that industry with its raw material. The new situation meant not only an increased demand for cloth, especially for the particular lines favoured by the foreign buyer, but – what was more important – a demand for more cloth to be delivered at an overseas market at a particular time. The export trade was essentially periodic. Cloth was shipped over to the Netherlands twice a year, for sale at the four great fairs of Antwerp and its neighbour Bergen-op-Zoom. This was the work of the Merchant Adventurers. But the cloth had previously to be collected from the makers and carried to

London, or to one of the 'outposts' engaged in the trade, in time for the half-yearly shipping, and this called for the services of another middleman, the cloth-dealer. Just as the wool-chapman had once toured the country collecting wool for the Staplers, so now the cloth-dealer bought cloth for delivery to the Merchant Adventurers at their head-quarters, Blackwell Hall, in London. Thus transmitted through this distributive 'grid', the power of the London demand penetrated the cloth-making districts throughout the country. The historic centres of the industry were the towns, and in 1485 there was hardly a town of any size which did not maintain the groups of craftsmen – weavers, fullers, tuckers, shearmen, dyers – whose combined labours went into the manufacture of cloth. But the industry had long since expanded into the countryside, and it was rural cloth-making which received the chief stimulus from the growth of the overseas market. The size of that market, and its distance, both in space and time, from the place of manufacture, favoured the growth of larger units of pro-duction, under capitalist initiative, and these fared better in the country than in the town, whose gild organization was the bulwark of the small producer, the independent craftsman. The foreign demand was, moreover, mainly a demand for unfinished cloth, for cloth which would be dressed and dyed after it reached the Continent. Such cloth the rural industry was both able and willing to supply whereas the towns preferred, in the interest of their own finishing processes, to market their cloth already dressed and dyed. It was, therefore, to the rising class of country clothiers, the entrepreneurs who had their spinning and weaving done at low piece-rates by village operatives, rather than to the town craftsmen working under gild regulations and at gild rates, that the dealer on London account looked for his supplies, and clothiers, dealers and exporters were soon linked together in a chain which stretched from the looms in English cottages to the show-benches at the Antwerp fairs.

But in truth that chain stretched a good deal further in both directions. It began with the wool on the back of an English sheep and ended, it might be, with the coat on the back of an Hungarian nobleman. What became of English cloth once it passed into foreign hands belongs to European rather than to English history, although whether an English weaver found himself in or out of work might ultimately depend upon how it fared with the Turkish invasion of Hungary. But whence came the wool with which the weaver satisfied that distant demand is a question which belongs indubitably to English history. For the answer is the English sheep, and at no time has the English sheep come nearer to making English history than in the half-century which followed the accession of Henry VII. To the men of the time sheep were synonymous with enclosure; and from 1487, when it first provoked legislation, until 1549, when it all but provoked revolution, enclosure was a great, if not the greatest, national issue. Statutes and proclamations penalized it, royal commissions investigated it, preachers and publicists denounced it. Seen through their eyes, enclosure was as simple as it was sinister. Thanks to the expansion of the cloth trade, there was an almost insatiable demand for wool, and everywhere land formerly kept in tillage was being put down to grass. The resulting 'dearth' – in the sixteenth century this noun still retained its original meaning of dearness – of victuals was not the least deplorable consequence, nor the only one. Tillage, or husbandry, called for many hands, sustained a thriving rural population, and ensured the maximum distribution of wealth. Pasture farming devoted wide tracts of country to sheep-walks, reduced the demand for rural labour, and drove the surplus population to roam the country in search of food and work. Its promoters and beneficiaries were the handful of landlords and merchants who sought only their own profit and who were prepared to sacrifice to it the livelihood of their fellows, the well ordering of society, and the safety of the state.

Modern research has modified this contemporary, and traditional, picture of the enclosure movement as the agency by which the landed and moneyed classes of Tudor England effected a widespread conversion of arable to pastoral farming in response to the changing needs of the market. It has been shown, first, that only a small percentage of the land of the country underwent enclosure at this time, and that contemporary accounts of wholesale depopulation are not to be trusted. Again, it is argued that by no means all enclosure was for pasture, but that the permanent fencing of portions of either the open fields or the common 'waste' was often undertaken as the indispensable preliminary to improved cultivation. Yet another modification relates to the classes of people responsible for the changes: the 'rich men' of contemporary indictments are joined by a host of lesser folk, and the peasant is revealed as the author, as well as the victim, of enclosures. It has to be confessed that what the picture has gained in truthfulness, it has lost in simplicity; and that each fresh contribution makes it more instead of less difficult to generalize with any confidence upon the subject. But we can hardly doubt that the growing demand for wool meant a serious aggravation of the problems involved in the growing demand for food, or that the large-scale conversions to pasture now being undertaken by enterprising landlords differed substantially in their nature and effects from the small enclosures which the peasantry had long been making in order to improve their own mixed farming.

We have been speaking of landlords and peasants, merchants and craftsmen, townsmen and countrymen, and it is time to say something of the society which these groups composed and to which they contributed labour or leadership. Early Tudor society was in some respects substantially more, and in others notably less, homogeneous than that of our own day. Against the smallness of the population – between two and three millions all told – as a factor making for social cohesion (and, incidentally, for that wide personal acquaintance with their subjects which characterized the Tudor sovereigns) we must set the relatively large area – Penzance then being as distant in time from Berwick as is London now from Sydney – over which that population was spread. Thus, while each local unit, be it village, town or county, was then closer knit than is its modern counterpart, these units were bound together more loosely, and felt less community with one another, than in our own day. It was to be at once a primary aim, and a major achievement, of the Tudors to weld together these local units into a larger whole, to supersede the smaller loyalties by a greater, in short, to create a nation. In doing so, they were helped or hindered by a variety of factors, physical, social and cultural; and it is some of the more important of these which we must now briefly review.

The English people which Henry VII and his successors ruled was of substantially the same racial composition as that which owes allegiance to Elizabeth II. But it lacked certain ingredients which have been added since, and those of which it was composed had yet to be thoroughly mixed together. The Tudors themselves, besides introducing Welsh blood into the royal line, also encouraged the first significant movement of Welsh immigration into England.

A century later James I was to perform a similar office for the Scots, although Scottish infiltration, too, had begun under the Tudors. (Of Irish blood, however, there was as yet scarcely any admixture; even the English aristocracy did not intermarry with the Anglo-Irish families.) The sixteenth century was also to witness the first great Continental immigration, that of the French, Dutch and German refugees from religious persecution. They would be followed in the seventeenth by the Sephardic Jews and the Huguenots, and in the eighteenth, nineteenth and twentieth by the flood of immigrants from Central and Southern Europe, as well as by the great influx from Ireland. Thus, whereas today there are few English persons in whom there flows no recent non-English blood, in the sixteenth century most of the English had a purely indigenous descent stretching back for many hundreds of years. But the make-up of the contemporary Englishman probably owes less to these subsequent additions than to the better blending of the older strains within him. Until the sixteenth century this blending process had, outside London and the larger towns, and below the governing class of society, made but slow progress. While we must not exaggerate the stationariness of medieval man, it remains true that most men and women lived and died where they had been born, and that the inhabitants of each district were thus in the main sprung from a local ancestry, an ancestry which in many cases reached back to the era of settlement, in the North-East to the coming of the Danes, in the Midlands and South to the arrival of Angles, Saxons and Jutes, and in the West to a past perhaps even more remote. We may therefore infer that the provincial and local characteristics which here and there still resist the averaging and unifying pressure of modern life were a good deal more marked in Tudor times. We might instance the two inches' advantage in height which is still enjoyed by the men of the North-East over those of some South-Western counties and which was presumably somewhat greater than that four hundred years ago, even though the national average has risen over the same period with the improvement in the standard of living. Similarly, the now all but extinct contrast between the fair-haired and light-eyed Easterner and the darker man of the Midlands and West must then have been more evident.

But, more than either his physique or colouring, it was an Englishman's speech which, like St Peter's, then betrayed his place of origin. By the fifteenth century England had ceased to be a bilingual country, in which official and polite intercourse was carried on in one language, French, and the mass of the people employed their vernacular English. But the spoken, and to some extent the written, English of the time still varied from one part of the country to another. Medieval dialects, like other regional characteristics, were a legacy of the early settlements, and the Northern descendants of the Danes used an English which was barely recognizable as such by Kentish descendants of Jutes or by the West Saxon stock of Dorset and Somerset. Language has always been one of the most powerful of unifying, and dividing, forces, and these regional differences of speech must have contributed much to the strength of local, and to the weakness of national, loyalty. In this respect, however, the sixteenth century was to mark a turning-point. For it was then that the English of London, itself an amalgam of three or more regional dialects (East Midland, Southern and South Eastern), began to exploit the prestige which it had been building up since the time of Chaucer and to gain recognition as 'standard' English. The notion of 'correct' pronunciation was, so our evidence suggests, born in the reign of Henry VIII, when men like

John Palsgrave, who tutored the royal offspring, and Sir Thomas Elyot, who produced that classic of educational literature, *The Governour*, first stressed the importance of teaching children to 'speak none English but that which is clean, polite, perfectly and articulately pronounced'. It was doubtless this 'Court' English which the Italian visitor of 1497 found 'pleasing enough' to his Romance-trained ear. Its emergence heralded the characteristically modern division of the spoken language, the horizontal 'class' division, and the gradual disappearance of the vertical division into regional dialects which had prevailed in the Middle Ages.

If the sixteenth century thus invented a new linguistic test of social status, it was content to take over from the Middle Ages both the conception of a stratified society, in which every class had a peculiar and, as it was believed, a preordained position and function, and the social strata thus evolved. In practice, this stratification had never been carried so far in England as on the Continent, and it gave way earlier before the unifying and equalizing effect of political, legal and economic development. Moreover, the Tudors themselves were to be responsible for blurring the lines of social cleavage to a far greater degree than any of their predecessors. But, in this as in so much else, the Tudor monarchs were innately conservative, and at the same time as they were releasing forces which beat ever more fiercely against the traditional barriers separating class from class, they were hard at work shoring up those barriers and striving to restore the lost social equilibrium. Tudor society therefore exhibits two kinds of inequality, the practical inequality springing from differences in livelihood, wealth and opportunity and the conventional inequality arising from the incorporation of these differences in the political, legal and social system; and the main interest of Tudor social history lies in the tendency of these two kinds of inequality to part company and in the efforts of the rulers to bring them together again.

In Tudor England, as in England down to very recent times, the inequality which affected the largest number of people was not a social, but a sexual, one. The woman of the time, whatever her rank in society, was treated as an inferior being, and her freedom of action was restricted at every turn. Prior to marriage she was an infant, to be watched over by parent or guardian. Her marriage, which was normally a business arrangement in which she had no say whatever, converted her into *feme covert* and submerged her legal personality in that of her husband. Only as a widow could she hope to enjoy something approaching equality with man in the disposal of her person and property. Such, at least, was the dictate of the common law. Municipal custom was rather more liberal, and the independent woman trader is a not unfamiliar figure of the period. But, indispensable as was their labour in house or field, at the treadle or the spinning-wheel, and capable as they might here and there prove in a business career, women were wholly ineligible for public office and for the professions, while those who took religious vows did so as almost the sole alternative to the more customary task of reproducing the species. This is not to say that the woman of the period had no opportunity of exploiting any gifts other than those called for in a wife, mother, or housekeeper. In particular, the Renaissance was to stimulate an interest in women's education which was to have no parallel until the nineteenth century. But any part which talented women played in the political or cultural life of the country was of necessity an unprofessional one, and the fact that, of the two women of Tudor England who through the accident of royal birth furnished its sole exceptions to this rule, one was to be outstandingly successful in the most exacting of all professions cannot but suggest that the subjection of its womanhood deprived the nation of much potential ability.

Of inequalities attaching to different classes of society, the most notable were those to be met with at opposite ends of the social scale, namely, the privileges of the nobleman and the disabilities of the villein. The privileges pertaining to the nobility had their origin in the special importance of the territorial magnate as the king's lieutenant in war and his counsellor in peace; and it was in these two spheres that the nobility remained pre-eminent in early Tudor England. During the fifteenth century these mighty subjects had indeed become over-mighty. They had stretched their privilege of commanding the king's armies to the point of commanding armies against him, and of Tudor achievements none was to be more salutary than their deflating of these swollen pretensions. The process was facilitated by the high death-roll which was the wages of the peers' sin against the state. Into the vacant places Henry VII and his son were able to introduce men whose loyalty to the throne would outweigh devotion to their dignity. For the Tudors had no thought of destroying the aristocracy; on the contrary, once they had tamed it, they made it an integral part of their system. Politically innocuous, the Tudor peerage was to remain socially supreme; and since land was the foundation of social ascendancy, the peers were expected to remain, as a class, the greatest of landowners. Indeed, those who fell below the required standard risked their titles or privileges. In 1477, and again in 1493, a duke was 'demoted' for lack of a sufficiency of land, and 'decayed' peers were sometimes not summoned to the House of Lords. Conversely, when new peers were created. they were often given lands to support their dignity. Apart from the royal duchies of Lancaster, York, Cornwall and Richmond, and the earldom of March (that is, the Welsh Marches), there were, during the half-century after 1485, four dukedoms and some fifteen earldoms, nearly all named after English counties. Their holders did not always hold the bulk of their land in the counties concerned; for example, the Stanleys, Earls of Derby, had their main estates in Lancashire and the Isle of Man, and the Greys, Earls of Kent, theirs in Bedfordshire. But a duke, earl or marquess was always the magnate of a particular region. while many of the fifty or so barons who followed them in the table of precedence fell little short of them in wealth and prestige. Such men formed the apexes of the social and political pyramids of each county. They 'lived like lords', maintaining establishments which were replicas in miniature of the royal household. They kept open house, and moved abroad followed by considerable retinues. The leaders among them lived in castles whose size and apparent strength bespoke their greatness. At Thornbury, in Gloucestershire, the Duke of Buckingham built, at the turn of the century, the immense pile whose ruins warrant its description as 'the final manifestation of the fortified house of the over-mighty subject'. In its great hall there regularly dined, so we learn from a set of accounts of 1507–8, between one hundred and two hundred persons.

But Thornbury has other associations for the student of Tudor society besides the magnificence of its lords. As late as 1586 Lord Stafford was to claim the natives of the village as his bondmen, just as his ancestor Buckingham had done in the early years of the century. Neither claim succeeded, but they remind us that, at the opposite end of the social scale from the privileged aristocrat, there remained a class of people burdened with legal disabilities. In 1586 there were not many such people left. But a century before their number may still have run into four figures. They were a survival from the past, a past in which unfree men and women had made up a large part of the population. The medieval bondman, or villein, occupied a status midway between the slave of the Ancient and the free labourer of the Modern World. Unlike the slave, who depended upon his master to keep him alive, the villein had to support himself and his family, and he did so out of the holding of land granted to him for the purpose by his lord. It followed that, whereas the slave's work was wholly at his master's disposal, the villein rendered to his lord only a part of his labour, devoting the remainder to his own subsistence. This was the tenurial aspect of villeinage. There was also the element of personal unfreedom, originally designed to ensure the supply of this form of labour for the cultivation of the lord's own estate. The villein was 'bound to the soil', he was not free to leave his holding without his lord's consent, and his person, family and property were more or less at his lord's disposal. But for a century or more before 1485 vellein tenure and villein status had been parting company. Villein status itself was tending to disappear and the number of people who bore the taint of servility became progressively smaller than the number who, personally free, continued to hold their land by the modified form of villein tenure then becoming general. By 1485 the separation was complete, and it was the accepted rule that 'no land holden in villeinage ... shall ever make a free man a villein'. The continuance of these tendencies under the Tudors would virtually extinguish personal villeinage in England. But the Tudors themselves could take little credit for the fact. No great emancipating statute, inspired by the growth of an enlightened opposition to villeinage, removed this stigma from the hundreds of families who bore it. Henry VIII certainly struck a blow at the remains of villeinage when he dissolved the monasteries, on whose lands it had lingered more than on lay estates. But it was left to the rebellious peasantry of 1549 to sound the note of freedom with their demand 'that all bondmen may be made free'. The call fell on deaf ears. So far, indeed, were the rulers of the period from heeding it that even the 'gentle' Somerset, when in 1547 he legislated against vagabondage, was prepared to make a slave of anyone presented to the Justices of the Peace as an idler. Neither liberty nor equality was a Tudor watchword.

But peers and villeins, besides being the extremes, were also the exceptions in early Tudor society. The vast majority of Englishmen neither enjoyed personal privilege nor suffered legal disability, and their position and prospects in society depended almost exclusively upon material considerations. The rural population – and that was nine-tenths of the whole – fell into two classes, those who derived an earned, and those who enjoyed an unearned, income from the land; the first category comprised the great mass of the cultivators of the soil, the second the much smaller number who lived on the rents or services rendered to them by the majority. The institution through which this system of rights and obligations was made to work was the 'manor'. It was in manors that land was 'held of' the king, and it was within the manorial framework that each parcel of land was 'sub-let' by the king's tenant to his own tenants, the peasants who farmed it. The manor thus furnishes the rough dividing-line between the two great classes of rural society, the 'upper' or landlord class and the 'lower' or tenant class; the first held manors and derived an unearned income from them, the second held land within manors and earned its livelihood by tilling the soil.

The holders of manors and their kin formed – if we exclude such of them as bore titles of nobility – the class to which the sixteenth century would apply the name 'gentry'. The English gentry never established itself as a legal entity in the way that the nobility had done. We may indeed see in the order of knighthood what might have become the official badge of gentility. If our medieval kings had succeeded in their ambition of conscripting into its ranks all with landed incomes of twenty (later raised to forty) pounds a year, the knightage might have come to form the Third Estate of the realm, and a commonalty separated from it have been relegated to fourth place. But the Crown regularly allowed those qualified for this unwanted privilege to evade it, and the dignity of knighthood thus came to be restricted to only a proportion of the rural upper class; it became more a personal honour, less an indication of status, and the attempt to assign to it peculiar rights and duties (such as the representation of the counties in parliament) gradually broke down. By contrast, the rank of esquire, originally limited to those standing in degree next below that of knight, suffered from over-popularity, and from soon after 1500 it began that expansionist career which has ended in suffixing it to the names of all sorts and conditions of men. In one respect only did the untitled landlord class acquire a formal mark of gentility, in the bearing of arms. With the reorganization of the heraldic establishment in the fifteenth century, the devising of their own insignia by nobles and knights gave place to a more orderly process of grants by the Kings of Arms. There was a heavy demand by the gentry for patents of arms, and between 1450 and 1600 the Heralds were kept very busy. Although the repeated complaints to this effect suggest that they showed some lack of discrimination, the general result of their activities was to create, in the grade of non-noble armigers, the nearest approach to an official register of the gentry.

The assumption of arms, and the compilation (which included the fabrication) of pedigrees, were part of the cult of gentility with which the rural upper class sought to meet the challenge of the times. Separated from the nobility by a clearly marked frontier of title and privilege – a frontier which could be crossed only at the behest of the Crown – the gentry could boast no such demarcation from the groups beneath, whose upward pressure was, moreover, intense and unremitting. The fifteenth century had dealt hardly with the gentry, and they answered it in kind. The over-supplied land market, and consequent fall in land values, undermined their position. Tenants were hard to come by, and had to be attracted by lower rents and reduced services, while the alternative, hired agricultural labour, was to be had only at higher wages. Not only was the national income falling, but its distribution was changing; tenants and labourers were getting more, and landlords and employers less, than they had before. Viewed against this background, some of the less attractive traits of the country gentleman take on the colour of a struggle for survival in a hostile world. His subservience to the nobility, whose protection was all-important in an age which knew no higher authority; his readiness to supplement his income from such dubious sources as illicit trade or piracy; his intense litigiousness, and his unscrupulous use of every trick known, or unknown, to the law to defeat a rival; and perhaps most of all, his devotion to the great business of match-making, the lifebelt of the sinking family, the ladder of the rising one – all these 'genteel' pursuits, which loom so large in the chronicles of the time, must have been matters of deadly seriousness to men whose social security was at stake. We can surely go further and discern in the restlessness which the threat of impoverishment induced in them one of the causes of that outburst of political gangsterism which we call the Wars of the Roses. Certain it is that when, a century later, faction aspired to succeed Henry VIII as king, the gentry were at once more prosperous and more law-abiding, with nothing to gain and much to lose by anarchy – and that this time there was no civil war.

If the gentry owed the mending of their fortunes during that century chiefly to the reversal of the trends which had earlier threatened them – to land-hunger in place of land-surfeit, to rising instead of falling prices, to a growing instead of a shrinking market – some credit must go to their own reinvigoration as a class. The ranks thinned during the 'time of troubles' were quickly filled by promotions from below. The newcomers were of diverse origin. A good many of them climbed by way of the royal service, receiving their grants of land as something between a reward and a salary. Others owed their rise to noble patrons, who also knew hardly any other method of payment. What such men earned by service, others acquired by their earnings in different fields. Lawyers were always prominent in the movement; their professional *expertise* and connexions must have stood them in good stead. (It was a lawyer, Sir Anthony Fitzherbert, who in 1523 published the first handbook of farming for the benefit of his fellow-proprietors.) Then there were the men of business, the merchants and industrialists. They had been thrusting their way upwards since the fourteenth century, and some of them, like the Poles of Hull, had already reached dizzy heights. In 1500 the tide of capital from town to country was running strongly, and a government which deplored its effects was beginning to make a vain effort to dam it. The assimilation of this urban-professional element to the established gentry was smooth and rapid; indeed, there was hardly any problem of assimilation. The landed class, encouraged by the operation of primogeniture, had long since been furnishing recruits to the trades and professions, while those of its members who remained on their manors often had a hand in trade and were for ever dabbling in the law. Between the squire turned merchant, and the merchant turned squire, there was no great gulf fixed; and if the new gentry brought anything of value to the class of their adoption it was not so much the 'business outlook' – that the old gentry already had – as the proven quality of success.

The same impersonal forces of supply and demand, and the same personal ones of individual enterprise or the reverse, which produced these changes in the genteel fortunes of the period were also at work among those lower down the rural scale. The fifteenth century had, as we have seen, proved favourable to the English peasantry, and there must have been many families which emerged from it with enlarged and consolidated holdings, increased flocks, and a higher standard of living. But even this spell of prosperity held the seeds of future misfortune. For by conducing to inequality of holdings and to individualism in their exploitation, peasant prosperity weakened that solidarity of interest and outlook which alone could have saved the peasantry as a class in the supreme test which lay ahead. As it was, the peasants faced that test with their ranks divided. True, their widening range of economic competence tended to coincide with, and reinforce, the historic division of the peasantry into free tenants, or freeholders, and customary tenants, or copyholders. It was the free tenant, holding his land in return for a fixed money payment, who was best placed to survive in the new conditions of competitive and commercialized farming. Not only did he enjoy the protection of the King's law courts in his tenure of his land, so that he was relatively immune from landlord-oppression, but as soon as prices began to rise the real value of his rent started to fall, and in many cases the rent itself disappeared and the free tenant became the freeholder in the modern sense. But freeholders constituted only a minority – perhaps one in five – of the tenant population of Tudor England; and although their economic position did not always correspond to their legal and political status – it will be recalled that they alone enjoyed full civic rights in their locality, including the parliamentary franchise – they must be regarded as a sort of tenant-aristocracy, who might, or might not, feel much community of interests with their humbler neighbours.

It was the customary tenants who accounted for the bulk of the rural population – about three peasants in every five belonged to this category – and who may therefore be regarded as more typical representatives of their class. Unfortunately, the very fact that they held their land by manorial custom, which varied from manor to manor, makes it difficult to generalize about their legal position while they clearly displayed the widest range of possessions and prosperity. (We must not overlook, either, the many cases in which the same individual held both freehold and copyhold land, and perhaps leased land as well.) But certain things we can say about them. As we have seen, the great majority of them had already achieved personal freedom, and were no longer beholden to anyone save the king. In the generation before 1485 the king's courts had even shown a disposition to extend their cognizance of the customary tenant's rights as a person to his rights in his land. This was a development which, if persevered in, might have immeasurably strengthened his security of tenure. But the courts did not persevere in it, and although the Tudors brought such cases within the purview of their new Courts of Star Chamber and Requests, the common lawyers' failure to handle them was in the long run to prove fatal. Thus protected, save for the royal prerogative which he often lacked the means to invoke, solely by the 'custom of the manor' from arbitrary interference with the terms of his tenure, the customary tenant was ill placed to resist a grasping landlord's demands for 'improved' rents or fines (that is, premiums on entry), for the compulsory substitution of leases for existing tenures, or for any of the other devices by which the increased value of the holding might be transferred to the lord's pocket; while he and his fellows were seldom better able to prevent those enclosure operations which made it difficult, or impossible, for them to go on making a living out of their holdings.

But in 1485 these were clouds no bigger than a man's hand, and the peasantry who made up the majority of Henry VII's subjects were still warmed by the golden rays of the medieval sunset. The most substantial among them had already gone some way towards achieving recognition as a middle stratum of rural society, between the knights and gentry above and the simple husbandmen below. These were the 'yeomen of England', famed in song and story. Like the term 'gentleman', the term 'yeoman' never became a legal definition, and its connotation varied a good deal both in place and in time. It was not a synonym of 'free-holder', for, although many, perhaps most, yeomen were freeholders, at least as to part of their lands, there were some who were customary tenants, and some, like the father whom Bishop Latimer immortalized in a passage of one of his sermons, who were only lessees of their lands. Let a peasant farm enough acres, and farm them so that they yielded him, as his leasehold yielded the elder Latimer, a modicum of the comforts and pleasures of the age, and he was free to call himself a yeoman. The name had yet to acquire the glamour which, originating with the

Elizabethans, was to reach its peak three centuries later in the extravagances of the 'Merrie England' School, and the yeomen of 1485 would doubtless have been hard put to it to recognize himself in that romantic reincarnation. But even setting aside their martial valour, which, exposed as it has been to legendary exaggeration, was nevertheless a fact, and on occasion, as we shall see, a decisive fact in national history, the qualities of the yeomanry, and the services which they rendered to the England of their day, were such as to command the attention, and earn the commendation, of posterity.

It remains to glance briefly at the urban side of the picture. The brevity may at least claim to correspond with the scale of the subject, for not more than one in every ten of Henry VII's subjects was a townsman. There is, moreover, a tendency to exaggerate the importance of towns and the distinctive characteristics of urban life in an England which had yet to be urbanized. The physical antithesis between town and country was certainly much less marked than today. The average Tudor town, with its two or three thousand people, was simply an overgrown village. Even the walls which had earlier delimited some towns were now either decaying or ceasing, with the growth of extra-mural suburbs, to mark their boundaries. A community whose houses and shops were set among plots and gardens, whose members gained their living, not simply by manufacturing and trading, but by cultivating these acres and by pasturing their livestock on the town's common fields, and whose streets were weekly filled with the din and and dirt of cattle coming to market, might indeed claim to be *rus in urbe*, a country town. It was, in consequence, a community with a strong sense of solidarity with the surrounding countryside, whose child it was and whose customer and salesman it remained; whose problems, too, it shared, like that movement to enclose common fields which provoked townsmen as well as countrymen to riot. The town had, of course, plenty of problems of its own: how to safeguard its supplies of food, water and fuel, how to dispose of its refuse without those indispensable accompaniments of modern town life, the water closet and the main drain, how to combat those outbreaks of plague which it owed to its filth and its rats and those outbreaks of fire which it owed to its ill-constructed chimneys and its reliance on timber. The larger the town, the more acute were these problems, and the more rapid the growth of a specifically urban outlook. But when the Venetian visitor of 1497 declared that, apart from London, there were only two towns in England, Bristol and York, he was not egregiously wrong, although he might have added the names of Norwich, Coventry, Chester and Exeter.

If the town had not entirely forsaken the occupations of the countryside, the countryside was, as we have seen, already encroaching upon the occupations of the town. In the sphere of local industry and trade, town and country still bore to one another their historic complementary relationship. But upon this aggregate of local market-patterns there was being imposed a new national one, in which the provincial town was replaced by a metropolis which took the whole country for its province. Much of the economic and social – and not a little of the political and religious – history of the Tudor century can be written in terms of the growth of London; of a London which fed its vast population (approaching 75,000 in 1500, and 200,000 in 1600) from an ever-widening area of the country, which called into existence new rural centres of industry and doomed old urban ones, and whose wealth brought the nation increasingly under its dominion. In 1500 these things were only in their infancy. But some of their social implications were already apparent, and they may serve to round off this sketch of early Tudor society. The social structure of the medieval town had been sharply distinguished from that of the countryside. The political emancipation of towns from the control of feudal magnates had coincided with their social emancipation from feudal bonds. In the town the villein became a free man, the tenant a burgess; society became more fluid, and the power which made it flow was the power of money. By the close of the Middle Ages, however, not only was urban society crystallizing into a pattern not dissimilar from that which was emerging in the countryside, but urban and rural society were, at least at the middle level, being rapidly reintegrated. The 'classlessness' of the medieval town was giving place, under the impact of economic change, to a twofold division, the division into a 'governing' class of merchants and industrialists, reinforced by lawyers and professional men, and a 'governed' class of small master craftsmen and journeymen artisans, petty traders and dependent servants. Retarded in the smaller towns by their diminutive scale and restricted scope for enterprise, as well as by the greater resistance offered by the gilds and by the claims of local magnates, this stratification proceeded more rapidly in the larger ones, and most rapidly of all in London, where it is symbolized by the rise of the Livery Company, the fraternity of the successful, as the dominant institution in the commercial, and an important one in the political, life of the capital. It was from this urban upper class, and above all from its large London contingent, that the 'new' gentry was largely recruited, and thus a community, if not an identity, of interest and outlook established between those who ruled the Tudor countryside and those who ruled the Tudor town; and it was with, and through, a ruling class which had its feet firmly planted on English soil and its hands stretched out to pluck the fruits of English industry and English trade, that Henry Tudor set out in 1485 to rule England.

II

HENRY TUDOR AND SON

BOSWORTH established, and his own political genius endorsed, Henry VII's right to rule a state which was one of the most considerable in Christendom. That state comprised, in addition to the Kingdom of England, a number of 'dependent' territories of varying size and significance: the Principality of Wales, the Lordship of Ireland, the Isle of Man, the Scillies and the Channel Isles, and the town and district of Calais. England herself had long since achieved statehood, but it was a more recent experience for her to be the centre of a political agglomeration. The nascent English State had been absorbed into a succession of ephemeral empires, Danish, Norman, Angevin, whose centres of gravity lay outside rather than within her own borders. But as the Middle Ages drew to their close these unstable combinations gave place to a clearer and more lasting pattern. The Hundred Years War had first re-knit and then again snapped the political tie between England and France, and Calais alone remained to challenge the conclusion that the Channel was too wide to be bridged by the political engineering of the age. Frustrated in their attempt at a Continental expansion which (as the Parliament which had helped Edward III to launch it had foreseen) held danger to English as well as to French national independence, the kings of England had also failed to extend their dominion over the British Isles. Wales they had bludgeoned into submission, but over Scotland they could show nothing but a paper suzerainty and over Ireland a sway which was effective only within the limited area of the Pale. The union of these territories still lay in a distant future. Yet it is likely that Henry VII's realm could have been larger only at the cost of being weaker. In an age when slowness of communication set a fairly rigid limit to the area which could be administered from a single centre, the unity of states was apt to bear an inverse ratio to their size; and the forcefulness of Tudor government owed not a little to the relatively short distances at which it was required to operate.

Nothing was to become Henry VII better in his kingship of this realm than his keeping of it. The twenty-four years which closed with Bosworth had seen three kings of England thrust violently from their thrones; the twenty-four which followed were to see one king ever more firmly seated upon his, and the twenty-fifth his son and heir succeed him amid perfect tranquillity. If Henry VII had done nothing more than remain king for life, he would have deserved well of his country. But, in truth, Henry could not have done that without doing much besides. For if his ability to keep his throne would be the ultimate test of his kingship, it was the quality of his kingship which would determine whether or not he kept his throne. In politics, as in life, nothing succeeds like success. In the politics of 1485 nothing could succeed but success.

It was certainly not to the strength of his title that Henry owed the security of his tenure. The diffusion of the blood royal in the fourteenth century, and its squandering and sullying in the fifteenth, had together created a situation in which no individual could boast an unimpeachable title. But there were better-looking claims than Henry's. Richard III had died childless, and Edward IV's two sons had first been bastardized and then murdered. But there were five

44

daughters and two nephews of Edward's living in 1485. If he had been lawful king, and if a woman could inherit the throne, then his eldest daughter, Elizabeth, was the rightful heiress, with her four sisters standing in line after her; if only men were eligible, then his brother Clarence's son, Edward Earl of Warwick, stood first, and his sister Elizabeth's son, John Earl of Lincoln, presumptively, second. In Lancastrian eyes, of course, both Edward IV and Richard III had been usurpers, and the last lawful sovereign was the deposed and murdered Henry VI. But Henry Tudor was a less indisputable heir of Henry VI than either Elizabeth or Warwick of Edward IV. It was Henry VI's mother Catherine of Valois – the victor of Agincourt's 'fair Kate' – whose subsequent (and clandestine) union with her Welsh clerk of the wardrobe Owen Tudor made her the mother of Edmund and the grandmother of Henry Tudor. We may perhaps wonder how it was that this child of Wales, born (in 1457) a few months after his father's death at twenty-six, came to be given the English and regal name of Henry. Was the name simply a thank-offering to the sovereign who had legitimized and ennobled Edmund Tudor? Or were these Tudors already raising their eyes to a throne which that feeble-minded monarch and his infant son seemed incapable of retaining? They were not likely to forget that this son of theirs had English as well as French royal blood in his veins. For Henry Tudor's mother was Margaret Beaufort, heiress to those earls of Somerset whose chain of descent led back, through John of Gaunt, to Edward III. Unfortunately, it was a chain with a weak link. The Beauforts were sprung from John of Gaunt's union with a mistress, and although subsequently legitimized they had been excluded from the succession. So long as there remained princes of the House of Lancaster above suspicion of the bend sinister, the sin of its founder would be visited upon his Beaufort progeny of the third and fourth generation; and it needed the tragedies of 1471 to enable Henry Tudor to live down his birth-taint and live up to his name by being recognized as Lancastrian claimant to the throne.

The same process of elimination which had helped to turn Henry Tudor into a king was to serve the great aim of keeping him one. Henry had begun to employ it when, during his preparations for the invasion, he had given an undertaking to marry Elizabeth of York; and the rapidity with which, as soon as Bosworth was fought, he had Elizabeth brought to London, stamped her as one of the spoils of victory. His capture made, however, Henry proceeded with his usual circumspection. To have married in haste might have been to repent at leisure, for it would have implied that Henry, the adventurer without title, had to marry to obtain one. So it was not until after his coronation and his recognition by parliament that Henry took Elizabeth to wife (18 January 1486) and not until after he had put down his first serious rebellion that he had her crowned (24 November 1487). We are tempted to wonder what would have happened if the first of Tudor royal marriages had been as luckless as most of its successors. In fact, the founding of the dynasty was blissfully unprophetic of its struggle to survive. Within thirty-five weeks of her marriage Elizabeth bore the child who more than any other heir apparent merited his title of Prince of Wales, and who received the 'British' name of Arthur in honour of the land of his fathers. Such marital fortune proved too good to last. Children there were in plenty. But of the seven who followed the first-born, one son and three daughters died in infancy. The heaviest blow of all was Arthur's own death on the threshold of manhood and marriage, a tragedy which united his parents in grief as his birth had united them in joy, only to separate them within a year when Elizabeth,

whose health had been affected, failed to survive the birth
of her eighth child. Even so, she left Henry VII with the
same sized family, a son and two daughters, as his six
queens were to leave Henry VIII. It was enough to secure
the succession and thus to fulfil the purpose of the match,
and Henry acknowledged as much with a splendid tomb.

The Queen's own early fecundity robbed her sisters'
marriages of some of their importance. But the King disposed of these princesses as 'safely' as possible. The eldest,
Cicely, became the wife of Lord Welles, a kinsman and
comrade-in-arms of Henry's, while Anne married Lord
Thomas Howard, son of that Earl of Surrey who was to
expiate, by cleaving to the new monarch, his father's death
fighting at Bosworth for the old. Neither marriage produced
a child to grow up and complicate the succession.* But
Katherine's marriage to Lord William Courtenay, son
of another of Henry's stalwarts, the Earl of Devon, which
produced a son, must be accounted one of the reasons
which, five years later, brought William Courtenay to the
Tower; and the offending child was himself one day to pay
the ultimate penalty of his cousinship of Henry VIII. The
kindest fate of all awaited the fourth sister, Bridget, whose
tranquil life as a nun at Dartford Priory closed shortly
before her nephew shattered the peace of that retreat. The
cloister was also the last home of these princesses' mother,
the Dowager Queen Elizabeth. Henry had begun by showing
his mother-in-law marked favour. But her political way-
wardness soon forfeited it, and in 1487, on the eve of
Lincoln's rebellion, he had her removed to Bermondsey
Abbey and transferred her property to his own Queen. The
Dowager's death in 1492 delivered her from an irksome
confinement and Henry from an embarrassing complication.

*The pretensions for which the Thomas Howard of this marriage and
his son (by another) were convicted of treason in 1546 were of independent origin.

The salvation which Elizabeth's female relatives found in the nuptial or the nunnery her male kin were forced to seek elsewhere. But the younger generation of them either made too little effort or received too little encouragement to redeem the original sin of their ancestry, and their 'liquidation' thus became indispensable to the stability of the régime. The names of the leading victims – Lincoln, Warwick, Suffolk, Courtenay – mark the steps up which the Tudors clambered to the safety of supremacy. The first to go down was Lincoln. The eldest son of the 'trimming' Duke of Suffolk, Lincoln had attached himself firmly to Richard III and by him had been chosen, in place of his cousin Warwick, heir presumptive. The loss of his regal prospects was too much for this restless young nobleman, and, after being probably implicated in the unsuccessful rising of Lovell and the brothers Stafford in the spring of 1486, he engineered the much more serious enterprise of 1487. Lincoln's rebellion resembled in pattern Henry's own successful one. Its Brittany was the Netherlands, where Lincoln's aunt, the Dowager Duchess of Burgundy, a Yorkist die-hard, raised German troops for the invasion, and its Wales Ireland, where there was as much sympathy for the Yorkist cause as there had been among Welshmen for Henry's. True, Henry had been fighting for his own claim, whereas Lincoln fought for Warwick's, transferred for the occasion to Warwick's 'double', the impersonator Lambert Simnel. But this picturesque embellishment should not obscure the real nature of the rebellion, which was a bid for power by the grandson of that Duke of York whose self-assertion had precipitated the Wars of the Roses. The battle of Stoke (16 June 1487) at which Henry overcame Lincoln's German-Irish army thus marks, more truly perhaps than Bosworth itself, the end of an epoch, and Lincoln's death on its field the elimination of the most perfect, and most dangerous, type of factious nobleman left over from the earlier contests.

The Earl of Warwick whom Lincoln championed and Simnel impersonated was a boy of ten when Bosworth was fought, and one of Henry's first acts as King had been to imprison him in the Tower. That grim fortress had bred so many mysteries of late that nothing was easier to believe than rumours of Warwick's death or escape, and it was one of these which prompted the Simnel imposture. But murder, unless it was the legalized murder of the state trial, had no place in Tudor political technique, and Warwick was to die, not in some dark corner of his prison, but under the sky on Tower Green. He had grown to manhood during his fourteen years in the Tower, and he might have been left to drag out his days there but for the repeated use of his name by those bent on overthrowing his captor. It is true that Simnel's successor in the role of impostor-claimant, the Flemish-born Perkin Warbeck, who for six years performed, to audiences which included most of the crowned heads of Europe, his masterpiece of impudent impersonation before mistakenly transferring it to the English stage, had been assigned the part, not of Warwick, who could so easily be brought out of the Tower to expose the fake, as he had been to expose Simnel's, but of one of the princes whose earlier fate there remained a black mystery. Save in so far as they sustained Yorkist hopes and thus courted Tudor revenge, Warbeck's antics spelled no harm to Warwick until 1498, when, after an attempt at escape from his mild captivity, he too found himself in the Tower. There he soon inveigled Warwick into a plot for their joint escape, and it was this indiscretion, combined with a fresh attempt to impersonate him by a young Londoner, Ralph Wilford, which sealed Warwick's fate. Henry had reluctantly reached the conclusion – which his granddaughter would one day reach even more reluctantly – that the safety of the throne was incompatible with the preservation of the pretender-in-chief; and in November 1499 Warwick was condemned and executed for treason.

Warwick's death certainly removed the best-qualified pretender, but the Spanish ambassador was over-sanguine when he wrote that it left not 'a doubtful drop of royal blood' in the kingdom. For the 'doubtful' blood of York still flowed in the dead Lincoln's brothers, the de la Poles, and it was to these young noblemen, and to their cousin William Courtenay, that there now passed the fatal cup of claimance. Edmund de la Pole had long fretted at the diminished inheritance – some sixty-four manors in Suffolk, Lincolnshire and Oxfordshire – and the reduced rank – an earldom instead of the dukedom of Suffolk – resulting from his brother's disgrace. In 1501 he fled abroad with his brother Richard, and under the name of the 'White Rose' quickly became the centre of a fresh web of Yorkist intrigue. His flight brought his brother William and his cousin Courtenay to the Tower and some of his intimates to the block. Five years later Suffolk himself was surrendered to Henry by Philip of Burgundy and he too finished his life in the Tower. His brother Richard found his way to the French Court, and on the outbreak of Henry VIII's first war with France he got himself recognized by Louis XII as King of England. This piece of folly doomed Suffolk, as Warbeck and Wilford had doomed Warwick, and in 1513 he perished on the scaffold. Finally, the adventurous Richard, after a dozen more years of romantic errantry, fell by the side of the French King at Pavia in 1525. So perished the de la Poles, after a family epic which, begun two centuries before in a Hull warehouse, had soared to within a fatal proximity to the throne. Of them there would be no echo, although their dukedom was destined,

in other hands and in another generation, to repeat its
vain challenge to the monarchy.* But their royal blood
would continue to haunt the Courtenays, sending one of
them to the block under Henry VIII and another, after
fifteen years in the Tower, into exile under Mary. Uneasy
lay the head that might have worn a crown.

But no more uneasy than the crowned head itself. The
futility of the Yorkist attempts to engineer revolution should
not lead us to underestimate their seriousness as a problem.
The government of Henry VII was but poorly equipped
to meet the challenge of arms. To attacks from abroad the
sea offered a natural obstacle, but hardly more. Englishmen might brag about their 'wall', but a wall so thinly
manned afforded scant protection; it had not kept out
Henry himself, and neither Lincoln nor Warbeck found
much difficulty in crossing it. Henry was certainly to show
himself sea-minded both in his creation of a miniature
fleet and in his encouragement of the maritime activity
which yielded ships and seamen for naval operations on a
larger scale. But it was left to his son to build upon these
foundations a royal navy capable of making good the English
Herald's boast that his master was 'lord of the sea'. Puny
at sea, the early Tudor monarchy was not much stronger
on land. We have with us still, in the Yeomen of the Guard,
a living memorial to Henry VII's establishment of the first
permanent military force in England. But a corps which in
peace-time never exceeded two hundred and fifty men,
however valuable as a safeguard against a *coup de main*, was
a meagre addition to a military power which for the rest
consisted of a few tiny garrisons at home and the more
substantial, but largely immobile, forces stationed in Ireland and at Calais. Nor did the professionalization of war,
that notable contribution of the age to a shifting balance

* See below, pages 165–6.

of power both within states and between them, make itself
felt either so early or so markedly in England as on the
Continent. Henry VII was soon to become wealthy
enough to have taken into his pay one of those mercenary
armies with which Europe abounded, but prudence and
parsimony alike counselled him to keep this form of
aggrandisement, and of expenditure, down to a minimum.
The development of artillery was certainly a matter of
interest to Henry, and still more to his son. But, again,
gunpowder was no atomic bomb revolutionizing warfare
at a stroke, and the cannon which from this time began
to figure in armouries and weapon-statements doubtless
looked more impressive there than they did in the field.

The defence of the realm therefore rested, not with a
professional army and navy disposing of a specialized
technique, but with the whole of its male citizenry using
such weapons, and such skill in handling them, as could
be acquired in the intervals of earning a living. Then, as
now, every able-bodied man was required, when called
upon, to fight for his king and country. But whereas today
no one may possess firearms without a licence, everyone
was then obliged by law to have weapons ready for use in
an emergency. The national weapon was, of course, the
longbow. The bow was no longer the queen of the battlefield, but for the swift and silent propulsion of death to man
or beast the steel-tipped arrow was still without an equal.
It was with dismay, therefore, that the Tudors observed the
waning of interest and skill among their subjects in 'the feat
and exercise of shooting in long bows', and by statute and
proclamation they strove to check a decline which seemed
to threaten national security. But if the defence of the
realm demanded universal preparedness to fight, the peace
of the realm called for control of the resulting military
'potential'. 'Nothing, perhaps, can govern a nation of armed

citizens,' wrote the moral philosopher Paley, 'but that which governs an army – despotism'; and nothing could have governed an English nation whose every male citizen was capable of being turned at short notice into a soldier but what we know as the Tudor Despotism. The keystones of the many-arched temple of the Tudor Peace were the noblemen and gentlemen of the kingdom. The feudal obligation under which these magnates had once held their lands, the obligation to furnish the king with troops, was now more formal than real, but they still enjoyed, with their estates, that command over men which made them indispensable to the mobilization and governance of the nation's armed strength. During the fifteenth century this 'bastard feudalism' had got completely out of hand, and local military followings, instead of forming subsidiaries of a national defence system, had developed into private armies which held different parts of the country, and at times the whole kingdom, in their thrall. The problem before Henry VII was how to suppress the magnates' abuse of their power while preserving the power itself. He could no more do without a ruling class than he could do with a class that refused to be ruled; and an aristocracy which had learned to obey must not have forgotten how to command. The two instruments by which this military aptitude could be harnessed to the national need were the commission of array and the signet letter. The commission of array was normally used for home defence: issued when an army was required to restore order or to repel invasion, it empowered a dozen or more of the notables in the counties concerned to raise the men needed and to conduct them to the scene of operations. For expeditionary forces, or for exceptional emergencies at home, the signet letter, a personal summons to a magnate to recruit among his own followers, was generally used. The levies thus mustered and

officered saw plenty of service during the first years of
Tudor rule. Between 1485 and 1497 Henry VII issued
eleven commissions of array, and the men of twenty-six
counties were embodied, many of them more than once.
It was the men of the Eastern Counties who won the hard-
earned victory of Stoke in 1487, and in 1489 and again in
1491 the Midlanders were called out to suppress local
insurrections in Yorkshire.

But it was the crowded year 1497 which put the severest
strain on the government's resources. In the spring the
King's best commander, Daubeny, set about gathering an
army for the invasion of Scotland, and his preparations
were already well advanced when rebellion suddenly
flared up in Cornwall. The two things were connected,
for it was resentment at the taxation imposed for the
Scottish enterprise which stung the county most remote
from Scotland into revolt. Led by a combination of brawn
and brain – a blacksmith and a lawyer – to which, as they
passed through Somerset, they added the blue blood of a
noble recruit, James Lord Audley, the rebels marched,
some 15,000 strong, right across Southern England as far
as Blackheath, on the outskirts of London – a striking
commentary this on the government's unpreparedness.
The Cornishmen had apparently hoped that Kent, a county
famed for turbulence (Jack Cade was still a lively memory),
would rise with them against the capital. But the Kentish-
men followed their magnates, Abergavenny and Cobham
(a cousin of Audley's), in supporting the government, and
they hemmed the Cornishmen in on the east while Henry
and Daubeny amassed a larger and better-equipped army
between the rebels and London. On 17 June the royal
forces attacked, and the Cornishmen's bows and bills
proved no match for the King's horsemen and cannon. By
midday the rebels had surrendered, and Henry made

his way back to London to receive the grateful homage of its citizens. The three leaders, Audley the peer, Flamank the lawyer, and Joseph the smith, were executed, but the mass of the rebels were, by an act of politic clemency, pardoned by proclamation and allowed to make their way back to their homes, farms, and mines. They had scarcely done so when Cornwall was thrown into fresh confusion by the arrival, early in September, of the impostor Perkin Warbeck, or, as he called himself, King Richard IV. It is eloquent of the disturbed state of the Duchy that ten days after he had landed Warbeck appeared before Exeter with 6,000 local adherents, and of their fighting spirit that, without siege-equipment, they breached one of the gates and penetrated some distance into the city. But the defenders thrust them out again, and the next day, after a half-hearted assault, the rebels moved off towards Taunton. Theirs was now a forlorn hope. The mock king's army began to melt away, while from all the neighbouring counties the nobility and gentry were obeying the real King's summons to join the advancing Daubeny. When the royal host was within twenty miles of him Warbeck bolted for the coast with sixty horsemen, leaving his rank and file to throw themselves on the royal mercy. The King was willing enough to avoid bloodshed, especially after the impostor himself was captured, and again there was only a small number of executions. Warbeck himself was put under that mild detention which his further attempts at escape were responsible for changing, first into closer confinement, and then into the hangman's noose. But the West Country kept its gallows empty at the cost of emptying its pockets, for during the next few years it had to pay some thousands of pounds in fines; and over half a century was to pass before Devon and Cornwall were again minded to indulge in the ruinously expensive game of rebellion. Even Exeter, whose loyalty the King rewarded with the sword and cap of maintenance which remain to this day the city's most precious insignia, must have found Henry's stay of nearly a month there, while he was restoring order, a burdensome honour.

The Tudors' lack of a standing army was matched by their lack of a civil service. The century of their rule was indeed to see the emergence of a professional governing class at the centre. But in the field of local government – and that was relatively a much wider one than today – Henry VII and his successors had to rely almost exclusively upon the part-time services of amateur administrators. To bear a share in the service of the community was as much a part of the ordinary Englishman's (although, as we have seen, not of the ordinary Englishwoman's) duty as to bear arms in its defence. Within each unit of local government – manor, parish, township, hundred or shire – there were offices to fill, juries to man, returns to make, taxes to collect, and all competent citizens were expected to take a share in these tasks. At the top Tudor rule might savour of despotism, but at the bottom it rested upon a broad basis of self-government; and under kings who were masters of their craft the English people went on quietly serving their long political apprenticeship. Both the despotism and the self-government were tempered, however, by a strong infusion of the aristocratic principle. The civil counterpart of the commission of array was the commission of the peace. The device of replacing an individual officer, the sheriff or coroner, by a committee, the conservators or justices of the peace, as the chief representative of the royal power in each county, dates from the fourteenth, or even from the twelfth, century. But the J.P., if not born, certainly came of age under the Tudors, who saw in his office the ideal instrument for their purposes. Frequently renewed, the commission of the peace ran no risk of founding either an irremovable clique or an independent power; carrying but trifling remuneration, it cost practically nothing to operate; largely local in personnel, it exacted obedience, not through force, but through respect; and overwhelmingly aristocratic in complexion, it typified that attachment of political obligation to social advantage which lay close to the heart of Tudor political philosophy. Little wonder that the Tudors worked this admirable institution for all – and indeed for more than – it was worth. To the J.P.s' primary task of preserving local law and order, sovereign after sovereign, and parliament after parliament, were to add fresh duties bewildering in their variety and back-breaking in their volume. In time the Justices came to be the censors of practically every other local official or institution, from the sheriff to the village constable, as well as the executants of Tudor paternalism in the fields of economics, morals and manners. The expanding scope, and rising prestige, of the office were reflected in the number of treaties and hand-books relating to it. The first of these, *The Boke of Justyces of Peas*, was published in 1506, the most famous, the *Eirenarcha* of William Lambard, in 1581.

When Lambard wrote, the chief threat to the efficiency of the J.P. was the weight and complexity of his duties. 'How many Justices', he was moved to ask, 'may now suffice (without breaking their backs) to bear so many, not Loads, but Stacks of Statutes, that have been laid upon them?' But this state of affairs was the outcome of nearly a century of Tudor pressure, and the official who in the 1580s earned sympathy as a willing horse struggling with a gigantic burden had been in the 1480s both a less heavily laden and a less docile animal. Nothing was more sympto-matic of the political decay of the fifteenth century than the erratic performance of their duties by the J.P.s. It was a

Tudor task to strengthen this weak link in the chain of government by inculcating new standards of integrity and efficiency. Something could be done by greater care in the choice of persons to serve, and Henry VII probably gave more attention to these appointments than any king before or since. He certainly helped to make nomination to the commission of the peace the recognized first step in a gentleman's public career, and the competent discharge of its duties the condition of his further progress. But to say that in these and other ways the Tudor monarchy raised the level of its local representation is not, after all, to say very much; and Tudor local government probably owed its success less to its own improvement in quality than to the skill and forcefulness with which it was handled.

For there can be no doubt that to the question *Quis custodiet ipsos custodes*, who should govern the governing class? Henry VII found the almost perfect answer. It was an essentially personal answer, since it consisted of the King himself and the small group of men who, under him, wielded power in the kingdom. There was, of course, nothing original about making government the concern of a handful of individuals chosen for the purpose; practically all the systems of government which have ever existed, under whatever names, have in fact been run by such dominant groups, and the system which Henry VII inherited was certainly no exception. It was, moreover, within the framework of a medieval institution, the council, that Henry organized his own key-group. The novelty consisted, first, in his choice of persons. Henry could call upon any of his subjects to aid him with 'counsel', either individually or in company with others, and it is clear that he always did a great deal of business in the most informal way. But the process had long since become institutionalized, and in Henry's day there were two main types of deliberate assembly, distinguished from one another in point of size and frequency of meeting. The larger and less frequent was the body which, according to its composition, ranked either as a parliament or as a 'great council'. Of parliaments we shall have to speak later; but we may notice there that the great councils which met four or five times during Henry's reign were composed of those of his subjects – peers, ecclesiastics, judges and royal officials, and leading townsmen – then regarded as best qualified to advise and support the King. The smaller and more regular assembly owed its existence to the royal need for more frequent consultation and to the practice of using for that purpose a few of the people who together would have made up a great council. It was the body thus evolved which is known to history as the 'council'. But just as the council was the product of more frequent meetings of fractions of the great council, so those 'of the council' can be further subdivided into the small number who received regular and frequent summonses, and the majority who attended only once or twice, or at long intervals. The longer list, which contains, for the reign of Henry VII, upwards of 150 names, including practically all the nobility and most of the bishops and higher clergy, does little more than demonstrate the persistence of the idea that these two groups constituted the 'natural' advisers of the sovereign. Far more important is the list of the regular attendants. For these were Henry VII's counsellors *par excellence*, and it is their names which reveal the extent of his breach with the past. True, the ecclesiastics among them, without whom, in view of the Church's continuing preponderance in society and pre-eminence in learning, any such body would have been obviously incomplete, gave Henry's council a medieval air. But, as we shall see, even this apparent continuity concealed a real change. And, among the laymen, the change was both apparent and real. In place of the great nobles who had previously dominated the council, Henry drew his leading counsellors from men of lower rank and smaller fortune. The few dukes and earls whom he thus leaned upon owed the fact less to their titles than to their kinship or fidelity to the King. In any case, with scarcely an exception, they yielded in importance to such minor peers, knights or squires, as Cheyne or Dynham, Bray, Conway, Edgcumbe, Guildford or Poynings. Henry's dependence upon these 'new men', who in turn were wholly dependent upon him for their position and prospects, has long since become a commonplace in the appraisal of his government. It did not pass unnoticed at the time, and one of the items in Perkin Warbeck's proclamation of 1497 denouncing the Tudor 'usurper' was a list of the 'caitiffs' whom he had admitted to his counsels. Henry, for his part, did not forget the rewards which would encourage his servants to scoff at scoffers. Among his thirty-seven nominations to the Order of the Garter, which during his reign gained new lustre from the completion of its magnificent chapel at Windsor, there appear, beside those of the princes of the blood, foreign potentates, and English peers, the names of a dozen of his untitled counsellors.

Henry's unfettered choice of counsellors was matched by his absolute control of their activities. The council was entirely dependent upon him. It could do nothing of its own motion. Under a Henry VI this would have meant that the council did little or nothing; under a Henry VII it meant that there was little that the council did not do. In origin, and still pre-eminently, an advisory body, the Tudor council came to discharge an almost unlimited range of duties, legislative, judicial, executive. It issued proclamations having the force of law, and from time to time punished breaches of them. It could make treaties and receive foreign ambassadors, dispose of the armed forces, appoint or dismiss officials. It was the obvious body to superintend the work of local authorities, and it was for ever prodding J.P.s and the like into renewed bursts of activity. Most important of all, it interfered on the grand scale with the administration, or maladministration, of justice. The twin characteristics of the council – complete dependence upon the king and omnicompetence under him – were together responsible for its rapid proliferation. The monarch upon whom it depended was peripatetic in his habits, and some at least of his counsellors therefore had to move about with him. On the other hand, much of the council's business could best be done by a stationary, and thus more accessible, body, while the volume of business soon became so great that no one body, wherever located, could handle it all. Hence the early and continuing tendency of the council to develop sub-units, each answering to a particular need. The counsellors with the King became the 'council attendant', as distinct from those who remained at Westminster. Then there were regional requirements to be met. The two parts of Henry's kingdom which it was at once most necessary and most difficult to familiarize with the stern blessings of his rule were Wales with its Marches and the North. The remedy applied in both cases was the conciliar one. In the North Henry inherited, and in the Marches he was soon to create, the prototypes of the Councils bearing those names, which eventually came to perform on the spot nearly all the functions which the parent body went on performing from its southerly headquarters.

But it was the conjunction of the conciliar system with the administration of justice which produced the council's most celebrated offspring, the Court of Star Chamber. The medieval council had always enjoyed a jurisdiction distinct from and superior to that of the king's ordinary courts, the courts of common law; and it was this residuary jurisdiction, this right and obligation to do justice which the common law courts could not provide, or to undo injustice which they could not prevent, that furnished the Tudor council at once with its greatest task and its greatest opportunity. The measure of the task was the extent to which the common law courts, threatened from within by the creeping paralysis of formalism and dilatoriness, and from without by the lethal pressures of corruption and intimidation, were no longer capable either of dispensing justice between subject and subject or of enforcing obligations between subject and sovereign; and the measure of the opportunity was the prestige which would accrue to any institution which could set these wrongs right, could pull down the powerful law-breaker and raise up the humble law-abider, wherever the king's writ ran. It was that miracle of comprehensiveness and flexibility, his council, which enabled Henry VII to perform this greatest of contemporary political feats, and the secret lay in another of those bifurcations to which the council lent itself so easily. It was once believed that a statute created the Court of Star Chamber in 1487 just as a statute abolished it in 1641. But here, as elsewhere, Darwinism has prevailed, and a creative act has been superseded by an evolutionary process. The so-called Star Chamber Act is now seen to have been merely an incident in the gradual concentration of the judicial work of the council in the hands of its stationary members and the consequent crystallization of the meetings under the star-spangled ceiling of one of the chambers in the Palace of Westminster into the Court of Star Chamber, the busiest, most formidable, and most popular law-court in the kingdom.

It was the twenty or thirty men sitting at the hub of affairs in Council or Star Chamber, and the six or seven hundred J.P.s covering the country in petty and quarter sessions, who were, at their respective levels, the chief agents of royal power in the early Tudor State. They belonged to the continuously working parts of the governmental machine. By contrast, parliament was an institution which functioned, and indeed existed, only intermittently. It is true that during the early part of his reign Henry VII summoned parliaments with a frequency which promised to give those assemblies greater continuity; between 1485 and 1497 there were ten sessions, with an average duration of six weeks. But the remainder of the reign saw only one session, that of 1504. The inference is clear – Henry availed himself of parliament when he had a use for it, and ignored it when he had not. His early parliaments certainly helped to buttress his régime. The first, meeting within ten weeks of his accession, recognized him as king, ensured him the wherewithal to carry on the government, and proscribed the vanquished party. Its members, lords and commons, also gave individual pledges of good faith by forswearing those evil practices which had done so much to thwart the rule of his predecessors. Subsequent parliaments further strengthened Henry's hand. The measures of 1487 included, besides the Star Chamber Act, a statute – obviously inspired by Lincoln's treason – for the better unmasking of 'compassings, imaginations and confederacies' in high places. Various statutes reinforced the campaign against the evils of embracery, maintenance and liveries, which if unchecked would have brought most of his other reforms to nought, while hardly a session passed without some addition to the powers and duties of the J.P.s who, in their turn, were kept up to the mark by such forthright exposures of their shortcomings as the act of 1488. But Henry's parliaments did no more than he asked them to do. They forged the legislative weapons which he needed and, that done, they dispersed again. They gave him the tools, but it was he who finished the job.

After a peaceful realm, Henry wanted a prosperous one; and with this end in view, he and his parliaments made substantial additions to the code of national economic welfare which, originating in the fourteenth century, was to reach its apogee in the sixteenth. The leading measures of their reign sprang directly from that complex of changes, agrarian, industrial and commercial, which, as we have seen, itself reflected the quickening tempo of the nation's economic life. Such were the protectionist and bullionist statutes of 1487 against the export of unfinished cloth and precious metal and the financing of foreign trade by bills of exchange; the two acts of 1489–90 against enclosure, and their corollary, the act giving priority in the purchase of wool to the native cloth industry; the act of 1495 against usury, or the taking of interest upon loans; and that of 1497 fixing the fees charged by the Merchant Adventurers. Other statutes dealt with weights and measures, prices, wages, and vagabondage – the last three a portent of the shape of things to come. It would be as easy, and as erroneous, to erect these measures into a conscious and coherent programme of economic reorientation, inspired by Henry's resolve (in Bacon's famous phrase) to bow 'the ancient policy of this estate from consideration of plenty to consideration of power', as to dismiss them as a miscellany of empty manifestoes, indefensible in theory and unenforceable in practice. Rather, these statutes are to be looked upon as the first strivings of that young Leviathan, the early Tudor State, to grapple with forces which gained in strength from its own existence and success; and few of the many paradoxes of the period are more penetrating than that which points to Tudor political mastery as a prime cause of Tudor economic ineptitude.

By the year 1497, that significant half-way mark of his reign, Henry VII had accumulated all the statutory powers that he needed, and, with the simultaneous defeat of the last armed challenge to his throne, he was free to apply himself to the satisfyingly humdrum task of making his system work ever more smoothly. He could also go on making it pay ever more handsomely. Henry VII was incomparably the best business man to sit upon the English throne. Beginning his reign, as is the lot of pretenders, in debt to his backers, he pinched and scraped his way, first to solvency, then to affluence, and finally to wealth beyond the dreams of any avarice less superlative than his own. A king who, after punctually repaying his own early loans, went on to amass enough money to cover his expenses, lay up a fortune in plate and jewels, and lend large sums to fellow sovereigns, needy nobles and enterprising merchants, such a one was as novel a spectacle in the England, and the Europe, of the time as a king who, without either an army or a bureaucracy, exacted an unsurpassed obedience from his subjects. Henry VII was the better able to do each of these things because he could do them both. Royal poverty had been both a prominent cause, and a major penalty, of the political troubles which he had set himself to surmount, and Henry knew that if he would have his way he must also pay his way. Here, as elsewhere, it was the early years which were decisive. Henry promptly put an end to the insidious evil of alienation, by which royal lands (and the income which they represented) had been passing from the Crown to its subjects, and replaced it by a vigorous campaign of resumption, which brought them back again. To the lands thus recovered he added the wide estates of attainted opponents and victims of his régime. The 'feudal incidents' of homage, wardship and marriage, now simply a form of land-tax, he enforced with a thoroughness which defied evasion, and the privilege of declining knighthood he sold to landowners at an 'improved' rate. The customs duties known as 'tunnage and poundage' yielded Henry an income which grew with commercial expansion and the administration of justice a profit which grew with its enhanced efficiency. The Star Chamber, with its heavy mulcts (not, however, always levied in full), was a particularly good money-maker, and such lapses of allegiance as Devon and Cornwall's in 1497 were redeemed by crushing fines. But Henry's flair for bringing money in was, if anything, eclipsed by his skill in preventing too much of it from flowing out again. His predecessors had recognized the need for a more flexible instrument than the antiquated and stereotyped Exchequer. Henry VII went further and fashioned such an instrument in the new office of the King's Chamber. By diverting from Exchequer to Chamber a mounting tide of revenue, including all the new revenues from land; by appointing as its Treasurer one of his most trusted servants; and not least by checking and signing almost every page of the accounts himself, Henry came to exercise over the royal finances a control to which English history shows no parallel. Indeed, we may well feel that these columns of figures, each subscribed with the initial 'H', are the most eloquent memorial to that infinite capacity for taking pains which made the first of the Tudors the most uniformly successful of English kings, and a millionaire into the bargain.

A demise of the Crown commonly points the contrast between age and youth, and the succession to Henry VII was no exception. The thirty-four years' difference in age between the two Henrys who on 21 April 1509 were both King of England was the difference between a wizened and toothless old man and a handsome and lusty young one. But father and son were separated by more than their years.

At eighteen the elder Henry Tudor had been a refugee in Brittany; between him and the throne there lay ten years of frustration and hardship, and beyond the twenty-four of ceaseless calculation which were the reward of victory. The younger Henry looked back from his eighteenth year upon a boyhood of even tenor and unbroken security. For the last seven years he had been the heir apparent, a position which, if it focused upon him his father's solicitude, also brought him the flatteries of all who shared the national weakness for worshipping the rising, to the neglect of the setting, sun. Henry VII was the man who, starting from next to nothing, had built up a great family business, but whose head remained conspicuously unturned and whose habits substantially unaltered by success. Henry VIII, inheriting a flourishing concern, was to display traits characteristic of second generations. He spurned the drudgery of the office-stool and aspired to cut a figure in the world. Young, virile and handsome, he coveted honour and glory; the business which paid for it all he was content to leave to expert, but subordinate, management. It is in some such terms that we shall seek to explain the striking contrast between the politics of the years before, and of the years after, 1509. Down to 1509 one man alone holds the stage, the King; after 1509 there will be two, a King and a Minister, and at times the Minister may appear greater than the King. Certainly, both will far outshine the unpretentious figure who has made way for them. Again, the new reign will bring a notable shifting in the centre of political interest, from England to the Continent, from state-building to diplomacy and war. The struggle for supremacy at home will yield place to the struggle for power abroad; Stoke and Blackheath will be followed by Thérouenne and Flodden, royal progresses through English shires by vast expeditions to the Continent, the homely dignity of parliaments by the flamboyance of the Field of Cloth of Gold.

If Henry VIII had died before he was forty, perhaps of that sweating sickness which killed several of his intimates in the summer of 1528, his reign might well have gone down as one of the Great Betrayals of English history. For during his first twenty years Henry did little enough to add to, or even to conserve, his heritage of power, and he can take small personal credit for the fact that it was able to meet the heavy drafts which he drew upon it. True, the most obvious of Henry's failures during these years, his failure to beget an heir, cannot be laid at his door. For his marriage in 1510 to Catherine of Aragon was a piece, not of his own, but of his father's, statecraft. Catherine was the widow of his brother Arthur, and it was the grasping Henry VII who had determined to retain the Spanish alliance, and the Spanish dowry, which she brought with her to that brief marriage, by betrothing her to Henry. Seldom has greed been more grievously punished. Loyal, courageous, and warm-hearted, Catherine was to prove, until he sickened of her, an excellent wife to Henry in nearly every way save the one that mattered. Within five years of their marriage she had borne five children, only one of whom survived as long as two months. And when in February 1516 she was delivered of her only normally healthy child, it chanced to be a female. The toss of Nature's coin, which in humbler circumstances or humaner times has often enough bred disappointment, was tinged for Tudor queens with tragedy; and the sex of Henry's first surviving offspring was to prove as fatal to Catherine's hold on the queenship as that of his second to her successor's hold on life itself. The birth of the Princess Mary was followed by further miscarriages, and each year made it more evident that the Queen would never produce a prince to

displace the heiress presumptive. Whatever the cause –
and where contemporaries saw the hand of the Deity our
own age looks for evidence of disease – the result was un-
deniably alarming. For a king without an heir portended
a kingdom without a king, and without a king the kingdom
would surely perish. Henry was certainly to move mountains in the averting of this peril. But that was only after he
had gratuitously darkened the outlook still further by his
extra-marital diversions. The reputed boast of Henry's old
age, that he had never spared a woman in his lust, was
perhaps as far from the truth as its demonstrably false
counterpart, that he had never spared a man in his anger.
But from soon after his accession, and despite (or was it
because of?) his father's strictness in the matter, Henry
began to make use of that *droit de signeur* which in fact if
not in theory formed part of his royal prerogative. There
was the young French girl whom he made his page during
his first trip to France; there was Elizabeth Blount; there
was Mary Boleyn. Is it a measure of Henry's limited endowments that these successive unions produced only one child?
But it was a male child, and in the circumstances its
solitariness spelled, not safety, but danger. The King
certainly advanced his son exactly as he would have done
his heir. Christened Henry, the boy was created in turn a
Knight of the Garter and Duke of Richmond (his grandfather's title), appointed to high office, and given precedence even of the Princess Mary. Clearly, if the King were
to die without an heir, his bastard son would be a strong
candidate for the throne. Equally clearly, his widow would
fight like a lion for her daughter's claim. The net result
of Henry's luckless marriage and reckless liaisons might
well be a succession struggle in which the fruits of Henry
VII's painful husbandry would be trampled underfoot by
warring factions. And there was in this not merely short-

sighted folly, but blind injustice. Henry VII had sacrificed noble lives to a succession which he did nothing to compromise. But Henry VIII went on sacrificing lives to a succession which his own conduct was simultaneously serving to confuse. So it was that he had Suffolk executed in 1513 and Buckingham in 1521. To the demands of his dynasty Henry was to show himself, as time went on, ready to sacrifice anything and anybody; to those, or any other, demands he had yet to show the slightest readiness to sacrifice himself.

If Henry's amorous propensity boded ill for the future, his martial ambition laid a heavy burden upon the present. The ambition itself is understandable enough. War was the sport of kings, and a sovereign who revelled in manly contests of all kinds could not resist the most honourable and exciting of them. There was, too, abundant incentive. The whole of Henry's reign of thirty-eight years was to fall within the period which history has labelled the 'Age of the Italian Wars'. Italian in origin, these wars were European in scope and well-nigh continuous in character. They were waged by the two greatest powers of the age, the Spanish and Imperial House of Habsburg and the French House of Valois, and their prize – never secured by either side – was the mastery of the Continent. The minor states perforce arranged themselves under one or other of the banners, and a Europe divided into two camps trembled in an unstable equilibrium. If Henry needed any further stimulus to martial adventure, it was provided by the accession, within ten years of his own, of two other youthful rulers, Francis I of France and Charles V of Spain and the Holy Roman Empire. The new monarchs incarnated the belligerence of their New Monarchies. Between Henry and Francis, in particular, there developed a personal rivalry which was to dominate their thirty years' relationship. For

it was with Spain, and against France, that England normally aligned herself throughout the early Tudor period. No
arbitrary choice this, dictated by the whim of the prince,
but one imposed by national needs and feelings. While
enmity towards France was kept alive by the retention of
Calais, by the vain attempt to preserve or recover the
independence of friendly Brittany, and by France's more
successful support of hostile Scotland, the new-found
friendship with Spain, rooted in a common antagonism to
France, was strengthened by economic ties, and above all
by the growing commercial intimacy with the King of
Spain's dominions in the Netherlands.

Henry VIII owed his Spanish alliance, like his Spanish
wife, to his father. But whereas Henry VII had looked to it
to strengthen his power at home, Henry VIII saw in it a
lever for raising his prestige abroad. The first Tudor had
engaged in only one Continental war, that war with France
which he had brought to a lustreless, but lucrative, end at
Étaples in 1492. The second was to fight, during his first
twenty years, two wars with France, and with France's
ally Scotland, and one with the Emperor. The war of
1512–14 certainly brought England renown such as she had
not enjoyed since Agincourt. On 16 August 1513 the Anglo-
Imperial army which, under Henry himself and the
Emperor Maximilian, was besieging the French frontier
town of Thérouenne, won the brilliant cavalry action
known as the 'Battle of the Spurs'. Three weeks later (9
September) the Earl of Surrey, the King's septuagenarian
general in the North, gained the tremendous victory of
Flodden Field over the invading Scots. The naval war also
had its spectacular episodes, and although some of them,
like Howard's impetuous attack on Brest, ended in defeat,
there was solid ground for satisfaction in the English fleet's
mastery of the Channel. But as a brilliant morning sky is

often overcast by noon, so the sun was soon to fade from English arms. When war came again in 1522, the younger Surrey gained no second Flodden while holding the Scots in check, and Suffolk achieved nothing with the largest expeditionary force to leave England for a century. It was the Emperor's turn to startle Europe by destroying a French army and capturing the French King at Pavia (1525). Henry's third war, the war of 1528–9, was waged in alliance with France against the Emperor. The fighting was confined to Italy, and for England it was purely an economic war, which entailed, as we shall see, serious economic loss.

Fewer victories meant smaller spoils. The Battle of the Spurs had gained for Henry the great fortress of Tournai, which France bought back in 1518 for 600,000 crowns. This was the game of war as Henry VII had played it, with his 750,000 crowns' worth of indemnity at Étaples. By contrast, Suffolk's futile record in 1523 was echoed in the failure to obtain, at the peace of 1526, anything save 'peace with dishonour', while from the war of 1528 the country had to get out on the best terms possible. But the costs of war did not fall with its profits; and they were responsible for thrusting a monarch who had inherited the greatest of royal fortunes swiftly and inexorably towards bankruptcy. Henry's first war absorbed his father's treasure and large parliamentary grants as well, his second called for still heavier taxation, and his third struck at the sources of wealth by paralysing the nation's industry and trade. What a contrast with the financial prudence of the previous reign! It is true that Henry VIII, after ostentatiously repudiating his father's methods by throwing to the shorn lambs those fleecers-in-chief Empson and Dudley, proceeded to maintain and even to increase the efficiency of the revenue-collecting machine. Lands, wardships, knighthoods, profits of justice, and the rest, yielded a mounting income, and the Chamber continued its expansionist career. But whereas Henry VII had used these things to make himself financially secure, Henry VIII was forced, after exploiting them to the full, to raise further huge sums from his subjects. The result was the unedifying spectacle of a government whose demands were obstructed in parliament and resisted in the country. There was some difficulty in extracting from the Parliaments of 1512–15 the balance of the cost of the first war. The Parliament of 1523, asked to foot the entire bill for the second, proved much more stubborn. Despite Sir Thomas More's skilful Speakership of the Commons, it took the unprecedented total of one hundred days to induce the Members to consent to part of the government's proposals. But the climax came in 1525, when the ludicrously misnamed 'Amicable Grant', an extension to the poorer classes of the 'benevolences' earlier levied upon the wealthy, threw the peasants of Kent, East Anglia, Lincolnshire and Huntingdonshire into a frenzy of resistance which provoked nervous comparison with the Peasants' Revolt then raging in Germany and revived searing memories of the Great Revolt of 1381. The men of Kent put the matter in a nutshell when they told Archbishop Warham that after all his wars the King 'hath not one foot of land more in France than his most noble father had, which lacked no riches or wisdom to win the kingdom of France if he had thought it expedient'. Before the threat of rebellion the government fell back, as it was bound to do, upon its greatest subjects. The Dukes of Norfolk and Suffolk helped to pacify their titular counties, the centre of the most violent agitation. And, as it was no less bound to do, the government withdrew the tax, and abandoned the campaign which it was to have financed.

The contrast between the Tudor monarchy in 1525, bent upon a glittering triumph but with a treasury bare of gold, and the same monarchy twenty years before, certain that no triumph could glitter half so convincingly as its own golden hoard, was ultimately the contrast between the two men who successively wore the crown. But it owed something to the influence of a third man, who in 1505 had been on the threshold, and in 1525 was nearing the end, of a career unique in English history. Thomas Wolsey served for nearly twenty years as the general manager of the great concern which Henry VII had built up and which the young Henry VIII had neither the temperament nor the experience to direct in person. During the first year or two of the new reign it had seemed not impossible that a board of directors might take control, composed of such leading counsellors as Fox, Warham, Surrey, Poynings and Lovell. But Wolsey quickly cast them all into the shade, and from 1512 it was clear that the principle of personal rule, firmly established by the old King, was also to prevail under the new. This was, from the constitutional standpoint, the capital decision. It meant that the King would exercise his office by deputy, not put it into commission. And, however powerful the deputy, his power would be all the King's. Instead of a council or committee, which might, in acquiring corporate responsibility, also begin to acquire corporate independence, there was to be a minister raised to supreme power by the King but remaining absolutely dependent upon him. This was the position which Wolsey achieved within three years of Henry's accession and which he held unchallenged during the next seventeen years of the reign. It was a position which no man could have attained, much less held for so long, who had not both consummate ability and colossal driving-power. 'He is,' wrote the Venetian ambassador of Wolsey in 1519, 'very handsome, learned, and indefatigable. He alone transacts the same business as that which occupies all the magistracies, offices, and councils of Venice, both civil and criminal; and all state affairs likewise are managed by him, let their nature be what it may ...' Wolsey made of his chief secular office, that of Chancellor, which he attained in 1515, an instrument similar to that which Metternich was later to wield in the Austrian, or Bismarck in the German, Empire. He concentrated political power, and the responsibility for its exercise, to a degree without parallel in English history, and his biography, between the ages of thirty-nine and fifty-seven, approximates to a history of England from 1512 to 1529.

Yet during these seventeen years Wolsey did nothing which can compare in creative significance with what Henry VII had done during the twenty-four years of his reign or what Henry VIII was to do in the remaining seventeen years of his. At home Wolsey's administration was a period of much promise, little performance. A first-rate administrator, he projected more reforms in the machinery of state than he carried through, and the English government at his departure was not substantially different from what it had been at Henry VII's. Nor did he consistently exploit his monopoly of power to any great national purpose. During his early years Wolsey did labour earnestly at tasks which would have earned Henry VII's approval. He taught the great ones of the land the 'new law of the star chamber', fining and imprisoning right and left for riots and retainers; he encouraged the small ones to bring their unredressed complaints to that other judicial novelty, the Poor Men's Court, or Court of Requests, where they found speedy and inexpensive justice. His greatest single effort at thwarting that 'conspiracy of rich men procuring their own commodities' which More diagnosed in early Tudor (and Marx rediscovered in early Victorian) England was his campaign against large-scale enclosure, a campaign in which he was to have but one emulator during the century. Had Wolsey stuck to his legal last, he, too, might have achieved a reformation. But the solid gains of these years, which won high praise from old governmental hands like Warham and Fox and shrewd critics like More and Erasmus, he sacrificed to the pursuit of shadows abroad, and the 'many great gifts' which More saw in him he prostituted to his insatiable pride and ambition.

But to express Wolsey's power simply in political terms is to miss half the significance of his extraordinary career, just as to concentrate, as we have so far done, upon the politics and economics of early Tudor society is to paint only half a portrait. For Wolsey was not only the viceroy of a King, he was the deputy of a Pope, and the England of his day did not live by bread and governance alone, but by the Word of God as Latinized by his Church. It is to the place of that Church in early Tudor England, and to the story of its displacement by Henry VIII, that we must now turn.

III

SUCCESSION AND SUPREMACY

THE most obvious way of measuring the difference in scale between organized religion in pre-Reformation England and in the England of our own day is to compare the number of people enrolled in its service. In 1951 there was one Anglican clergyman for every 2,200 of the adult population, and perhaps one priest or minister of any denomination for every 1,400. On the eve of the Reformation there may have been one cleric for every fifty, and there was almost certainly one for every hundred, of the adult population. A city such as York, with 10,000 inhabitants, then had 500 clergy; present-day York has 90,000 inhabitants and perhaps 150 ministers of religion. But such figures, if they are not to mislead, must be tested for their comparableness. Today the designation 'clergyman' carries an occupational as well as a sacerdotal meaning; most of those who bear it spend their lives, and earn their livings, in a particular way. Not so with the pre-Reformation cleric. Many of his kind were men in minor orders who engaged in secular occupations and had no intention of becoming priests or exercising the priestly function. Again, the ordinary parish priest was often a small farmer, cultivating the thirty or forty acres of glebe-land belonging to his church, while the higher clergy were to be found in almost every occupation, public and private – they were secretaries, librarians, teachers, lawyers, authors, doctors, civil servants, diplomats, statesmen. The Church was, indeed, not one profession but the gateway to all professions. It still wielded a virtual monopoly of education, from the village school to the university, and its Latin was the passport to the civilized world. It occupied a leading place in every branch of human activity, political, economic, charitable, cultural. It rendered great services and received great rewards. And it distributed its rewards, if not by any means equally, at least with much less of an eye to the accidents of birth and breeding than did the secular world. The Church threw open to talents not one career but many; and up its ladder a Wolsey might climb from the depths to the stars.

But if the clergy were less of an occupational category, they were more of a caste. The priest was not as other men. Dispenser of divine grace, and officer of the international institution which was the repository of that grace upon earth, he lived his life under different rules from his lay fellows. Two things in particular set him apart: he was debarred from marrying, and he enjoyed a privileged status at law. Although only the regular clergy – monks, nuns and friars who lived under a Rule – took the vow of chastity, all clergy were subject to the canons of the Church, and these, despite occasional campaigns against the prohibition, forbade them to marry. The ban did not prevent large numbers of the clergy, from parish priests to Popes, from having concubines and begetting children, and it is open to question whether the Church did not lose more than it gained by its insistence upon celibacy. The Continental Reformers, from Luther onwards, were all certain that it did, and the Anglican Church, once freed from Henry VIII's conservatism in the matter, was to fall into line with them. Whatever may be thought of the effects of clerical marriage on the life of the Church, there can be no doubt of its value to the life of the nation; and pre-Reformation England could show nothing corresponding to the impressive catalogue of men and women who, since the

English parsonage has been permitted to house a family, have gone forth from it to win distinction in every field. Clerical 'nephews', like Wolsey's Thomas Winter, although often given a flying start, seldom stayed the course. The drawback of celibacy was offset by the privilege of legal immunity. Whereas the lay criminal was punished by the King's courts, the criminous clerk could only be handed over to his bishop to receive what was invariably lighter punishment. During the Middle Ages, it is true, 'benefit of clergy' had been stretched to cover almost anyone who could read, to the frustration of efficient and impartial justice. Henry VII's statute of 1489, by differentiating between those actually in orders and those not, tended to reduce the size of the problem, but at the cost of re-emphasizing its ecclesiastical character; it may even have encouraged the practice of taking minor orders mainly or merely to insure against the consequences of crimes which the individual might then be less fearful of committing. Wolsey made a half-hearted attempt to tackle the subject, but 'benefit of clergy' remained one of the scandals which the parliament of 1529 was to be summoned to reform.

Segregated from the laity by the conditions proper to their estate, the clergy were divided amongst themselves by deep gulfs of function, status and outlook. The lower strata included the parochial clergy who catered for the day-to-day needs of the living, the chantry priests who interceded for the souls of the departed, the friars who were the itinerant traders in spiritual wares, the monks and nuns wholly or partially withdrawn from the world ostensibly to pursue the contemplative life. It was in England's nine thousand parishes that her popular religious life was principally carried on, and our ancient churches, living witnesses to the parochial piety of our forbears, were then centres of an intense spiritual-cum-social community life. Foreigners regarded the English as a devout nation, and the restriction, at least in the countryside, of churchgoing to Sundays and holydays reflected, not the familiar modern contrast between weekdays and Sundays, but the difficulties of work and distance. Feasts and ales – bucolic equivalents of our bazaars and sales of work – and morality plays were regular parish occasions, as were the festivals which, whether pagan or Christian in origin, remained the landmarks in the farming year. Behaviour in church was as 'natural' as it was outside, and included much that we should find unseemly. But even this had its obverse: it flowed from that identification of religion and life which helped to purify life by vulgarizing religion. The lower clergy bore the stigmata of this identity. Living close to the soil, they shared the virtues and vices of the folk from whom they came and whose fortunes they shared. Few of them could have felt much zeal for a calling which few of them had chosen. Many were too ignorant to perform its duties competently. Some lived better lives, some worse, than those which were lived around them, but most of them probably conformed well enough to the accepted standards. If they were mercenary, it must be remembered that most of them were peasants, and that most of them were poor. They are to be regarded as the victims rather than the villains of pre-Reformation society.

The higher clergy present a very different picture. Where the rank and file were largely drawn from peasant stock, their superiors came increasingly from that 'middle class' of yeomen and small gentry, merchants and professional men, which was everywhere thrusting its way to the fore. The practice, so common on the Continent, of appointing noblemen and even royal persons to high office in the Church, while not unknown in England (Henry VIII, it is said, might have become an archbishop if he had not had to become a king), was never common here. It was ability, nurtured by a university education and ripened by legal or administrative experience, which carried off the prizes of the English Church. And glittering prizes many of them were. The two archbishoprics were each worth about £3,000 a year, the seventeen bishoprics ranged from perhaps £1,000 to £2,500 – large incomes in a society whose greatest landowner had about £6,000. Then there were the diocesan pyramids of deaneries, archdeaconries, canonries and prebends, and the rich benefices with enough of which a determined pluralist might net as much as a bishop; the highly complex, and highly lucrative, apparatus of ecclesiastical jurisdiction, with its monopoly of matrimonial, testamentary and eleemosynary affairs; and the mass of miscellaneous perquisites which in a largely priest-run, if not priest-ridden, society was bound to accrue to the possessory caste. To the people who had to pay for it all this prosperous hierarchy might well appear parasitical, and the service rendered incommensurate with the tribute levied. Its critics had long been saying so, and in the hands of the Reformers their charges would become a trumpet to smite the walls of this opulent Jericho. But we must remember, what they were inclined to forget, that in paying for its Church the community was paying for everything that its churchmen did, and that, as we have seen, was much more than was comprehended by even the wide contemporary connotation of religion. In particular, the community was contributing heavily, by way of its ecclesiastical, to the cost of its secular, government. For the rulers of the English Church were the servants of the English King, and it was because they served the King that they were allowed to rule the Church. The Crown used the large number of ecclesiastical appointments, including all the bishoprics, which were in its gift to pay the many clerics whom it employed. That was why, save in those cases, like Durham, where secular and ecclesiastical duties coincided in location, an early Tudor bishop was usually to be found anywhere but in his diocese. He might be attendant upon the King, or permanently stationed in London (where the leading bishops all had houses, commemorated in such street names as Ely Place and Winchester Square), or abroad upon an embassy; while if, as was not uncommon, he was a foreigner whose support the King had purchased with a see, he need never have set foot in England at all. The Crown had taken over the heads of the English Church long before it took over the Headship; and bishops who drew their pay from the Church but who earned it by service to the King were unlikely, when the piper played, to refuse to dance the royal measure.

It is against this background that we must set Wolsey's ecclesiastical career and ambitions. His rise to pre-eminence in the Church differed only in degree from that of other royal servants. Ordained priest in 1498, Wolsey was first dependent upon private patronage for his advancement. But in 1507 he became chaplain to Henry VII and in 1509 almoner and counsellor to Henry VIII. Political supremacy lifted Wolsey straight into the archiepiscopal class. He became in quick succession bishop of Lincoln and of the captured French town of Tournai, and then archbishop of York (1514). Canterbury, which he coveted, eluded him to the end, owing to Archbishop Warham's longevity, but in 1518 he got Bath and Wells, in 1523 Durham and in 1528 Winchester, and from 1521 he was also abbot of St Albans, the richest monastery in England. This combination of a province, a diocese and an abbey, together worth nearly £10,000 a year, would in itself have made Wolsey by far the richest man in the kingdom. But he heaped upon it his fees from Chancery, the profits of his legatine jurisdiction and of his administration of sees held by absentee foreigners, his pensions from foreign powers, and the gratuities showered on him by all those, great and small, who needed his favour. His total income, towards the end, was perhaps little short of £50,000 a year. This was the wealth which built his most permanent memorial, Hampton Court, and his three other palaces, and which sustained a magnificence that has passed into legend. But an archbishopric, especially the inferior one of York, was not the limit of Wolsey's ambition or achievement. In 1515 the Pope made him a Cardinal, and in 1518 Legate *a latere* or Papal Viceroy in England. This last dignity, hitherto of a temporary and extraordinary character, Wolsey received first for a term of years and finally for life. It made him as supreme over the English Church as Henry's favour made him over the English State, and he was soon superseding the traditional constitution of the Church by an autocracy as novel as it was unwelcome. But if in the secular field Wolsey did no more than wield the power which Henry VII had built up, in the ecclesiastical he did no more than build up the power which Henry VIII was to wield. Wolsey certainly shared the almost universal desire for reform, and there is no knowing what he might have achieved – and what he might have prevented Henry VIII from achieving – if he had bent himself to the task. He might have multiplied and remodelled the bishoprics and hacked a way through the jungle of canon law, reconstructed the universities as the prelude to a great educational drive, reincorporated in the national fabric a purged and reinvigorated monasticism, and burnished instead of breaking the bonds between England and Rome. All these things passed through Wolsey's intensely active mind, and some of them he set his hand to. But between the nature of his authority and its application to such ends there was a fundamental contradiction. The Church's greatest pluralist was not the man to suppress pluralism, its greediest money-maker not the man to stamp out avarice, its most arrogant upstart not the man to preach longsuffering and humility. The physician must have begun by healing himself; and there was no way out of this doctor's dilemma but the way of suicide.

Wolsey's career was to end, however, not in resignation but in dismissal; and it was not his failure to reform the Church but his failure to remarry the King which brought him down. From 1527 Henry VIII wanted one thing above all else from the Pope, a release from the marriage which could no longer give him an heir and freedom to marry his last mistress's sister, the young Anne Boleyn, who he was sure would do so. The 'Gospel light which dawned from Bullen's eyes' had begun to add its baneful gleam to the angry dawn of the Reformation. According to the notions of the time, Henry's request was not an unreasonable one, and the new Pope, Clement VII, had no doubt of his power to grant it. Wolsey was clearly the man to make the arrangements. But the subject who had been able to get almost everything for himself proved unable to get the one thing demanded by his sovereign. There was, of course, an obvious stumbling-block. The Pope was politically in the pocket of the Emperor Charles V, and Charles V was the nephew of the Queen whom Henry intended to abandon. Granted that the papal dispensation was essential to Henry's purpose, there were thus two courses open to him: to strike a bargain with Charles by which England would accept his control of Italy in exchange for his consent to the dissolution of the marriage, or to break that control and free the Papacy to dissolve the marriage in defiance of Charles. Left to himself Henry VIII might have followed the first course and reached his goal. He cared much more for Anne than for Italy, Charles much more for Italy than for Catherine, and on this basis a deal might have been done. But what to Henry was an open door was to Wolsey a closed one. Wolsey could not for a moment contemplate a solution which meant abandoning to Imperial control the institution from which he derived so much of his power and which he had always cherished the ambition of one day making his own. To Wolsey, as to Charles, the real struggle was for control of the Papacy, and it had to be fought to a finish.

It was this struggle which first broke Wolsey and then forced Henry to break with Rome. Its dreadful overture was the sack of Rome by the Emperor's army in May 1527, a deed in which Protestants saw the fall of Babylon and all Europe the start of a new Babylonish Captivity, with Clement VII the pawn of Spain as the Avignon Popes had been of France. Wolsey hurried abroad, made an alliance with France against Charles, and strove to extort, first from the Cardinals, and then, after his release from confinement, from the Pope himself, the powers necessary to the hearing of the marriage-suit in England, where the result would be a foregone conclusion and where even Charles' long arm would not be able to save his aunt. The wretched Pope turned this way and that, clutching at every expedient, but at length, in April 1528, with a French army carrying all before it in Italy, he commissioned Cardinals Wolsey and Campeggio (the latter an absentee bishop of Salisbury) to try the case in London. It was the nearest that Wolsey was to come to success in his desperate gamble. Everything now turned on the fortune of war, and war proved, as always, a fickle jade. By June Wolsey was forced to abandon his part in it because of its disastrous effects on trade and industry. By September the French army in Italy capitulated, and by the winter the Pope had resolved 'to live and die an Imperialist'. A final effort by

France in the spring of 1529 was beaten before it got under weigh, and in June the Pope made his peace with Charles at Barcelona and in August Francis I did the same at Cambrai. It was the end of Wolsey's hopes. It was the end of the Legatine Court. With every month bringing its suspension nearer, Campeggio had contrived to spin out the thread of its proceedings until the papal shears were ready to cut. Opened in May 1529, the court provided the nation with the unique spectacle of its King summoned before a tribunal set up in his own capital by a power other than his own. But it lives in the national memory as the platform from which an ill-used princess uttered that cry from the heart which, clothed with Shakespearean elegance, still speaks for all those who were called upon to suffer that the Tudor commonwealth should not perish.

Yet even Catherine had her hour. On 22 July it became known in London that the Pope had revoked the suit to Rome, and on the following day Campeggio, declaring that the court must adhere to the Roman legal calendar, adjourned it until October. His adversary supreme in Rome, his ally humbled, and himself about to be summoned before a foreign court – all these mortifications Henry owed to Wolsey, and Wolsey had to pay the penalty. On 9 October 1529 he was indicted in the Court of King's Bench under the Statute of Praemunire for alleged misdeeds in his legatine capacity. Given the option of answering either before that court or before Parliament, the Chancellor who had exalted Chancery over the common law, and the Legate who had denied the jurisdiction of lay courts over clerics, submitted himself to the judgement of the common law. That law duly condemned him, but its penalty of imprisonment and confiscation of goods was commuted to honourable retirement to his own house at Esher and a partial loss of property. Wolsey lost the Chancellorship but kept his Archbishopric. In December Parliament hurled an avalanche of accusations at him, but the King did not choose to punish him further; he might yet have need of that fertile brain. In April 1530 Wolsey went north to enter, for the first time, the province which had been his since 1514, and it was on the eve of his belated enthronement at York, six months later, that he was suddenly arrested. What the precise charges against him would have been we do not know, but they were doubtless connected with the obscure manoeuvrings by which he had been scheming to recover favour and power. He was not called upon to meet them, for he died at Leicester Abbey on his way south on 29 November 1530.

Wolsey paid the penalty not, as he claimed upon his deathbed, of having served his King better than his God, but of having served himself better than his King. None the less, he had served Henry VIII better than he could have known or claimed. Not only had he, by the herculean labours of close on twenty years, preserved inviolate the principle of one-man rule, he had also paved the way for that great extension of monarchical power which before his death Henry had begun to realize. Instead of hiding in the earth of a pedestrian prudence the talent of secular authority entrusted to his keeping, this royal servant had traded his talents abroad and with them earned the huge dividend of the legatine authority; and Wolsey's lord, although his gratitude compared ill with that of the parable, was to prove almost as quick to pocket both principal and interest as the man who travelled into a far country. Wolsey had done even more. By virtually domiciling the papal power in England he had rendered it so obnoxious to his fellow, or subject, clergy that they would regard the Royal Supremacy as the lesser evil; while by simultaneously inflating priestly power and flaunting priestly pomp, to a degree never before seen in England, he had ensured Henry the whole-hearted support of the laity for his programme of secularization. And it was to an institution which Wolsey hated, and which brought together the people, bishops and abbots, noblemen and well-to-do commoners, who most hated him, that Henry promptly turned to repair the colossal blunder of Wolsey's closing years. Within a fortnight of Campeggio's suspension of the Legatine Court, the writs went out for the most important of all the parliaments which have helped to make English history.

The first four sessions of the Reformation Parliament, which were spread over the two and a half years from November 1529 to May 1532, were designed to do three things: to mass the laity solidly behind the King, to overawe the clergy into acquiescence in his demands, and to frighten the Pope into yielding to them. The first two aims Henry completely achieved, the third he as completely missed. Parliamentary cooperation was enlisted from the start by the attack upon ecclesiastical abuses which Wolsey's lay successor as Chancellor, Sir Thomas More, foreshadowed in his opening speech, and which absorbed much of the first session. Nothing was better calculated to please the Commons than to be allowed, nay, incited, to vent their anti-clericalism, and they went to work with a will. By the end of the session three substantial reforms had been carried, a Mortuaries Act and a Probate Act limiting clerical fees for funerals and wills, and an act against the grosser forms of pluralism and non-residence. Thirteen months later (January 1531) Henry mustered his parliamentary forces again for the first major trial of strength with the Church. The two Convocations of the Clergy, meeting at the same time as Parliament, were confronted with nothing less than a threat of praemunire against the whole body of the clergy. Their offence lay in their recognition of that legatine authority which had brought Wolsey within the provisions of the statute of 1393, and the penalty incurred was imprisonment and loss of goods. It mattered not that, if the clergy had so offended, the King had offended even more, at least, it mattered not to this King or to the lawyers who acted for him. Only his pardon, enshrined in an act of parliament, could spare the clergy the consequences of their wrong-doing, and only a suitably large gratuity could evoke that act of grace. The example of Wolsey was more cogent than the exhortations of the Papal Nuncio, and both Convocations agreed to pay, Canterbury £100,000, York nearly £19,000. But when the pardon bill came before the Commons its restriction to the clergy provoked suspicion and criticism. Did not laymen stand in equal need of exoneration for their acquiescence in the legateship? After momentary hesitation, the King took the point, and a free pardon to the laity was embodied in a separate act. The next year, 1532, saw two more sessions, lasting for over one hundred days, and more aggressive legislation. Several acts further circumscribed 'benefit of clergy'. More important, the so-called 'Supplication against the Ordinaries', a catalogue of lay grievances against episcopal officials which, if inspired and even drafted by the government, found support readily enough in the Commons, gave Henry the excuse to bully Convocation into promising to make no fresh canons without his permission and to submit all existing canons to his scrutiny. But the big measure of this year was the Act of Annates, which reduced these commission fees to Rome to a mere five per cent (instead of the previous hundred) of the first year's income from ecclesiastical preferments and also arranged for the 'domestic' consecration of archbishops and bishops in the event of the requisite papal bulls being withheld. This hint of the shape of things to come was deftly worked into the pattern of the present. The Act was not to come into force for a year, and Henry was to spend that time seeking some amicable arrangement with the Pope. There could have been no clearer indication of its motive, to convince the Pope of the consequences of non-cooperation.

For three years Henry waged his 'cold war' with Rome. There was as yet no open breach. Papal relations with the English Church, and with the King himself, continued with scarcely any interruption. But to all Henry's attempts to secure a favourable decision in the great matter Clement VII, prompted by Charles V, turned a deaf ear. Early in 1530 an English embassy headed, oddly enough, by the father of Anne Boleyn, returned with nothing better than a writ citing Henry to appear before the Roman Court. In the course of the same year Clement took steps to counter the King's energetic canvassing of the universities of Europe in support of his thesis, politely but firmly rejected the round-robin which, at Henry's instigation, eighty magnates of the realm despatched to Rome, and replied with yet another *non possumus* to a direct approach by the King himself. During 1531 the outlook grew slowly, and during the early months of 1532 more rapidly, worse, with the Emperor trying to force a hostile decision in Rome and Henry carrying one after another of the ecclesiastical outworks in England. But when the fourth session of the great parliament ended in May 1532 the breach was still far from irreparable.

It had come much nearer to being so when the fifth session opened in the following February. The turning-point can be placed with fair certainty in the autumn of 1532. On 1 September Henry created Anne Boleyn Marquess* of Pembroke and settled upon her £1,000 a year in

---

*Not Marchioness as is often stated. Anne was to enjoy the dignity in her own right.

land. It was the public registration of a private bargain and sale. For six years Anne had done what no other individual or institution in the country could do, she had balked Henry of what he wanted. Now, choosing her moment with the exquisite skill which the ages would extol in her daughter, she gave it to him. Before the year was out she was with child. Few pregnancies have been so doom-burdened as this one, and Anne Boleyn's child was to wield from the womb a coercive power greater than it was ever to wield in the world. For if this child were to be the answer to Henry's, and the nation's, prayer, it must be born in wedlock; and that meant unmaking one marriage and making another within the seven or eight months which would elapse before its birth. No question now of further futile manoeuvrings at Mantua or at Rome. The thing must be done quickly and it must be done in England. Archbishop Warham's death in August, which had helped to time Anne's decision, paved the way for the management of its consequence. In November Henry recalled from Italy the forty-three-year old (and twice-wedded) cleric whose tireless championship of the King's cause had earned him the succession to Canterbury, and Thomas Cranmer set his hand to the plough which was to cut the fateful furrow of schism. In January 1533 Henry and Anne were secretly married, and simultaneously Rome was asked to issue the eleven bulls requisite for Cranmer's promotion. The motive behind the appointment was an open secret, and a more resolute Pope might have rejected the application and the small sum in lieu of annates which accompanied it, and driven Henry to resort to the revolutionary method of making an archbishop forecast in the recent act. But the bulls were forthcoming with unusual speed, were rushed to England, and in March Cranmer was consecrated in traditional fashion. What might have proved, with a man of greater – or less – devotion to his ideals, an even bigger difficulty, the oath of fidelity and obedience which Cranmer had to take as a condition of receiving the papal blessing, was got over, or got round, by his prior construction of this oath as in no way inhibiting him from the work which he had been promoted to do.

Upon an archbishop thus vested with all the powers which a Pope could bestow, there now had to be conferred another, and inimical, power by a parliament. The conferment of this power, by the statute 'For the restraint of Appeals', was the main item of the session of February–April 1533. It was, as we shall see, a statute remarkable for the scope of its theoretical claims. On the practical plane, which is what concerns us here, the Act against Appeals provided that henceforth in spiritual suits appeals should lie, not to Rome, but to the Archbishop of Canterbury or, in cases touching the King, to the Upper House of Convocation. Already Convocation, acting as a kind of grand jury, was in process of returning a true bill against the Aragon marriage, and the way was clear for the Archbishop to exercise his new jurisdiction. On 8 May he opened proceedings in the decent obscurity of Dunstable. Queen Catherine, only four miles away at Ampthill, ignored a summons to appear, and was pronounced contumacious by a court which could have felt nothing but relief at being spared the embarrassment, or worse, of her intervention. On 23 May the Archbishop pronounced the marriage null from the beginning. Five days later its successor was declared lawful, and on 1 June Anne Boleyn was crowned Queen of England. After more than six years during which he had thought of little else Henry had got his way. Anne Boleyn was, at least to his own satisfaction and with his own kingdom's consent, his lawful wife and queen, and her child would be his heir. Three months more had to pass before Henry, and the world, knew that, as far as this child was concerned, it was all wasted effort. The infant born on 7 September 1533 was a girl. She was given the Yorkist name of Elizabeth. Only if Nature could have held the mirror up to Art, and the real Cranmer have possessed the prophetic eye of his Jacobean simulacrum*, might the King have felt less regret at his misfortune and the new Queen less despondency at hers.

The series of swift moves which had brought to a close the first phase of the Henrician Reformation was also the starting-point of its second. The quickened tempo communicated itself to Rome, where in July the annulment of the Aragon, and contraction of the Boleyn, marriage were alike declared invalid, Cranmer and his fellow judges excommunicated, and Henry VIII given a month's warning of the same penalty. Eventually the King's sentence was pronounced in September and published in the Netherlands, the nearest 'safe' territory to England, in November. Henry replied to this papal declaration of war with the legislation of the winter of 1533–4, which severed the remaining links with Rome and made the Church of England as independent of the Pope as the Crown of England was independent of the Emperor. The principle of national self-sufficiency had already been asserted in the Act against Appeals, in whose preamble it was trumpeted that 'this realm of England is an empire ... governed by one supreme head and king ... unto whom a body politic, compact of all sorts and degrees of people, divided in terms and by names of spiritualty and temporalty, be bounden and ought to bear, next to God, a natural and humble obedience', and the wearer of its imperial crown 'institute and furnished, by the goodness and sufferance of Almighty God, with plenary whole and entire power pre-eminence authority

*King Henry VIII, Act V, Scene IV.

93

prerogative and jurisdiction to render and yield justice and final determination to all manner of folk ... in all causes ... without restraint or provocation to any foreign princes or potentates'. But it required the measures of January–March 1534 to make this sonorous boast a reality. There were four of them. A new Annates Act forbade the introduction of any bulls or briefs from Rome or the payment of any first-fruits there; in default of these indispensable incidents of papal preferment, archbishops and bishops were in future to be elected by deans and chapters after nomination by the king, and instead of an oath of fidelity to the Pope they were to take before consecration an oath of fealty to the crown. The Act against Papal Dispensations transferred, under certain safeguards, to the Archbishop of Canterbury the dispensing power formerly exercised by the Pope, and abolished the payment called Peter's Pence, and all others, hitherto made to Rome. Another act declared it no longer heretical to inveigh against the 'bishop of Rome or his pretended power'. And finally the Act for the Submission of the Clergy gave statutory force to the control of convocations and canons which the King had enjoyed since 1532.

Papal Supremacy had been repudiated in principle before it was destroyed in fact; Royal Supremacy had become a fact before it was erected into a principle. Practically everything which the legislation of 1529–34 had taken away from the Pope – jurisdiction, prerogatives, revenues – it had given or would give to the King or to institutions dependent upon him. The law gave what the law had taken away, and blessed in the King's sight was this rain of the law. But the powers which Parliament had rained upon the King, or, to put it more accurately, the powers which the King-in-Parliament had declared himself to possess, he had taken unto himself as King. If Henry had only had Parliament to consider he might have been content to let it remain so. It was his relationship with that other parliament, the Convocation of the Clergy, which convinced him of his need for another garb than the robe of majesty; and it was this need which he satisfied with the notion, and the name, of the Supreme Headship. The title had first been used officially in the document which, with the £119,000, he had extorted from the clergy in 1531 as the price of their discharge from the pains of praemunire. Convocation had then acknowledged, amid a glum silence which was taken for consent, that the King was their 'especial Protector, single and supreme lord, and, as far as the law of Christ allows, even Supreme Head.' It was with this precedent (but omitting the meaningful saving clause) that the preamble of the Act of Supremacy, the outstanding measure of the second session (November-December) of 1534, supported its assertion that the King 'is and ought to be the supreme head of the Church of England', and the act its declaration that he possessed all the powers, privileges and profits pertaining to that dignity. Unlike most declaratory acts, however, this one was more than a constitutional formula, it was a statement of fact. For Henry had already begun to exercise most of these powers and privileges and he had certainly begun to take the profits. Thus the Act of Supremacy did hardly more to make Henry VIII the ruler of the English Church than the Act of Recognition had done to make Henry VII the ruler of the English State.

Stripped to its essentials, this tale of England's breach with Rome has taken little time to tell. And, indeed, that breach took little enough time to make. The air of inevitability which hangs about the great events of these years is the inevitability, not of gradualness, but of breakneck speed; and the fact that they took place so quickly goes far to explain why they took place at all. Their tempo was, as we have seen, largely determined by their object, an object which, to be attainable, had to be attained within a given time. But challenge does not necessarily evoke response, and the relentless speed of this response is at once an explanation and a phenomenon to be explained. Something must be ascribed to the forcefulness of the royal personality which inspired it. Henry VIII is not, to most people, an attractive figure, although he was far from being, even in his later degeneracy, the human monster which one legend has made of him. But he was beyond question a masterful one. 'If a lion knew his own strength,' so ran More's celebrated metaphor on the monarch who was afterwards to rend him, 'hard were it for any man to rule him.' And whether, or in what proportions, the King owed his strength to the man, or the man found strength in the King, mattered less to those who knew him living than it does to those who dissect him dead and gone. Henry certainly brought to the labours of his middle years a set of qualities which, good and evil alike, added up to extreme effectiveness, and of him, no less than of his great father, could it have been written that 'What he minded, he compassed.' Not the least of his master craftsman's secrets was his eye for a tool. The sovereign who in his youth, when he lusted after glory, had discerned the nearly perfect instrument in the ambitious ability of a Wolsey, now with riper judgement made choice of a Thomas Cromwell to serve more realistic ends. Henry owed Cromwell to Wolsey, who had brought him forward and leaned much on him during the later twenties; and it was from the Cardinal's service that this son of the people, this self-made solicitor from Putney and self-taught student of Machiavelli, had passed with practised ease to the King's. Great ability, boundless ambition and self-confidence, and insatiable greed, all these Cromwell shared with his first patron. But they drove him forward by a rather different road. Where Wolsey had been a priest, Cromwell was a priest-hating layman; where Wolsey craved the pomp of power, Cromwell was content with its substance; where Wolsey mistrusted parliaments, Cromwell managed them. It was, indeed, Cromwell's commanding of the parliamentary front which was his outstanding service to the generalissimo during these years. It was a political achievement without precedent, because this was a parliament without precedent. No parliament had lasted nearly as long, or needed so much replenishing of its casual vacancies. It was Cromwell who grasped the importance of the regular bye-elections and busied himself promoting the return of reliable men. Again, no parliament had ever been given, with so long a span of life, such incentive to acquire corporate experience and confidence, potentialities which, if exploited in the King's interest, could prove as valuable an asset to him as, if not, they might have proved a serious drawback. It was in the Reformation Parliament, and with Cromwell as its adept, that there was first developed that technique of managing the House of Commons which, handed down from generation to generation of Tudor privy councillors, was to enable Crown and Parliament to maintain for so long the fruitful cooperation begun in 1529. And finally, of no parliament before this one had so much been required in the form of legislation – one hundred and thirty-seven statutes, thirty-two of them directly concerned with the great national issue. Once again it was Cromwell who, under the eye of the King, and with the expert help of the judges and bishops, drafted and redrafted these long and complicated documents – some of them as long as a chapter of this book – until every claim had been pegged out, every contingency provided for, every loophole stopped. It is not only as a breaker of religious houses, but as the architect of a Church, that Thomas Cromwell deserves to be remembered; and like the earth upon Vanbrugh, Cromwell's own act of attainder might well be conjured to lie heavy upon one who had in his day laid so many heavy loads upon the statute book.

Parliament needed a good deal of managing. But it needed little coercion. The fact that here and there the royal policy met with opposition is proof enough that, however much or little influence was brought to bear upon its composition – and that was probably less than is often alleged but more than can ever be proved – the Reformation Parliament was no mere instrument for registering the royal will. In this, as in all branches of public policy, the initiative lay with the King. If Henry VIII had not led the Reformation Parliament, it would not have achieved the Parliamentary Reformation. But equally, if – *per impossibile* – Henry had attempted to use this, or any other of his parliaments, not to fortify, but to weaken, the State against the Church, the layman against the cleric, he would have found Parliament uncooperative to the point of hostility. His 'faithful commons' did what he asked them to do, not simply because he asked them to do it, but because it was what they themselves would have done if they, and not he, had been responsible for shaping policy. The House of Lords, with its large ecclesiastical element, naturally showed less enthusiasm for his programme. But already – and Henry's parliaments were to be a landmark in the process – the parliamentary centre of gravity was shifting from the Upper House to the Lower. Bills might originate in the Lords, and those brought up from the Commons were certainly susceptible of amendment or even rejection there. But King and Commons were too formidable a combination for the Lords, just as King and Parliament were too formidable for the Church.

It is as easy to find reasons why the English Church succumbed so easily to the English State as to find reasons why it should not have done. A Church Militant led by men who had put on the whole armour of God, and commanding the devotion of followers who could wield the weapons of earth, would have fought the good fight and, if need be, have finished its course in the Death which would have been also the Victory. But neither the Church in England, nor the Church of which it formed part, disposed any longer of the will or the wisdom to wrestle with principalities and powers. The faith which had once moved mountains had been corrupted by the life of the plains; a clergy which had growing difficulty in leading the flock looked in vain for leadership from dignitaries who set their dignity before their duty, and their duty to Caesar before their duty to God; and a Church which had ceased to stand immovable upon the rock of principle was betrayed among the shifting sands of a delusive expediency. The trumpet gave an uncertain sound, and there were few who prepared themselves for the battle.

The trumpet quavered, but here and there the still small voice spoke clear. There were not lacking in England men and women who knew what they fought for, and loved what they knew, and whose part in it lifted this struggle far above the plane of power politics. They were a small company, and a tragically divided one. For they fought under hostile banners, and in their zeal they mistook one another for the enemy. Had the Henrician Reformation been an isolated phenomenon, it would have made fewer martyrs than it did. It was an act of state, and of a state which embodied, to a degree perhaps never equalled in English history, the collective will of the nation. It was a revolution, but a revolution directed against a hated foreign authority rather than against authority within the realm. It involved no soul-searching challenge to cherished dogma or ritual. And it was carried through with a speed and a skill which gave doubt little chance to harden into hostility. Only those of the toughest moral or intellectual fibre could have withstood this aggregate of strains, and it was only such who did. But they were to include not only those who refused to be wrenched from positions long held, but also those who could not be restrained from forging ahead to new. It was here that the Continental Reformation first impinged upon the native and insular movement. The movement which Luther had launched in Germany in 1517, and which had quickly spread across half Europe, had enough in common with what Henry VIII started in England in 1529 to entitle them to a common name. But they had different leaders and starting-points, they followed different routes, and they moved at different speeds. Where Luther plunged impetuously forward into the quagmire of doctrine, Henry refused to budge from the firmer ground of organization. Henry had first encountered the Lutheran innovations as heresies against a Faith and a Church with which he had as yet no quarrel; and the encounter had drawn from the theologically-trained and conservatively-minded King the counterblast which earned for its author the Papal title *Fidei Defensor*. Refutation was reinforced by destruction. The year of Henry's book (1521) saw the first great burning of Lutheran books in England. But so long as Wolsey wielded power – and we must set the fact to his credit, although his own age blamed him for it – there was no burning of bodies. That was to commence, or recommence, after his fall. The spectacle of their sovereign at grips with the Roman Antichrist must have warmed hearts which drew their inspiration from Luther or from the native tradition of Lollardy. And, indeed, Henry was not above a calculated flirtation with the new doctrines to fill the Pope with fears for his orthodoxy. But Henry's Church was to remain as orthodox as the Pope's. The King himself wanted it so, and on political grounds it was, at least at this stage of the struggle, the only possible decision. Safety lay in unity, and unity was only to be found in the traditional creed. Nothing stung the Reformation Parliament into sharper protest than the imputation of heresy – and this, we may feel, not simply out of righteous indignation. For heresy in the twenties and thirties was not only spiritually damnable, but socially dangerous. The German Peasants' Revolt, and still more the rise of Anabaptism, awakened fears which Luther's own repudiation of social radicalism had by no means dispelled; and, as we shall see, the first generation of English Reformers was to be remarkably outspoken in its criticism of the social order. The same considerations which moved his subjects moved the King, and the years which saw him break with Rome also saw him persecuting those who had broken with the Roman Faith. Between 1531 and 1534 nine or ten persons were burnt for heresy, many others forced to abjure. More than one of the victims came from that Cambridge group which had been for ten years the centre of 'German' studies in England, and which had produced Tyndale and Coverdale, the founders of the English Bible, Cranmer, the maker of the Prayer Book, and Latimer, the Voice of Revival and of Reformation. Latimer had to stand a trial for his opinions in 1532 but escaped, with a good-humoured warning from the King, the fire which was to claim him nearly a quarter of a century later. The Lutheran had some hope of escape, the Anabaptist had none. In 1535 twenty-five Anabaptists were burnt in one day.

The challenge which Henry's allegiance to the old

doctrine threw down to consciences which had embraced the new, his new doctrine of allegiance threw down to those which remained faithful to the old. This issue, already implicit in earlier legislation, was fairly joined with the passing of the Act of Succession, the last major item of the parliamentary session of January–March 1534. That act gave statutory sanction to the dissolution of Henry's first marriage and to his contraction of a second, and declared the succession vested in the children of this second marriage. All the King's subjects were required to take an oath to abide by these decisions, and refusal to do so, or questioning of their validity, was made treason. The Succession Oath was the first of the series of such probes by which, during the next few years, the government located the few pockets of resistance to the new order. It brought immediate results. Within a month of its fashioning two outstanding figures, one a churchman, the other a layman, refused to take it. They were John Fisher, Bishop of Rochester, and Sir Thomas More. Both had already marked their disapproval of royal policy, Fisher by his bold championship of Queen Catherine, More by his resignation of the Chancellorship. Both had been implicated in the *cause célèbre* of Elizabeth Barton, the Nun of Kent, whose visions (real or imaginary) threatening death to the King for his marital inconstancy led her to the gallows in April 1534. Their refusal of the oath brought More and Fisher to the Tower. Then, in November 1534, came the Supremacy Act and a new Treasons Act, two more strings to the whip which Henry was preparing for such offenders. The trouble which the Treasons Act gave Cromwell in Parliament – it was said that 'there was never more sticking at the passing of any act' than this one – may have owed something to sympathy with these two universally respected men. But the same parliament passed acts of attainder against them, thus plunging More's household at Chelsea, that model to all ages of domestic felicity, into destitution and despair. Six months later the two underwent their final ordeal. Charged with high treason under the Acts of 1534, they were found guilty and sentenced to death. They were both beheaded on Tower Green, Fisher on 22 June and More on 6 July 1535. A few weeks before, Tyburn had been the scene of a yet more brutal deed, the hanging and quartering of three Carthusian priors and a monk for denial of the Royal Supremacy.

A world which ever ceases to cherish the memory of Sir Thomas More will not only have mislaid its measure of human greatness, it will have forgotten the most important lesson which, with so much blood and tears, it has ever struggled to learn. But the world in which More died, and, indeed, More himself, had yet to learn that lesson. For More was the victim, as he had been an exponent, of the stubborn illusion that any human institution possesses a monopoly of truth or the power to impose its dogmas upon all who are subject to its man-made authority. In More's case the offending institution was a Parliament. 'I will put you this case', so ran the famous passage between More and Rich, the solicitor-general, which crystallized the issue, 'Suppose the Parliament would make a law that God should not be God, would you then, Mr Rich, say God were not God?' 'No, sir, (quoth he) that would I not, since no Parliament may make any such law.' 'No more (said Sir Thomas More, as Mr Rich reported of him) could the Parliament make the King supreme head of the Church.' That was well and bravely spoken. But had More's Church any greater power of making the bread and wine change into the Body and Blood of Christ for those who did not, in their own hearts, know that the change had taken place? In both cases dogmatism compassed itself about with a cloud of wisdom and witnesses, and the Old Church, because it was older and wiser than the New Monarchy, achieved the greater obfuscation. But the trappings concealed a nakedness, and it was the nakedness of fear. Churchmen feared the wrath of God, statesmen feared the curse of anarchy, and both obeyed that instinct of self-preservation which is the first law of Nature. The Church strove to preserve the unity of Christendom of which it was both creator and guardian, Henry VIII the unity of a kingdom of which he felt himself the highest expression. So long as both confused unity with uniformity, so long would they provoke that clash of loyalties which would inflict such grievous casualties. And who fell in the conflict was largely the sport of chance. 'By God's body, Master More,' Norfolk had warned the greatest of them before he went into action, 'the wrath of the Prince is death.' 'Is that all, my lord?' answered More. 'Then in good faith the difference between your grace and me is that I shall die today and you tomorrow.' Not until both States and Churches had learned to cast out the fear, and with it the wrath, which had been death to so many valiant warriors for truth, would humanity be delivered from the curse of religious persecution and freedom of conscience take its place among the freedoms which are the Light of the World. It is not in the More who condoned the burning of Protestants, nor even in the More who so gracefully submitted his own head to the axe, that the hard-pressed humanism of our own day finds a kindred spirit. It is in the More who could escape from his own world into a Utopia whose religion was an undenominational theism, whose priests were chosen for their holiness, and whose citizens pursued the good life together unhindered by the clash of creeds.

The executions of 1535 were the product, not of a king's baffled rage, but of his fixed determination in the face of an uncertain outlook. There were some clouds in the sky in that summer of 1535. The English could in the main be relied upon, as could the Welsh; although the North was restive, and the decision to assimilate Wales, by the great statutes of 1536–42, to the English system of government, was not unconnected with immediate problems. But the Irish, under Kildare, had begun to kick against the prick of their old enemy's new religion; the Scots were held in check only by Henry's friendship with France; and from all sides the Emperor was being exhorted to launch a crusade against the royal divorcee and schismatic. The fate of More and Fisher showed that what Henry had taken he was determined to hold. And he had already determined to take a great deal more; the turn of the monasteries had come. It had, of course, been coming for a long time. The monasteries had been shaken by medieval gales; Wolsey's gust had blown down some of the frailer houses; and from 1532 the Henrician hurricane had begun to blow. But it was Cromwell's appointment as Vicar-General (the usual title of a bishop's deputy, applied in this instance to the deputy of the Supreme Head) which spelled death to the monastic system in England, and the two great inquests of 1535 – one into monastic habits and morals, the other into Church revenues – which supplied, the first the ostensible, the second the real, grounds of the sentence. Few people now believe that the monasteries were the dens of iniquity which Cromwell's ruffians described, few that they were any longer the haunts of holiness which they might once have been. Monasticism was not the only medieval institution which had lost its original justification without finding an adequate substitute. Establishments whose resources were chiefly used, not to spread light and learning, nor to sub-sidize laziness in luxury, but rather to provide convenient dumping-grounds for unwanted men and surplus women, profitable posts for needy younger sons of the nobility and gentry, pensions and perquisites for innumerable hangers-on, and board and lodging for travellers who, like the kings who so often availed themselves of it, took for nothing what they should have paid for, such establishments constituted almost as clear a misappropriation of funds as did Henry's action in dissolving them, or the ingenuity with which some of the monks and interested laymen attempted to defeat his purpose.

The smaller monasteries, nearly 400 of them, were dissolved by statute (many having been already surrendered) in 1536; the remainder were seized by various methods during the next four years and their confiscation ratified by statute in 1539. The major result of the process, the transference, first to the Crown and then to private hands, of the vast monastic estates, will find a place in our next chapter. Of its other aspects, the treatment of the ejected personnel, nearly 10,000 strong, is the least discreditable. There were a few tragedies, like the hanging of the Abbot of Glastonbury at his own gateway, and the act of ejection was doubtless often carried out with gratuitous brutality. But once it was over, there were compensations: everyone was given a pension, many monks in time received benefices, many nuns married, and for heads of houses there were bishoprics, deaneries and the like. Buildings and furnishings fared less well. The government was chiefly interested in the plate and jewellery, which went straight into its coffers, and in the lead from roofs, which it used or sold. The stone and timber structures met with varying fates. Some, as we shall see, became industrial establishments, some mansions for their despoilers. But many were exposed to pillage for the sake of their building-stone, and the picturesque ruins of a Fountains or a Glastonbury are what remained on the plate after the neighbourhood had eaten its fill. The most

grievous loss was undoubtedly the destruction or dispersal of
the monastic libraries, the full extent of whose riches is only
now being revealed by laborious research. A little restraint
would have preserved them intact. But they were cast out and
trodden under foot by greedy philistines, and it was left to
antiquaries like Leland, Camden and Cotton to salvage what
they could of these manuscript treasures and in so doing to
lay the foundations of English historical scholarship.

The juggernaut which had put to flight the Pope, crushed
More and Fisher and pulverized the monasteries had one
further obstacle to surmount before it came to a grinding
halt after ten years of relentless motion. That was the
rising in Lincolnshire and the North known as the Pilgrimage of Grace. This took place in the second half of 1536,
and its main purpose was to halt the campaign, then getting
under weigh, against the monasteries. The North set
greater store by its monasteries than the South, and if they
were to find champions it would be there. But the dissolution was the occasion rather than the cause of the
rebellion, which served to unite diverse, and some of them
contradictory, grievances generated over a good many
years. In the North, as elsewhere, there was plenty of mass-
discontent waiting to be mobilized: discontent fomented by
taxation, by rising prices, by enclosure and rack-renting.
And in the North there were people able and ready to
mobilize it: magnates who resented the Wolseys and the
Cromwells, gentry and towns becoming conscious of their
under-representation in Parliament, traders jealous of the
hegemony of London. In the history of England Tudor rule
meant the rule of the South over the North, just as later in
American history the federal system was to mean the rule
of the North over the South; and as the American South
was beaten in the four years of the Civil War, so the
English North went down in the thirty-four years which

opened with the Pilgrimage of Grace and closed with the Rebellion of 1569–70. The rising of 1536 brought out the best and the worst in Henry, his resolution, his sureness of touch, his lack of scruple, and the combination was too much for a movement which had numbers but which lacked a real leader and a real programme. In the upshot, the rebellion failed in more than its professed objects, for its chief results were to give to the dissolution of the monasteries added speed and to the Council in the North Parts, that branch office of the Tudor firm in the region beyond the Trent, added power.

The Henrician Reformation had begun with the fall of a minister and been quickened by the birth of a child; it was slowed down by birth of another child and brought to an end with the fall of another minister. Anne Boleyn had not lived up to the King's expectations, and he was soon seeking diversion. Catherine of Aragon died in January 1536, and on the day of her funeral Anne gave birth to a stillborn child. It was a fatal combination of events. Nothing now stood between Henry and a third, and indisputable, marriage with the young woman of his latest choice but the life of a Queen whose magic had fled. Where a Borgia would have used poison, a Tudor used the law. Within four months Anne was dead, executed for crimes which her prosecutors could not prove and which posterity can only speculate on. Her successor, Jane Seymour, was also to pay for her crown with her life. But she died of giving birth to the third, and last, Tudor Prince of Wales. Prince Edward's birth on 12 October 1537 was worth more to Henry than all the wealth of the Church – but he did not give any of that back. Instead, he heaped gratitude upon the Seymours, who for the next ten years were to reap a rich harvest of their dead sister's sowing, and thereafter, as we shall see, a harvest of another kind.

The world which saw the Seymours rise saw Cromwell
fall. Here, too, policy and personalities were inextricably
interwoven. Cromwell had made almost as many enemies
as Wolsey. He was hated by the Church he domineered
over, by the Northerners he had humbled, by the fellow-
counsellors he riled. Like Wolsey, he could snap his fingers
at them all so long as he did not make an enemy of the
King. But this is what Cromwell did, at first gradually and
insensibly, at last with terrifying speed and fatal issue.
Like Wolsey, too, Cromwell fell because he sponsored a
policy which ended in making a fool of his master. At home,
it was a policy of gradual concession to the steadily infiltrating Protestant party. In 1536, besides the act formally
abolishing the Pope's authority, and the dissolution
of the smaller monasteries, the Reformers, who already
included six bishops (Latimer among them), secured
the first slight modification of Catholic doctrine in the
Ten Articles of Faith promulgated by Convocation.
In 1538 Cromwell's Injunctions to the Clergy, with their
provision for teaching basic religious texts in English, for
sermons and for the removal of images, marked a further
advance, and acts of desecration like the plundering of
Becket's shrine at Canterbury made a powerful impression.
But Cromwell's greatest service to English Protestantism –
and to English civilization – was the support he gave to the
publication of the English Bible. The first authorized
translation, Coverdale's, appeared in 1535, the revised
'Great Bible' in 1539. It is largely to Cromwell that we owe
the fact, with its indisputable if immeasurable consequences,
that in England the Scriptures thus early ceased to be the
forbidden handbook of the agitator and became, under
some light safeguards, the common property of the nation.
With this domestic programme of cautious protestantiza-
tion there went a foreign policy of alliance with Protestant

Europe against the menace of a Catholic coalition, and it was this policy which produced Henry's fourth marriage, the tragi-comic affair with Anne of Cleves. Like his first, but unlike the two succeeding marriages, this one was pure diplomacy, into which the question of mutual attraction could hardly be expected to enter. But it was the King's revulsion from his bride, and the absence, since Edward's birth, of the compulsion to beget a child, which made it so short-lived. With the marriage there collapsed the diplomatic structure which it was to have cemented, and the shock of that fall smashed the foundation of internal policy. During the early months of 1540 conservatives and radicals contended furiously with one another, and Cromwell's stock oscillated violently. In April a Parliament assembled, and in a last blaze of glory the doomed minister was made Earl of Essex and Lord Chamberlain. But as soon as he had extracted from the Houses, with a rigour born of desperation, the supplies which the King needed, he was struck down. Arrested on 10 June, he was attainted on the 29th and executed a month later. The Cleves marriage had already been dissolved, and on the day of Cromwell's execution Henry married for the fifth time. His new Queen was Catherine Howard, and she was the niece of that Duke of Norfolk who had led the assault on Cromwell.

The fall of Cromwell marked the end of the Henrician Reformation. Supreme Head of his Church and master of its wealth, Henry VIII had everything that he had fought the Pope, killed More and Fisher, and looted the monasteries to obtain. He was monarch of all he surveyed and surveying it he found that it was good. Eleven years had he laboured to create this brave new world, and now he would have it remain just as he had fashioned it. But it was a living, not a dead, world that Henry had created. Cromwell he could kill, Latimer he could silence, Parliament he could persuade to frame an Act of Six Articles against the heresies which Cromwell and Latimer had fostered, and his Church he could trust to condemn those who went on dabbling in them. But could he lull back into spiritual and intellectual torpor a nation which he had so violently aroused? Would his power be as effective in checking thought as in stimulating it? Could Henry VIII stop the revolution which he had begun?

IV

COMMONWEAL AND COMMOTION

'By the beginning of the year 1538 Henry had established his kingdom, established his church, established his line. The rest of the story of his reign, if not without colour, is relatively without significance.' In these words, embodying the mature judgement of a leading student of the period, we recognize the traditional, and still generally accepted, version of the decade which followed the breach with Rome. That version springs from the view of Henry VIII as a king with a mission, to assert the undisputed supremacy of the State in his own person and posterity. Since Henry had substantially achieved this end before the thirties were out, the closing years of his reign necessarily take on the character of an epilogue, and none of their happenings can be held to rank in importance with what had gone before. To see the reign according to this pattern is to see it solely in terms of politics and religion. If, instead, we look at it from the economic and social standpoint, the pattern undergoes a marked change; what was a mere appendage now becomes the focal point of a new disposition. For in the history of the Englishman's getting and spending the fifteen-forties are as pregnant with change as are the fifteen-thirties in the history of his governance and creed; and in the last seven years of his reign Henry VIII and his counsellors did things which helped to shape their country's future hardly less than did the statutes of the Reformation Parliament.

It is a commonplace that Henry inherited an overflowing

treasury from his father and bequeathed an empty one to his son. If it be asked where the money went, the answer lies in the one word – war, beside which all the other items of royal expenditure, the upkeep of the king's household (including the wives, ex-wives and mistresses) the new palaces, the trips to the Continent and the foreign embassies, are of insignificant account. In particular, Henry's closing years were full of wars and rumours of wars, and it was then that his finances came to grief. There have been few wars which were worth waging in a material sense, and Henry's wars were not among them; they were wars of ambition and *amour propre*, and materially they were a dead loss. The first of them was sufficient to wipe out Henry VII's hoard of treasure; thereafter they had to be financed out of a compound of taxation, confiscation and depreciation.

Of that compound taxation was the least noxious element, especially as the bulk of it was levied directly upon property and income. With what vigour and success the government exploited this source is shown by the revenue-figures. Whereas under Henry VII the yield of direct taxes had averaged £11,500 a year, under his son it averaged £30,000, while during his last seven years Henry VIII raised nearly £700,000 in this way; and this is to ignore such extra-parliamentary items as forced loans and benevolences, and the taxation of the clergy, which together must have brought the last figure to over a million. If his ability to tax upon this scale is the best proof both of Henry's power and of his people's overwhelming acceptance of his rule and policy, the country's capacity to pay without serious difficulty testifies to a substantial increase in national wealth. The one section of the community which found the burden too heavy was the old corporate towns, which were not sharing in the general progress, and in course of time they would have to be given tax-remissions. In much the same way the weight of the customs was proving too much for the wool-trade, and a shifting of the load from over-taxed wool to under-taxed cloth was one of the needed reforms which would soon be made.* But with these exceptions the national economy does not seem to have suffered from the king's repeated exactions.

It was otherwise with the two expedients to which Henry was driven by the failure of even this unprecedented tax revenue to cover his mounting charges. The dissolution of the monasteries had brought to the Crown property worth well over £100,000 a year, and in capital value it made Henry a wealthier king than his father had ever been. If he and his successors had contrived to retain any sub-stantial part of this vast property as a permanent addition to the royal domain, and at the same time have kept their expenditure within reasonable limits, they would have been able to 'live of their own' to a degree unapproached by any of their recent predecessors, and on this financial bedrock they might have erected a more massive despotism than England had yet known. Cromwell may have dreamed such a dream, and while he remained in power the sales were mainly confined to the movable property, furniture, books, plate and jewels. But in 1540 there started the wave of selling which by the end of the reign had swept two-thirds of the monastic lands out of the hands of the Crown into those of a thousand or so of its subjects.

This gigantic transfer of land has no parallel in English history, at least since the redistribution which followed the Norman Conquest. Between 1536 and 1547 the Crown received through the Court of Augmentations, the depart-ment set up to handle the business, about £1½ millions from the sale or leasing of monastic property. The average figure of £130,000 a year, although considerably larger

* See below, page 144.

than the Crown's previous normal revenue, was not much more than it might have drawn in income by keeping the property intact – a sorry comment this on the financial fecklessness which promoted the sales. The Crown did, in fact, receive far less than the market value of the land disposed of – and this on the eve of a sharp rise in land-values. The meagre yield was only to a very limited extent the result of royal openhandedness; the picture of a Prince Bountiful showering abbeys upon sycophantic servants and courtiers, or staking them at cards and dice, belongs, like most stories of monarchical extravagance, more to the realm of fiction than of fact. A certain amount was given away or used in payment of debts; but the great majority of those who acquired monastic property paid – at least until Henry debased the currency – good money for it. The main reason why they did not pay more was that the land-market was almost from the outset – and as time went on became more and more – a buyer's market; the Crown as seller or lessor stood in greater need of money than its customers did of land and was therefore constrained to accept what they were willing to pay.

There is a well-known analysis by the Russian scholar Savine of the thousand individuals and institutions who first acquired the land from the Crown. Of property worth £90,000 a year, nearly a quarter went to spiritual corporations (which gave the Crown other lands as well as money in exchange); of the remaining £70,000, about a quarter went to peers, a seventh to royal officials, a tenth to courtiers, a twelfth to industrialists, and smaller fractions to the king's servants, lawyers and physicians, lay corporations, and clerks and yeomen. As a rough guide to the people who benefited by the initial share-out this is a useful list; but what, of course, it does not reveal is which and how many of these people retained all or most of their shares, and which parted with them fairly soon after their acquisition. Where the land was bought by a corporation we can be fairly certain that it was for investment; it is equally clear that the groups of London business men who acquired estates scattered all over the country were speculators who intended to resell them at a profit in smaller parcels. Moreover, the quickened tempo of land-transfer which now began was something which would go on and increase with the passage of time; it was not a case of a single great shake-up in ownership followed by another period of repose, but of the beginning of a motion which went on uninterruptedly and at increasing speed during the rest of the century and far beyond. While it is thus misleading to talk or think of a final destination for the land of the monasteries, it seems clear that of the two classes of people chiefly concerned in the original transaction, the peers and the gentry, it was the gentry who not only kept what they then received but added to it a good deal of what had gone to other groups as well as of the new land which the Crown continued to throw in great quantities on to the market.

Parallel with this distinction between the first halting-place of the monastic lands and their more permanent destination runs the distinction between the shorter- and longer-term effects of their disposal upon the rural economy. In the long run the monastic property, supplemented by the other Church and Crown lands brought into the market during the following century, would be absorbed into that system of medium-sized estates which was the economic basis of the rule of the gentry. There they would be prudently managed and efficiently farmed by owners who lived on, and to no small extent for, their estates, and by lessees who had to find their rent or quit; and with the striking of a new equilibrium in the demand for grain and wool they would, by the operation of natural selection, rearrange themselves into that pattern of cornland and grassland which would last substantially unchanged until the mid nineteenth century. But it was not into such a calm sea that Henry VIII had launched the monastic booty upon its exciting voyage. At that time the whole rural economy was being wrenched and twisted into a new and unfamiliar shape by the powerful and undisciplined forces of competition and the market. The monastic estates had been by no means immune from these pressures under their old management, but it can hardly be disputed that their transfer to lay-ownership increased their exposure. Among these disruptive forces none was stronger or more unremitting than the strain imposed by the expansion of the cloth trade. We have seen that one of the knottiest points in the history of sixteenth-century enclosure is the extent to which it was bound up with the spread of sheep farming. Whatever may be true of the rest of the century it is safe to assert that in the thirties and forties the real driving-force behind the movement was the insistent demand for more wool; indeed, it is the unanimity with which its critics then denounced the all-devouring sheep which had fastened that character upon the movement as a whole. Of the many deleterious aspects of enclosure the encroachment of sheep-rearing upon crop-raising, with its tale of filched fields, overstocked commons and deserted villages, was as certainly the most vicious at the time as it has proved the most poignant to posterity; and perhaps the worst circumstance attendant upon the release of monastic lands for fuller exploitation was the fact that it took place at a time when that so often meant the substitution of pastoral for arable farming.

The sale of those lands was not Henry's sole, nor even

his chief, contribution to the furtherance of the agrarian revolution. Simultaneously he was embarking upon an even more desperate expedient to stave off bankruptcy, the debasement of the coinage. The essential facts of this operation can be shortly set down. Between 1542 and 1547 about £400,000 worth of silver coin of the standard of fineness known then, as now, as 'sterling' was reminted into £526,000 worth of coin, each piece of which contained less than one-half the previous quantity of pure silver. The metal thus extracted from the coinage, valued at £227,000, represented the king's gross profit on the operation. It is one which possesses a certain topical interest to a generation which has seen the country's silver coinage replaced by one of cupro-nickel and the silver so released devoted, as in Henry's day, to the discharge of pressing State obligations. But there is no real parallel between the two cases. The silver coinage of which we recently took leave had long been a 'token' coinage, that is to say, its nominal value bore no relation to its intrinsic value as metal, and its composition might therefore be altered at will without any effect upon its face value or purchasing power. By contrast, in the sixteenth century the only sound currency was one in which the face value of the coins corresponded fairly closely to their intrinsic value, and for a government to interfere with the metallic content was thus to upset not only the currency but the values and prices expressed in it. This is not to say that such action was never justified. On the contrary, throughout the later Middle Ages the ever-widening disparity between the available stock of precious metal and the volume of business transactions which it was called upon to 'carry' made the periodic reminting of this metal into a greater sum of money, and a corresponding reduction in the metallic content of each coin, practically unavoidable. Edward

IV's recoinage of 1461 had been the last of this series of enforced debasements. Wolsey, when he debased the coinage in 1526, could scarcely plead the same exigency; but even his alteration of the weight (although not of the fineness) of the silver coins can be looked upon as a defensive measure dictated by a war-time fall in the exchanges and the resulting drain of metal out of the country. Neither plea, nor indeed any other, can be put in with regard to the Great Debasement of the forties. The country was not short of silver; indeed, the amount in circulation had lately been augmented by a considerable quantity of monastic silver. Nor was the exchange-outlook unfavourable; the pound sterling had been steadily appreciating for a decade, and the tendency was for silver to flow into, not out of, the country. Henry VIII's bedevilment of the currency, which would itself reverse these favourable trends, answered to no national interest save that which attached to governmental solvency.

Whatever its share in warding off a State bankruptcy – and this cannot have been decisive – it is open to question whether the remedy was not more lethal than the disease. For the debasement had two immediate consequences, each harmful in itself, and each more so in combination with the other. The first was a sharp rise in prices. To increase the volume of money in circulation, as Henry had done, with no corresponding increase, at least for the time being, in the volume of goods produced, is infallibly to send up the price-level. At Henry's death prices had risen by one-quarter; two years later, under the influence of further debasement, they had nearly doubled. It was the process with which our age is familiar under the name of 'inflation', and we, who have suffered from its effects, do not need to be reminded of their extent or acuteness. It is true that, initially at least, those effects were confined to a smaller, and on the whole a different, section of the community than present-day experience might lead us to suppose. To begin with, money played a much smaller part in the ordinary man's life then than now. Whereas today the mass of people who earn their living do so in return for salary or wages, and any movement of prices is thus immediately reflected in the real value of their earnings, in Tudor England the bulk of the population derived its livelihood, at least in the matter of necessities, direct from the soil and to that extent remained unaffected by changes in the market-value of their produce. Even those who laboured in industry were not so wholly dependent upon their weekly earnings as the modern wage-earner; not only was much of that industry located in the countryside and its labour part-time or seasonal workers drawn from the rural population, but even the town-worker remained both physically and economically near enough to the soil to supplement his earnings by raising crops or livestock. Again, to such people as these a rise in prices would not be the unqualified evil which it is to most of us. The surplus produce which they disposed of in the local market or to the travelling broker would fetch so much the more, and even if their own necessary purchases also cost more the net result might be to leave them no worse, if no better, off than before. The more divorced from the soil the harder they would be hit, and in the case of a metropolis like London the situation would not differ materially from its modern counterpart.

If the predominantly agrarian character, and the prevailing types of rural and industrial organization, of Tudor England served as a cushion against the direct impact of the price rise, they proved little protection against that phenomenon as soon as it manifested itself in new and severer stresses in the economic and social structure. It is always those whose incomes are fixed or inelastic who stand to lose most from rising prices. Today it is the pensioner and the annuitant, the stockholder and the *rentier*, who find it most difficult to make both ends meet. They had their sixteenth-century counterparts in such figures as the widow living out of a small rent-charge, the ex-monk pensioned off at the Dissolution (although most of his kind had exchanged their grants for benefices) or the schoolmaster allotted a fixed stipend when his school was disendowed in 1548. But by far the most important category of 'fixed income' people were those who received customary rents from land. The gentleman who in the face of rising costs can no longer maintain an establishment becoming his station is a familiar figure in the literature of the time. So, doubtless, he was too in real life, but not for long. For unlike his smaller and weaker brethren the landlord could, if he chose, break out of the shrinking circle of his fortunes by shedding outworn customs and conceptions and putting his affairs on to a strictly commercial basis. Enterprising landlords had been doing so, with varying degrees of thoroughness, for a generation or more, and the technique had been improving all the time. Now it was *sauve qui peut*, and everywhere landlords cast doubts aside, seized the proffered weapons and hacked their way through to solvency.

Less familiar a result of the debasement than the rise in the domestic price-level is the fall which took place in the value of sterling abroad. In 1542, on the eve of the debasement, the pound was worth about twenty-seven shillings Flemish; by 1547 it was down to twenty-one shillings. Initially it was Henry VIII's heavy buying of foreign currency to meet his war-expenses abroad which turned the exchanges against sterling; what the debasement did was to take the brake off this downward movement by lowering the point to which it could go without being checked by an outflow of metal. Thus currency debasement and exchange depreciation proceeded coincidently, and the value of English money abroad underwent roughly the same reduction as at home. One of the first effects of a fall in the exchange-value of a country's money is to encourage its export-trade. The fact that the pound sterling became cheaper to foreigners meant that English goods, for which they had to pay in sterling, grew correspondingly cheaper, and therefore that they could afford to buy more of them. (We must not, of course, forget that the rise of prices in England was continually tending to offset this downward trend, but especially at first there was a sufficient time-lag between the two movements to ensure the foreign buyer an advantage.) The article of which the Englishman had most to offer, and which the Continental most desired from him, was woollen cloth, and it was the cloth trade which received the main thrust of this monetary stimulus. English cloth-exports had been growing steadily since the opening of the century; they now leapt to record heights. Most striking was the expansion of the trade passing through London; when Henry VIII died London was exporting more than twice as many shortcloths as at his accession, and half as much again as ten years before. What these figures really mean is that Henry was paying for his Continental operations out of the increased export of cloth; the percentage of the national output which went to wage those wars actually crossed the Narrow Seas in the holds of the cloth merchants' ships. This was the reality of which the huge and complex deals between the king and his foreign bankers were but the outward show.

It was the unremitting pressure of this overseas demand, reaching its climax during the later forties, which was the main factor in producing the rapid and continual expansion of the cloth industry. The resulting scale of that industry was something for contemporaries to marvel at or shake their heads over. One of them guessed in 1533 that half the population depended directly or indirectly upon the trade with the Netherlands; like all such estimates this was a gross exaggeration, but it is certainly true that the country was coming to depend upon its foreign markets to a degree which bears comparison with the situation today. In the mid twentieth century England must export or die; in the mid sixteenth she had to export or fall dangerously sick. Already in 1528, when Wolsey's rash war with the Emperor closed the Netherlands market, the result had been catastrophic. In the great cloth-making districts mass-unemployment had brought with it serious disturbances; in London, where trade was at a standstill, the situation was nearly as grave. Before two months were out Wolsey was forced to come to an arrangement exempting the Antwerp trade from the embargo, and within another three this had been expanded into a formal truce.

If the mere size of the industry, with its weighty implications in politics and diplomacy, rightly commands attention, so do the changes in organization which accompanied its growth. As we have seen, cloth-making was carried on both in the towns and over wide stretches of the countryside. The urban industry was old-established, highly organized on the medieval pattern, and essentially conservative; the rural industry was younger, more elastic in structure, and largely innocent of tradition or inhibition. The cloth-towns had long passed the stage when they could readily respond to a call for bigger and speedier output, and it was the rural centres which therefore received the main stimulus of the overseas demand. Village after village developed into industrial as well as agricultural units, and the traditional division of function between the town which manufactured and sold and the countryside which raised and reared was still further obscured. It is not to be supposed that the rural artisan, often only half-trained and dividing his time between the loom and the plough, could vie in workmanship with the urban crafts-man with his years of apprenticeship and specialization, and the spate of complaints, both at home and abroad, of the faulty workmanship in English cloth suggests that the increase in output was not achieved without some lower-ing of standards. But if in the field of technique the increas-ing 'dilution' of labour meant retrogression, in the field of organization it helped to make possible a major advance. One of the great obstacles to increasing production had always been the lack of coordination between the various processes involved in cloth-manufacture. Under the old system by which the craftsmen who carried out these pro-cesses owned the material upon which they worked the cumulative effect of innumerable small checks and delays at successive stages was a considerable reduction in the rate, and therefore in the volume, of production; if the weaver were held up for yarn or the fuller for cloth the productive chain was broken and output suffered. To step up the tempo of production by reducing this friction was the chief service rendered to the industry by the capitalist *entre-preneur*.

The master clothier was no new figure in the mid sixteenth century, but in the genial warmth of that indus-trial springtime he blossomed out into a luxuriance which quite eclipsed the smaller and frailer members of the *genus*. He might commence operations at any point in the multiple business of cloth-making. The prosperous sheep-master might have his wool spun and woven for him instead of disposing of it in the raw, or the enterprising weaver engage spinners to furnish him with yarn or fullers and shearmen to finish his cloth. But whatever the source of this intruding capital its function was everywhere the same, to coordinate and expedite the manufacturing processes by ensuring the requisite supply of labour and material. It was now the clothier who owned the material and the spinner, the weaver and the fuller who exercised their crafts upon it at agreed rates of payment; by controlling the volume of material which underwent each process the clothier could both maintain a smoother productive flow and adjust its volume more exactly to the changing demands of the market. The scale upon which these men conducted their operations varied very greatly. At the bottom they shaded off imperceptibly into the still numerous class of independent craftsmen; at the top they reached an eminence which earned them a place in popular legend and story. Most famous of all was John Winchcombe, who as 'Jack of Newbury' is commemorated in Deloney's ballad of 1597. A weaver who, so runs the legend, started by marrying his late master's widow, Winchcombe built up one of the greatest clothing businesses of the time and died in 1520 a very wealthy man. He specialized in the coarse cloths known as kerseys, for which there was an insatiable demand at the Antwerp fairs. A son, John Winchcombe II, succeeded to the business, but his ascent of the social ladder brought other interests and ambitions; in 1541 he signalized his arrival in Berkshire society by being put on the commission of the peace, and in 1545 he sat in Parliament for Great Bedwin.

To such magnates as Winchcombe, Stumpe of Malmesbury, and the like, the dissolution of the monasteries presented a unique opportunity. What it offered them in land, land which would put money in their bulging purses and an aureole of gentility around their hard plebeian heads, we have noticed on an earlier page. But there were also exciting

vistas of business development. This is how Thomas
Cade, one of Thomas Cromwell's agents in the dissolution,
supported an Oxfordshire clothier's application for the
property of Abingdon Abbey: 'My lord, ye shall not fail
to approve him a very substantial and just man in his
dealings both in word and deed, and he setteth in occupation daily 500 of the king's subjects of all sorts, and if [by
acquiring the abbey] he might have carding and spinning
he would set many more in work than he doth; for this I
know for truth, my lord, that if ye be good lord to him he
will set the inhabitants of the king's town of Abingdon if
they will work, on occupation, as that they shall gain more
in few years coming than they have done in twenty years
past. For this I know, my lord, that weekly need con-
straineth him to send to Abingdon his cart laden with wool
to be carded and spun, or else many times his workmen
should lack work, and like wise he sendeth to Strodewater.'
More than one monastery was thus acquired by enterprising
business men. A few of them included manufacturing plants
which were going concerns; at Cirencester, for instance,
the last abbot had built two fulling mills at a cost, it is
said, of nearly £500. But even buildings consecrated to the
service of God could readily be adapted to the service of
industry. Built to last until Judgement Day, their spacious
halls, outbuildings and mills enabled the industrialist to
concentrate in one establishment workmen and processes
previously dispersed in many small units over a wide area.
The word 'factory', in its modern sense, would not enter
the language for another century, but the thing itself first
came into being in these converted monasteries of the
fifteen-forties. One advantage, indeed, they lacked which
has made the factory supreme in modern industry. The
rows of looms in a modern weaving-mill are driven by
energy supplied from a single power-house; those which

Stumpe installed in Malmesbury Abbey depended upon the muscles of their individual operatives. In this respect sixteenth-century factories offered no improvement on the existing system under which the weavers worked in their own homes, and it was for this reason that they did not come to stay. But while they lasted they were a phenomenon of no little importance, and that not merely in the economic sphere. The men who daily served their masters in such establishments could handle other tools than those of their trade. The clothier who coveted Abingdon Abbey had, as his sponsor reminded Cromwell, 'twenty tall men at his leading to serve the king's highness at your command-ment'. Tradition has it that Winchcombe led one hundred, equipped at his own expense, to Flodden Field. That may be legend, but when in 1545 the government surveyed its man-power for the French war it put down William Stumpe as able to supply one hundred men. With the countryman's readiness to follow his landlord when war or civil commotion threatened the Tudors were both familiar and content; it was part of the established order to which they could conceive no alternative save anarchy. But the growth of a similar allegiance among industrial workers to the men who employed them was something new in English society, and something which the Tudors, with their keen eye for any shift in the balance of power within their realm, would have been quick to observe and to allow for in their calculations.

Changes of the nature and magnitude of those we have been discussing reck little of the death of kings, even when, as in this case, their momentum is in no small part the result of royal action. There was, as the event proved, little that Henry VIII's successors could have done towards neutralizing the results of his policy. Certainly no one in authority could have meant better in this respect than the

Duke of Somerset, who in the role of Protector of the young Edward VI took over the royal functions on Henry's death. But the excellence of Somerset's intentions was not matched by the singleness of purpose or the freedom of action necessary to carry them out; above all, his policy was fatally compromised by the near-bankruptcy of his government. At the same time as he was embracing far-reaching schemes of reform Somerset was adding to the evils which they were designed to remedy by large new instalments of spoliation and debasement. It was under his direction that the chantry lands, which Henry had earmarked for seizure but had not lived to receive, followed the monastic estates into the Court of Augmentations and began to follow them out again, along with much land from other sources, into the waiting hands of the well-to-do. It was his authority, too, which sanctioned the issue in 1549 of a large quantity of silver coins of the standard of 1546, the last important step in the Great Debasement. Under its influence the exchanges took a further plunge and cloth-exports a further leap, and with domestic prices rocketing the twin demands for higher rents and more wool reached a new level of insistence.

If the new régime thus did little or nothing to check the mounting tide of economic change, it did allow men to speak their minds on the resulting problems with far more freedom than the old. Everywhere tongues were loosened to utter, and ears bent to catch, things which men had long wanted to say or hear said. And to the gift of freer speech there was added a freer press. The censorship, which had weighed so heavily for close on a generation, was now relaxed, and minds long restricted to an austerity diet of approved reading-matter, supplemented only through 'black market' trafficking in forbidden books, were now able to indulge in a much more plentiful literary fare.

The staple item of the new diet was religion, but writings concerned with, or inspired by, the pressing economic problems of the time also bulked large in it. The sixteenth century did not know those problems under that name, for they had not yet achieved that separate identity which would entitle them to a name of their own. On the one hand they were still widely regarded, as they had been throughout the Middle Ages, as a branch of applied religion, and a good deal of the 'economic' literature of the age set out to uphold or reassert the claims of religion in this field; on the other, they were coming to be treated more and more as a branch of politics, and when early Tudor writers felt the need of a word to denote this aspect of national life they adopted one with a distinctly political flavour.

This word was 'commonweal' or 'commonwealth'. It originally meant either the body politic or the general good, and in the second of these senses it had been the *leitmotiv* of many early sixteenth-century treatises. But it was in the years of Somerset's Protectorate that the word came into its own as the name given to a body of opinion which sought to define the commonweal and to devise and carry through a policy for its promotion. The term 'commonwealth's man', afterwards appropriated by the revolutionaries of 1649, was first applied to adherents of this movement; they were not a party or even a clearly defined group, and their views were shared, at least in part, by many who would have denied the appellation. Those who made it famous or notorious at the time, and who are remembered under it, were either the writers and preachers who publicized these views or the politicians who sought to translate them into policy. The ideas of 'commonweal' enlisted such fluent pens as those of Henry Brinkelow, the ex-friar who wrote ballads under the pseudonym of

Roderigo Mors, and Robert Crowley, an Oxford man who was the first to print that classic of social criticism, *Piers Plowman*. But the day was yet far distant when the press would rival the pulpit as a public platform. For everyone who read Brinkelow or Crowley, a hundred must have listened to Hugh Latimer. Latimer's voice had not been heard in public since he resigned his bishopric in 1539, but when he began preaching again in 1548 he quickly reached the top of his form. Whatever the audience or the occasion, whether in court sermons before the boy-king at Westminster or in open-air addresses at the Cross of St Paul's, Latimer could be trusted to lash the evils and evildoers of the time with a racy vehemence which still has power to stir the heart even when congealed into the frigid pages of a modern reprint. Latimer was over sixty when he delivered these famous sermons; Thomas Lever, a rising star at Cambridge, was not yet thirty when summoned to the Court pulpit. Neither religious ardour nor social conscience was the monopoly of any one age-group. While the divines were busy lending the cause of 'commonweal' the sanction of the Gospel, the politicians were striving to enlist for it the support of the government. Here the outstanding name is that of John Hales. A minor government official (he was Clerk of the Hanaper, one of the departments of the Chancery), Hales was not only its champion in parliament but also the chief architect of the enclosure commission of 1548 which was its first-fruit. Through Sir Thomas Smith, the eminent civil lawyer who was Somerset's Secretary of State and the movement's most powerful friend at court, Hales came to enjoy the patronage of the Protector.*

Differing in many respects, the apostles of 'commonweal' had two significant things in common: they were all

* It is now thought much more likely that Smith wrote the 'Discourse of the Commonweal' than that Hales did.

Protestants and none of them was a Londoner. The combination of radicalism in religion with a conservative social philosophy was characteristic of the first generation of English Reformers. Not for them the callous creed which would suffer the landlord to manage his estate or the employer his business after his own good pleasure, and with no veto of church or state to obstruct his pursuit of profit. 'If the possessioners,' wrote Crowley, 'would consider themselves to be but stewards and not lords over their possessions, this oppression would soon be redressed. But so long as this persuasion sticketh in their minds: It is mine own, who should warn me to do with mine own as myself listeth? it shall not be possible to have any redress at all. To the commonwealth men the new technique of money-making was abhorrent; it stood condemned alike by the evil passion which nourished it, the lust of gain, and by its fruits, the destruction of that 'right order of commonweal' which they were pledged to uphold. Posterity was to see in it only one facet of that individualism, that bursting of the human ego out of its medieval confines, whose first great triumph was the Reformation itself; but to these early Reformers, denied the enchantment of the more distant view, the scene was as ugly as the sin by which it was suffused.

Nowhere were the tendencies in contemporary life which they condemned more in evidence than in London. The neglect of the Christian virtues and the surrender to materialism, the decay of public morals and of business ethics, the ostentatious luxury and the grinding poverty, the vice and the crime – all these London displayed then, as London is wont to display everything, on a scale which compelled attention. Latimer, who knew it well, declared that there was more pride, covetousness, cruelty and oppression in London than in Nebo. But it was not only

its iniquities which earned for London the condemnation
of the commonwealth school; the very existence of such a
metropolis appeared to many Englishmen, especially to non-
Londoners, incompatible with the national welfare, and the
provincial affiliations of the commonwealth leaders –
Hales a Kentishman domiciled in Coventry, Latimer the
son of a Leicestershire yeoman – may well have reinforced
their hostility to the capital. There were cogent reasons for
that hostility. Tudor London devoured people – life in the
city was so unhealthy that the population showed scarcely
any natural increase but grew almost entirely by immigration; it devoured foodstuffs, pushing the tentacles of its
victualling organism ever further along the coasts and up the
river-valleys and raising prices wherever they penetrated;
it devoured trade so greedily that by the middle of the
century it was handling four-fifths of the country's commerce, while the outports languished; its merchants allied
with the rural cloth-industry against the provincial cloth-
towns, and at the same time imported those foreign
wares, like the fashionable felt hats, which drove other
native craftsmen out of business. Provincial producer, trader,
consumer, all were threatened by this monstrous growth,
which cancer-like seemed to doom the country to slow
economic extinction. We know now that the pangs were
those of birth, not death, and that the national economic
unity, under the supremacy of London, thus being pain-
fully gestated, would one day help to give England the
economic leadership of the world. But the men of the sixteenth century could not foresee the good that would come
out of this evil; they saw only the evil and denounced it.

Of the concrete programme of reform in which Hales and
his fellows attempted to realize their ideas two items are of
outstanding interest: the Subsidy Act of 1548 and the Enclosure Commission. The Subsidy Act, the sixteenth-century

equivalent of our annual Finance Act, was the measure in which a Tudor Parliament voted the Crown revenue from taxation, and on this occasion it included the novel provision for a tax upon sheep. The immediate object of the new tax was to enable the government to dispense with purveyance, the system by which the Crown purchased supplies from its subjects at low prices and on long credit; purveyance had always been unpopular and its evils were now aggravated by the rise in prices. It was to compensate the Crown for the loss of purveyance that Hales put forward his scheme for taxing sheep and cloth. He calculated, in a memorandum remarkable for its statistical approach to the problem, that a tax of one penny upon every sheep, of one halfpenny upon every pound of wool used in cloth-making, and of three shillings and fourpence upon every broadcloth exported, would yield £112,000 a year, a sum about equal to the whole normal revenue of the Crown. The scheme was not only a bold enlargement of the incidence of taxation, it was an early essay in the use of taxation as an instrument of economic planning. In Hales's view, the phenomenal expansion of the cloth-industry, and the concomitant growth of pasture-farming, were making the whole national economy lop-sided; they were diverting more and more of the country's output into a single channel, a channel moreover which, since its main outlet lay overseas, could be blocked or interfered with by forces largely independent of English control. The government had fought this tendency so far with every weapon save one; let us, said Hales, see what taxation can do. His plan was endorsed by the Protector and rather surprisingly accepted by a parliament which had given short shift to Hales's many other reforming bills. Doubtless the prospect of putting an end to purveyance helped to reconcile that assemblage of landowners to a tax on the most profitable use of land; so also, perhaps, did the reflection that such a tax would not be difficult to evade.

Hales's other principal achievement in the sphere of remedial action had not required parliamentary sanction; this was the issue, in June 1548, of a commission to inquire into the progress of the enclosure movement. Originally limited to the seven Midland counties where enclosure was most in evidence, the inquiry was later extended to other areas. The commissioners were instructed to discover what villages had been affected since 1489, the date of Henry VII's statute on the subject, and who were responsible; what individuals kept flocks of two thousand sheep and upwards (a useful list this, when the sheep-tax came to be levied) or had appropriated common land; and whether the grantees of monastic lands kept as much of them in tillage as before the Dissolution. By 1548 four statutes had been passed, and many proclamations issued, against enclosure; but, as Latimer said, 'in the end of the matter there cometh nothing forth'. Without more efficient machinery to bring evasions to light these acts would continue to be a dead letter; such machinery the commission was intended to provide. The memory of the prosecutions and compulsory disenclosures which had followed Wolsey's commission of 1517 was fresh enough to make that of 1548 at once a threat and a promise: a threat to the encloser that the government meant business, a promise to the peasant that at last he was to be given more than verbal protection. The Protector himself certainly saw it in the light of a crusade and was prepared to stake – as destiny exacted that he should – his authority on its success. His rousing defiance – 'maugre the devil, private profit, self-love, money, and such-like the devil's instruments, it shall go forward' – was the more notable as coming from one of the greatest landowners, and withal one of the greatest spendthrifts in the country, a man, that is, peculiarly liable to the temptation which was daily turning so many of his kind into enclosers and rackrenters. In this at least Somerset, the king in all but name, bore himself right royally; for the Crown had yet to smirch its championship of the oppressed peasant by exploiting its own estates on modern lines.

When Somerset pledged his support of the 'poor commons', they were already staging the opening moves of what was to become their greatest mass-demonstration since the Revolt of 1381. The oppressions of the last dozen years had not passed without protest. Since 1536, when the North had risen for the old order in Church and countryside, almost every year had added to the tale of local riots and disturbances, some against the despoiling of cherished shrines but more against rising rents and encroaching pastures. That sooner or later these little revolts would be gathered up and synchronized into a big one seems fairly certain; whether the rapid deterioration which set in during the forties would in itself have provoked an outburst we cannot say, but nothing could have combined more effectively with it than Somerset's decision to intervene. The appearance of the commission in the Midland shires in the summer of 1548, far from pacifying the peasants, aroused in them a mixture of elation and exasperation which vented itself in a crop of disturbances. But it was not until the commissioners resumed their task in the following spring, after the winter recess which Hales, their leader and spokesman, had spent campaigning in parliament, that matters came to a crisis. In vain Hales pleaded with the peasants not to take the law into their own hands and warned them that they were imperilling the good cause. Soon the whole of Southern England, from Land's End to the Wash, was in an uproar.

The initial widespread confusion crystallized into two

clearly defined and largely independent risings, the Western Rebellion based on Cornwall and Devon, and the rebellion in Norfolk led by Robert Ket. The Cornish rising stands rather apart from the general movement. Originating in a protest against the new Prayer Book, it retained throughout an essentially religious character. But it, too, had its undertow of class antagonism, running sometimes with and sometimes against the main current of religious zeal. In Cornwall only two gentlemen identified themselves with the movement, which was chiefly in the hands of priests and peasants; others were torn between sympathy with its religious aims and suspicion of its social implications, while the few who were known to be Protestants were naturally marked men and bore the brunt of the commons' ill-will. Again, the towns held aloof, and the city of Exeter, which once more proved itself, as in 1497, the government's bulwark in the West, took its stand on the side of authority under the leadership of men who 'howsoever they were affected otherwise in religion yet they were wholly bent and determined to keep and defend the city'.

In the Norfolk rebellion there were no such cross-currents. Apart from Ket himself, a man of some wealth and breeding whom the accidents of circumstance and personality threw into the lead, the rebels were all common folk, and hatred of the gentleman was one of their strongest bonds of union. They had no religious grievances to air; the new Prayer Book which had stung Cornwall into revolt was put to regular use by the men of Norfolk at what must have been some of the largest open-air services yet seen in England, and they had a 'new preacher' as one of their chaplains. The punctiliousness of their religious observance was matched by the orderliness of their behaviour. Until the government showed its hand there was little violence or bloodshed. Instead, a great concourse of country-folk, reinforced by many sympathizers from the ranks of the town-artisans, settled down in a vast *laager* on the outskirts of Norwich and there organized themselves into a miniature and rudimentary state on communistic lines. They had for governors Ket himself and two city-fathers, one of them the mayor, whom they pressed into office, and for council an assembly composed of two delegates for every hundred represented and a representative of Suffolk. This revolutionary 'county council' observed a due form and decorum in its acts: its commissions and orders were issued in the king's name and from 'the King's Camp', and were couched in the language of Westminster. A rude court of justice dealt with offenders, including such of the gentlemen as were unlucky enough to be caught; but contemporary rumours of daily executions do not seem well-founded.

Hardly less remarkable than the orderliness of the Norfolk rebels was their immobility. The Cornishmen, mobilizing two hundred miles from London, had lost no time in moving into Devon and but for the resistance of Exeter would doubtless have pushed on towards the capital; the men of Norfolk, less than half that distance away, were content to overawe Norwich and to make a feeble gesture against Yarmouth, probably in the hope of adding fish to their staple diet of mutton. The decision to turn the demonstration into a great sit-down strike may have been Ket's; it certainly fitted in with his notion of what that demonstration was meant to achieve. He seems to have shared the peasants' conviction that the government was on their side and that it would approve, or at least condone, their striking a blow in what was a common cause; how otherwise could he have wound up the Articles embodying the rebels' agrarian programme with the extraordinary request that the government should appoint him and his nominees to the commission for seeing them carried out? If

Ket really did believe that the government would look upon him not as a dangerous revolutionary but as an ally in the struggle against reaction, then his failure to adopt a more positive strategy appears less suicidal. For in that case he had nothing to gain by marching on London or even by raising the neighbouring counties; his task was to teach the gentry of his own county a lesson and thus to smooth the path of reform.

If Ket had only had to reckon with Somerset, his optimism would have been less fatal. His rising had confronted the Protector with the most painful problem which can face any statesman, how to deal with a threat to order which springs from genuine grievances and which he himself has fostered, but which no government can tolerate if it is to survive. It is to Somerset's credit that he did his best to soften the blow which the Council, under the leadership of Warwick, the apostle of force, was preparing to deal; but his authority, already compromised by the outbreak of rebellion, was still further weakened by his reluctance to put it down, and the decision passed out of his hands. It was the more tempting to rely on force in that the government had at its disposal, what it lacked in every other major crisis of the century, a professional army. Without the 1,500 German and Italian mercenaries then in the country on their way to the Scottish war it would have been far more difficult to wage the two campaigns needed to restore order. Russell, the commander in the West, made little headway until he received his Italian reinforcements, while Warwick, who marched against Ket, entrusted most of the fighting, including the final slaughter at Dussindale, to his Germans.

The rebellions spelt the doom of Somerset's Protectorate, and with it of the 'commonwealth' programme of reform. When Parliament reassembled in November 1549 Somerset,

Smith and Cecil were in the Tower, and Warwick and Wriothesley, champions respectively of social and religious reaction, held power. Hales still sat for his borough, but his credit was gone, and with it went the fruits of his earlier labours. The Subsidy Act was repealed as the result of vigorous lobbying by clothiers and sheepmasters. The Enclosure Commission lapsed, and instead of attempting to check enclosure Parliament, for the first and only time during the century, gave it positive encouragement by re-enacting the medieval Statute of Merton which empowered landlords to appropriate common land. Organized opposition to enclosure, to higher rents or to dearer corn was made treason or felony according to the number of individuals involved. Mindful of what it had owed in 1549 to the fortuitous presence of the mercenaries, the government also took measures to create a standing army; selected noblemen and gentlemen were empowered to raise and maintain squadrons of fifty or one hundred horsemen at the public expense, and the military powers formerly wielded in each county by the sheriff were transferred to a new authority, the lord-lieutenant, specially commissioned for that purpose. Henry VII had established the Tudor Peace by putting down armed retainers; it was now to be preserved by reviving them.

Silenced in the council chamber and the parliament house, the voice of social conscience still muttered in the press and thundered in the pulpit. It was in 1550 that Crowley set forth his *Way to Wealth*, which included an apologia for the Norfolk rebels, and his collection of epigrams, with its portraits of the enemies of the commonwealth. Meanwhile, 'that commonwealth named Latimer' – so his enemies called him, and he was indeed a host in himself – continued to hammer away at the government, as did his fellow critic Lever. Powerless as they were to effect any real change of heart, they that laboured in the Lord did not labour wholly in vain. Lever's indictment of the failure to refound the schools disendowed under the Chantries Act was followed by the re-establishment, in 1551-2, of a dozen or more schools with endowments which, adequate at the time, have since grown a hundred-fold with the value of the properties. That there are so few Edward VI Grammar Schools we owe to the rapacity of the boy-king's ministers of state, that there are any at all to the tenacity of his ministers of religion.

Yet it was Warwick's government which made the first serious effort at ending the monetary chaos which had cost the country so dear. Since 1549, when Somerset further debased it, the coinage had lost value more heavily and rapidly than ever. The exchanges had slumped in drunken fashion, and by May 1551 the pound sterling was worth no more than fifteen shillings Flemish. At home prices were touching levels about twice as high as those of 1547, and the government's campaign to keep them down only had the result, familiar enough to our generation, of driving goods off the open market into the 'grey' market of concealed trading. Already in 1550 the increased cost of producing cloth, combined with the first signs of saturation in the Antwerp market, had begun to check exports, and merchants were complaining of over-production. It was the beginning of the end of the great boom. The following year saw 'boom' give place to 'bust'. Between May and August the government carried out a fifty-per-cent devaluation of the coinage by calling the coins down to half their face-value. This drastic act of deflation, so necessary to restore a measure of stability at home, dealt the export trade a stunning blow. The exchanges took a sharp upward turn, carrying with them the prices of English cloth to the foreign buyer, and sales fell off alarmingly. From the record figure of 132,000 in 1550 the London shortcloth trade dropped to 112,000 in 1551 and 85,000 in 1552.

The resulting slump in the cloth industry presents a familiar pattern. With full warehouses and few customers, the merchants cut their purchases and their prices, and the clothiers found themselves selling at a loss. They in turn set about lowering production-costs; wages were reduced and standards of manufacture, already relaxed in the scramble to increase output, were now further sacrificed in the effort to cheapen it. But even at the reduced prices much cloth was unsaleable, and everywhere looms and wheels came to rest and those who served them proffered their nimble hands in vain. Apart from the export-figures, there is no basis for any quantitative estimate of the severity of the depression, but how seriously it was regarded by contemporaries is shown by the spate of discussion and of legislation aimed at mitigating its effects and preventing its recurrence. The twin objects of these measures were to 'rationalize' production and to stabilize trade. The parliament of 1552 saw a number of bills brought in, and two acts passed, to reduce the swollen cloth industry to normal and manageable proportions. The first of the acts laid down detailed regulations designed to maintain standards of manufacture, the second forbade anyone to weave broadcloth who had not served an apprenticeship or been engaged in the trade for seven years. Applying to town and country alike, these measures did nothing to redress the balance between the urban and rural industries. In 1553, therefore, the towns were exempted from the 'seven years rule', and in 1555 the comprehensive Weavers' Act further penalized the rural industry by imposing drastic limitations upon the size of its units and the scope of their activities.

There was, of course, little or nothing new in this restrictive legislation. But in the sphere of trade and finance the crisis had other and more novel repercussions, which may be illustrated by the career and ideas of one of the best-known figures of the period, the Sir Thomas Gresham who gave his name to a City college and a City street and whose sign of the grasshopper still adorns a City bank. Gresham came of a distinguished merchant family, and until 1549 he assisted his father in the family business. Then he hitched his wagon to the rising star, Warwick, and in 1551 he was appointed 'King's merchant' or royal agent at Antwerp. He retained the post almost continuously for sixteen years, surviving two sweeping changes of government and becoming one of the most important men in Europe. Gresham's principal task at Antwerp was to manage the royal debt, and although his legendary fame as the financial wizard who saved three English sovereigns from bankruptcy will hardly survive critical examination, he certainly handled the business entrusted to him with rare skill and success. In particular, it was mainly due to his grasp of the essential truths that credit rests upon confidence, and confidence upon the punctual fulfilment of obligations, that English royal credit soon came to stand higher at Antwerp than that of any other princely house and that both Mary and Elizabeth could borrow there several per cent cheaper than the ruler of the Netherlands himself. But to Gresham the successful floating and renewing of loans was only the beginning of what he could do for his country if he were given the chance. It was natural that in the fifteen-fifties Englishmen should come to think that prosperity was bound up with the rate of exchange. The exchanges not only loomed very large in royal finance, they appeared to govern the course of trade and thereby to exert a determining influence upon the whole national economy. A man like Gresham, who was handling it every day, was bound to see in the exchange mechanism one of the most potent instruments of economic control. In this he was typical of the new age into which England and the world were moving. Money had long been recognized as the root of all evil; it was now coming to be recognized as the root of much else, and its mysterious power and eccentric behaviour were made the subject of intense study and discussion. Thus, whereas the important economic thinkers of the previous generation had been reformers like Hales who thought instinctively in terms of agriculture and industry, that is, in terms of production, the men who mattered in the fifties and sixties were the experts who thought in terms of money and trade.

The exchange-rate with which Gresham was most familiar, and which he was chiefly concerned to control, was the London-Antwerp rate. Apart from governmental action in the form of royal borrowings and currency manipulations, the main factor determining this rate was the flow of trade between the two countries, of English cloth to Antwerp and of foreign wares to London. The cloth trade was already dominated by the Merchant Adventurers, and it was through the medium of this Company, of which he was himself a member, that Gresham planned to bring the Netherlands trade, and with it the exchange relationship, wholly under the control of the Crown. As he saw the matter, three things were necessary: the Company must be given a monopoly by the suppression of trade not amenable to its control; within the Company itself power must be concentrated in as few hands as possible; and the Crown's financial interest in the cloth-trade must be strengthened by an increase in the customs duties on cloth. Gresham was to see two of these three objectives substantially achieved before the death of Mary. In 1552 the only important alternative channel of trade with the Netherlands was blocked by the withdrawal of the centuries-old privileges enjoyed by the merchants of the Hanse; among them had been one by which the Hanseatics paid lighter customs upon outgoing cloth than even native exporters, an arrangement clearly incompatible with Gresham's scheme. The increase in taxation followed in 1557. It will be recalled that Hales had attempted this with his cloth subsidy of 1549; it was now done by raising the customs duties. Although Gresham's third objective eluded him until 1564, when the Merchant Adventurers were reconstituted along oligarchic lines, that did not prevent the Crown from making extensive and high-handed use of the Company during the preceding decade. It more than once dictated to the merchants, under the threat of refusing to allow their ships to sail, agreements for the transfer to the Crown of the proceeds of their sales at Antwerp in return for payments in London at a fixed rate of exchange. This device for ensuring the Crown the foreign currency needed to meet its obligations abroad was claimed by Gresham as his own discovery; it had in fact been used at least as far back as the reign of Edward IV. Indeed, Gresham's whole conception of the role of the Merchant Adventurers, as a privileged mercantile corporation vested with a mono-poly of a key-export in return for fiscal and diplomatic services to the state, is one which is familiar to all students of medieval economic history. For this is what the Company of the Staple had been from the end of the fourteenth to the beginning of the sixteenth century, and it was the decline of the Staple which had created the vacuum in govern-mental finance which the Merchant Adventurers now came in to fill.

Monopoly and state-control, these were the leading features of Gresham's 'plan of the English commerce'. But already in his day English commerce was shedding the habits and prejudices of the past and reaching out to a freer and fuller future. In this movement, too, we may trace the influence of the crisis of 1550. It is no accident that the years which followed that crisis were the years of England's resumption of maritime enterprise. Since the initial effort under Henry VII, there had been few voyages of exploration undertaken from English ports. John Rastell's abortive expedition of 1517, John Rut's quest of the North-West passage in 1527 and Master Hore's in 1536, and several trips to the coast of South America, these make up the meagre total for the reign of Henry VIII. The commercial initiative behind them came almost exclusively from the south-western ports; London took little interest, and that little chiefly out of curiosity or love of adventure, not out of business sense. Court and government were equally lukewarm. Roger Barlow, the Bristol merchant, saw action postponed again and again on the project which he had worked out with the better-known Robert Thorne, and died in 1554 with nothing accomplished. Both the King and the Londoners had their gaze too firmly fixed upon the Continent, which long afforded as plentiful scope for the political pursuits of the one as for the profit-making propensities of the others. Nothing was better calculated to induce a change of heart in the Londoners than the sudden coldness of the mistress who had so long held them under her spell, and nothing could have been more conducive to the success of the new maritime programme than the enlistment of the Londoners in its support. Thus the voyages of the fifties, which marked the effective beginnings of English overseas enterprise, were the immediate and direct outcome of the collapse of the Netherlands market which had so long monopolized London's – and that meant increasingly the nation's – attention and outlook.

This chapter opened with a *caveat* against the disposition to regard the closing years of Henry VIII as a comparatively unimportant epilogue to his reign. Its development involves a similar remonstrance against the view which sees in the eleven years separating his death from the accession of Elizabeth only a hiatus in the otherwise majestic sweep of Tudor history. For it is clear that, in the story of the 'work, wealth and happiness' of the English people, these years are of central and crucial importance. They saw the economic and social fabric stretched and distorted as perhaps never before. They saw the manufacture of cloth expanded until it overshadowed all else in the national economy, and then catastrophically deflated. They saw the revolution in agriculture touch new records in rapidity and magnitude. They saw prices rise at a rate never equalled before or since. And, as a result of these things, they saw an ominous shuddering in the social framework and they heard the rumble of revolution. In English economic and social history these years were a 'dangerous corner'. Once past it, the nation entered a broader and straighter road, and ahead were new vistas to beckon it on. But the margin of safety had been small, and the test a gruelling one. It was all the more severe because it coincided with two others. These were the test of a royal minority and a disputed succession, and that of a religious revolution and counter-revolution. These further afflictions of the years from 1547 to 1558 will form the subject of the next chapter.

V

LEFT INCLINE AND RIGHT
ABOUT TURN

THE birth of Prince Edward, which gave Henry VIII a male heir, also made it practically certain that this heir would succeed as a minor. It was a disquieting prospect, for every royal minority in English history had been the occasion of faction and turbulence, that is, of the negation of Tudor government. How could Henry best insure against these consequences when his own strong hand was removed? He could designate a regent or protector to exercise the royal authority. This had usually been done in the past, and in a state which depended so much for its efficient working upon individual control it might well have appeared, as indeed it was to prove, the only practical solution. But if history furnished precedents it also uttered warnings. Henry would not have forgotten the fate of the last Edward at the hands of the last Protector. Again, the office called for other qualities besides integrity, and among Henry's counsellors there were few who had them in sufficient measure to warrant the trust. Tudor infecundity meant that there was no one of royal blood to exercise it. Several leading noblemen could claim kinship with Henry; but only one of them, Edward Seymour, Earl of Hertford, brother to Queen Jane and uncle of the young Edward, had any real claim to consideration. Hertford was one of the two men – the other was John Dudley, Viscount Lisle – whom the former Imperial ambassador Chapuys named as alone fit to govern the realm on Henry's death. As Dukes of Somerset and Northumberland they were indeed to do so, but they came to power by their own effort, not by the fiat of the dead king.

These personal considerations apart, what chiefly shaped Henry's decision were his hopes and fears in the matter of religion. Since the overthrow of Cromwell the king had held steadily to the *via media* of his own choosing. Supreme Head of a national church which was independent alike of Rome and of Continental Reform, he had consistently refused to countenance any tampering with Catholic dogma or discipline. At first sight the religious history of these years seems to be summed up in Luther's comment: 'What Squire Harry wills must be an article of faith for Englishmen, for life and death'. As a statement of constitutional principle, this was irrefutable. The King was not only the source of all ecclesiastical power but also the final authority in matters of doctrine, ritual and discipline, and in this sense, therefore, every word and act of religious observance was uttered or performed because Henry willed it so. Yet to see in his doctrinal policy simply the determination of a despot to impose his own faith upon his subjects would be to misunderstand both the king and his kingship. Much as Henry hoped to keep his realm orthodox he was still more determined to keep it united, and just as in the interest of national security he had broken with Rome so in the interest of national unity he would, if necessary, break with Catholicism. The essentially secular aim of his religious policy also conditioned its execution. A thoroughgoing programme of religious uniformity would not have left so theologically 'unsound' a Primate as Cranmer in office; it would have made more systematic use of the Act of Six Articles; above all, it would not have allowed the Bible to reach even those classes (among men, from yeomen upwards; among women, only those who were noble or

gentle) permitted to read it in 1543. Moreover, the fact that
in this, as in every branch of Tudor government, so much
depended upon the individual authorities concerned –
within each diocese the bishop and his officers, within each
country the justices of the peace – was in itself a well-nigh
insurmountable obstacle to uniformity. Bonner's harrying
of Protestants in London contrasted with their treatment
by some of his brethren.

Henry's measures certainly did not put an end to religious discord. They did not even drive it underground. The
King admitted as much in the famous speech of Christmas
1545 to Parliament, in which he pictured the Bible as
'disputed, rhymed, sung and jangled in every ale-house
and tavern'. This was not the behaviour of a people living
in daily terror of the rope or the fire. And out of this welter
of argument and invective there was slowly crystallizing
the new faith, a faith which brought man and God into a
communion where neither king nor priest might obtrude.
Of the theology of this new vision there were already con-
flicting versions, and where a Primate could only grope his
way the simple parson or layman would soon be lost. But
amid the encircling gloom of dogmatism the kindly light
led on, and the company which followed it grew in number
and fortitude. A few, like the heroic Anne Askew, it beck-
oned almost at once to a martyr's death; others, like Foxe
the martyrologist and his friend Crowley the ballad-writer,
it drew away from cherished prospects of preferment.
Before the end of Henry's reign the Reformers included
some of the greatest in the land, among them the two
future Protectors. Had the reign lasted a little longer Henry
might himself have been numbered among them. It is
fairly clear that before the end the King had come to
recognize the need for a shift in officially-sponsored doctrine.
He confided his son's tuition to three Reformers, and in his

last months he was meditating the crucial step of converting the Mass into a Communion. One thing alone could have prompted this change, his realization that the old faith no longer satisfied enough of his people to serve as a bond of national unity. His nomination of the council which was to govern in the name of his son showed that what Henry did not live to do he expected to be done after his death. The council he chose was not ill-fitted for the task. It was neither small enough to become a cabal nor so large as to be unwieldy. It had a preponderance of laymen. Above all, while few of the councillors were men of conviction and none was a fanatic, both in number and quality the Protestant element was considerably the stronger. The only Catholic who could have made a fight of it, Gardiner of Winchester, was significantly omitted.

Whether this plan to put the Crown into commission would have worked we cannot say, for no sooner did Henry's death (28 January 1547) bring it into force than it was upset. At its first meeting the Council chose Hertford as Protector of the realm and governor of the King's person. Six weeks later, now as Duke of Somerset, he shook himself free of it by getting himself appointed Protector by patent, that is, nominally by the King. Thus vested with as much authority as anyone who did not wear the crown could wield, Somerset began his 'reign' of two-and-a-half years. His position was as stern a test of character as of ability. A man of finer metal might have resisted the temptation to clutch at power, one of baser would certainly have stooped lower to retain it. Having grasped the Protectorate, Somerset disdained to tighten his hold. He made as little use of his right to appoint new councillors as of his opportunity to fill offices with his henchmen. His colleagues he treated with an hauteur which contrasted with the warmth of his friendships and of his generosity to enemies. Honest himself, he was slow to suspect others; and in the jungle-warfare of sixteenth-century politics this soldier-statesman was completely out of his element.

While not averse from having a tyrant's strength, Somerset was resolved not to use it like a tyrant. He abhorred the methods by which Henry VIII had attempted to pulverize opposition, and in their place he sought to enthrone persuasion and gentleness. His most striking effort was the great act of his first Parliament repealing the treason and heresy laws of the last reign. Henry VIII had created more treasons than all his predecessors put together. Somerset's act not only eliminated nearly all these accretions but also tightened up the procedure in treason trials as a safeguard against tyranny. With regard to heresy it was even more sweeping, for it repealed all doctrinal legislation, including the Six Articles, as well as all restrictions on the printing and use of the Scriptures. The moral effect of this surrender of the government's sharpest weapons of coercion must have been great, and the homely metaphor of its preamble, which spoke of the 'lighter garment' suitable for the warmer weather now prevailing, doubtless kindled an answering glow in many a heart. This preamble went on to describe the new reign as 'more calm and quiet' than the old. But nothing could have less deserved those adjectives than the religious situation which was fast developing. Where Henry's heavy fist had failed, Somerset's gentle hand was not likely to succeed, and instead of quietness there came mounting uproar. The focus of controversy was the Eucharist. Dignity and restraint were not the hall-marks of sixteenth-century controversy, even when carried on at the highest levels, and the eucharistic battle was fought along a front which ranged from the bishop's palace down to the tavern and the street-corner, where its weapons were the language, the humour and the gesture of everyday life.

And into the torrent of argument and abuse the youthful press, revelling in its new freedom, dipped its bucket deep and often, bringing forth ballads, satires and libels in an unending stream. Images and relics were another fertile source of disturbance. The iconoclasts got to work with a will, and the distinction previously made between lawful and unlawful objects was soon lost sight of. In February 1548 the Council was driven to order their indiscriminate removal. The work then went apace, although there were still enough images left in 1550 to warrant the passing of an act for their destruction.

It was amid the sound and fury of this doctrinal hurricane that Somerset cast off from the Henrician mooring and sought a better and less exposed anchorage. He and his pilot, Archbishop Cranmer, believed that it was both right and necessary to do so. Cranmer was in many ways the ideal man for the task. He was not a born leader, but in that age of leaders this was a gain rather than a loss. A more generous endowment of that quality might have led him to the scaffold under Henry, his life's work scarce begun, instead of to the stake under Mary, his mission accomplished. While men and women were dying for beliefs which the Archbishop privately shared, he subscribed to the ruling orthodoxy and imposed it upon others. Yet we cannot dismiss Cranmer simply as a man who lacked the courage of his convictions, for one of his profoundest convictions was that in his public capacity he must conform to the doctrine prescribed by the Supreme Head of his church. It was essentially the same approach as the King's, and their identity of outlook was one of the strongest links between the two men. His person and place secured by the King's favour, Cranmer could indulge freely in those studies and contemplations which were to carry him further and further from his starting-point. He had little originality of mind, but he was an omnivorous reader and hearer of other men's views, and the development of his ideas owed much to the influence, first of Luther and Melanchthon, and afterwards of the Swiss Reformer Zwingli. Yet, although the raw materials came from a variety of sources, it was Cranmer who tested, refined and compounded them into a theological system so complex and subtle that it still furnished matter for learned disagreement.

The first liturgical innovation of the new reign was the Order of the Communion. The new service contained little or nothing clearly inconsistent with Catholic doctrine. At the crucial points its phraseology was ambiguous, and the statute embodying it explicitly renounced any intention of condemning rites used elsewhere. We can trace Cranmer's hand here. Himself deeply attached to the traditional forms, he was led naturally into modes of expression which might satisfy the same emotion in others. The new service came into use at Easter 1548. It was compulsory when lay worshippers were present, but the clergy themselves continued to celebrate the Mass, and even masses for the dead were not yet abolished, although the suppression of the chantries greatly reduced their number. Such piecemeal reform, however desirable as a means of accustoming people to change, was in itself a source of confusion. The co-existence of the Mass and the Communion, of private confessions and the new general confession, of Latin services and English ones, was bound to provoke invidious comparison. In vain the government strove to check the flood of argumentativeness which was sweeping the country. With every month bringing some fresh change or incident to elate some and infuriate others, and with press and pulpit both echoing and adding to the din, the 'grand national debate' gathered momentum. National it was to remain, although it had a European significance which explains both the attention with which it was followed abroad and the enthusiasm with which the many foreign refugees in England threw themselves into it.

In this situation the government decided that it must reimpose uniformity of observance. In September 1548 it took the drastic step of silencing the pulpit by suspending all licences to preach. At the same time Cranmer laid before an assembly of bishops his draft of a new prayer book. From the bishops the draft went straight to Parliament. The decision to ignore Convocation, regretted by many modern writers, was probably unavoidable in view of the urgency of the matter. But the book's immunity from criticism in Convocation was offset by its rough handling in Parliament. The original draft had to be withdrawn, and it was a modified version which eventually passed, although even then eight bishops voted against it on the third reading. *The booke of the common prayer and administracion of the Sacramentes, and other rites and ceremonies of the Church after the use of the Churche of England* combined in one volume three of the old liturgical books, the Breviary, the Missal and the Ritual. Cranmer's Breviary reduced the eight divisions of the Catholic daily office to the familiar two, Matins and Evensong. The Missal became the Book of the Communion, and the new service, while retaining large portions of the Mass, began the transformation of what had been a sacrificial act into a commemorative one. The Ritual showed many traditional features. Both auricular confession and Extreme Unction were preserved, as were the Lenten Fast and Friday abstinence. Taken as a whole, the Prayer Book was a skilful blend of the old and the new. It clung wherever possible to the ancient forms for the sake of their time-honoured beauty, but purged them of what was to Reformers their idolatrous character. Its keynote was compromise, and in that it faithfully reflected the personality of its chief author.

It also reflected his mastery of the language. Melanchthon had once told Cranmer that 'in the Church it is more proper to call a spade a spade than to throw ambiguous expressions before posterity'. But posterity has been more than willing to forgive Cranmer's prose its occasional obscurity of sense for the sake of its habitual majesty of sound. In one thing only Cranmer failed. He could not render the hymns of the Catholic Breviary into singable English, and three centuries were to pass before *Hymns Ancient and Modern* was to complete, with the Prayer Book and the Authorized Version, the splendid trilogy with which the Anglican Church has endowed the English-speaking world.

In compiling his Prayer Book entirely in English Cranmer had yielded, not without some lingering regret, to the arguments in favour of a language understood of the people. But there were a good many of the king's subjects whose vernacular was not English, and in their case the new liturgy was designed to serve an educational as well as a religious purpose. Both the Welsh and the Irish were given special editions, and the first Act of Uniformity thus took its place among the measures designed to promote political unity by the universalizing of the dominant language. This linguistic aspect of the Prayer Book had a small share in fomenting the one serious outbreak of popular resistance to it, the Western Rebellion. Over most of the country the introduction of the Book on Whitsunday 1549 passed off smoothly enough. But at one Devon village the parishioners were so incensed that on the following day they compelled the priest to don his vestments and celebrate Mass in the old fashion. Neighbouring parishes followed their example, and before the end of the month large parts of Devon and Cornwall were in open rebellion against the new dispensation. Although, as we have seen, economic and social grievances played some part in it, the Western Rebellion was essentially what it purported to be, a violent protest against the religious policy of the Protectorate. The Articles put forward by the rebels summed up in admirably terse and simple language the Catholic demand for a return to the 'good old days' of Henry VIII, although not, be it noted, to those of Papal Supremacy. They demanded the Latin Mass, communion in one kind, all the old ceremonies and images, and the Act of Six Articles to safeguard these things in future. The new Prayer Book they likened to a 'Christmas game', and they rejected both its content and its English, a language which some of them professed not to understand. They made no attempt to argue the theological issues, and it is doubtful whether even the priests among the rebels would have been either much interested in or conversant with these. What had stirred them and their flocks to anger was the sudden and, to them, unwarranted suppression by a remote and unfamiliar government of the rites and symbols which made up so large a part of their religion.

Although the news of the Western Rebellion came on top of the first reports of widespread agrarian disturbance, and was quickly followed by tidings of the great upheaval in East Anglia, the Protector met it with the same humanity and forbearance, and withal the same obstinate optimism, which had marked all his doings. 'Content yourselves good people. See our shires of Devonshire and Cornwall well in order. See the corn and the fruits of the earth, which God hath sent of His most great clemency, gathered now in time, whereby ye shall be sustained in winter. Do not with this rage and fury drive yourselves to the sword, your wives and children to famine and hunger. If anything be to be reformed in our laws, the Parliament is near at hand ...' It was the same language that he was to use towards the Norfolk rebels. Unfortunately he no longer spoke for his colleagues, who were determined to teach the turbulent commons a lesson. The brothers Carew went down to Devon with harsh orders of which Somerset knew nothing, and as soon as Russell, the royal commander, received his reinforcements, including the foreign mercenaries, he cut through the peasant ranks at St Mary Clyst, relieved hard-pressed Exeter, and finally annihilated the rebels at the same village from which, two months before, the signal for revolt had been given. By the end of August it was all over in East and West. Some thousands of peasant households mourned their menfolk slaughtered on the battlefield, some hundreds those who expiated their treasons on the gallows of a dozen counties.

There remained the last and most august victim of the tragedy. In the course of his brief reign Somerset had earned a place in popular esteem at the cost of alienating most sections of influential opinion. His religious policy, acceptable as it was to the indifferent majority, displeased those of strong views on either side. To devotees of the old faith he was the promoter of heresy, the persecutor of stalwarts like Gardiner and Bonner, and the pillager of the chantries, while zealous Reformers deplored his reluctance to go either as fast or as far as they wanted. His efforts at social reform, and his patronage of the 'commonwealth' men, had ranged against him two great vested interests: the landlords, who saw in him a traitor to his class, and the business magnates, who resented his denunciation of their profits and still more his attempts to tax them. But it was the Council which overthrew Somerset, and while these varied grievances all had their spokesmen in the Council, they could scarcely have produced the degree of resolution and unanimity which it displayed against him. What did that was the growing conviction that his experiment in 'liberty' was a betrayal of government, which if persisted in could only lead to the subversion of all order and authority.

The case for demoting Somerset seemed to receive its final justification from the ease with which the job was done. In the first days of October 1549, when he was with the King at Hampton Court, the Protector learned that the Council was meeting in London and that his authority was at stake. His first impulse was to make a fight of it. After issuing a proclamation calling upon all men of goodwill to rise in his support, he withdrew with Edward to Windsor and from there summoned Russell, who still lay with his army in the West, to his aid. His appeal to the people produced some thousands of armed peasants, but Russell ignored his command and so turned the scale decisively against him. Somerset's resolution did not survive the blow, and on 14 October he and his only remaining friends in office, Smith and Cecil, were sent to the Tower. Ten days had been enough to topple the Protector from his pedestal, but more than two years were to pass before the rival who had directed that operation completed it by procuring his execution. During that time Somerset's fortunes, and his relations with Warwick, underwent a curious cycle of change. In February 1550 he was released from the Tower, in April he re-entered the Council, and in June he gave his daughter Anne in marriage to Warwick's eldest son. For a time it appeared that the two might have agreed to rule the country between them. But in politics it is seldom true that two heads are better than one, and if the rule of Somerset had meant lack of government the duumvirate of Somerset and Warwick meant misgovernment. Warwick was master in the Council, but Somerset still had a following in the country, and it was fear of strengthening his position which led Warwick repeatedly to postpone the meeting of Parliament, although a session was urgently needed to deal with pressing economic problems. This sacrifice of national to factional interests was everywhere becoming the rule, and the country reeled under its plethora of troubles. Foreigners thought that England was done for. 'They do take us all for damned souls', wrote an English diplomat from the Netherlands, and the King of France was tempted to seize the moment to declare war.

The judicial murder of Somerset was but one step in Warwick's carefully-planned advance to supreme power. Its starting-point was the boy-king himself. So far Edward had been a mere childish figurehead in his country's government. But he was a forward lad, and it was his precocity which Warwick now turned to account. During 1551 he succeeded in gaining a remarkable ascendancy over the boy's mind, and that autumn he initiated Edward into his new role, bringing him to sit at Council meetings and instigating him to dispense with countersignatures upon his documents. In this way Warwick gradually freed Edward from the restrictions of his minority and at the same time bound him closer to himself. But so long as Somerset lived there was always the danger of his regaining his former influence over his nephew, and for this reason alone Somerset had to die. On 11 October 1551 Warwick procured his own creation as Duke of Northumberland and the ennobling or knighting of several of his supporters. It was at once the signal of victory and of vengeance. Five days later Somerset re-entered the Tower. In December he was tried by his peers upon a trumped-up charge of attempting to overturn the government, and although he was acquitted of treason his conviction of felony was sufficient to bring him to the block. His execution on 22 January 1552 was carried out with an eye to avoiding popular disturbance and preceded by one day the assembling of a Parliament which might have striven to save him.

Many mourned the death of Somerset, none wept for Northumberland when seventeen months later he too went to eternity by way of Tower Green. Posterity has endorsed the contemporary verdict. The historian, who can praise Somerset's intentions if not his statesmanship, finds little to relieve the black record of Northumberland's iniquities. And yet he, too, was in some sense the victim of circumstance. If Henry VIII had lived longer, or dying had left a grown man to succeed him, Northumberland might be remembered as one of England's best soldiers instead of as one of her worst rulers. In no setting would he have been other than a 'bold, bad man', but it was the peculiar maleficence of the Tudor interregnum that it encouraged him to indulge his ambition and practise his villainies at the expense of a kingdom.

Northumberland did not share Somerset's belief, or illusion, that government could be carried on in kid gloves, and the years of his ascendancy saw a reversion to the methods of Henry VIII. True, the ferocious Treasons Act of 1549 was a panic measure which owed more to the vindictiveness of a property-owning Parliament than to the personal severity of Northumberland. It was largely his influence, however, which brought about the revival of the old harshness towards opponents of the régime. The Tower stood full of them, the axe and the rope claimed a heavy toll of victims, and the fires of Smithfield, not seen since Henry's death, were rekindled in 1551 to consume two alien heretics. But those who had hoped, or feared, that the reversal of Somerset's policy would extend to his patronage of Reform were soon proved wrong. In their ecstasy of relief ardent Protestants waxed loud in praise of the 'faithful and intrepid soldier of Christ'. But it was not the good fight that Northumberland fought, and behind his championship of the godly cause there was less of conviction than of calculation. He used it, as he was prepared to use anything, to strengthen his own position and following, and before the end even his Protestant allies had begun to see through him. Yet Northumberland served the cause of Reform better than Reform served him, and it was under the protection of this unscrupulous cynic that English Protestantism took up the positions which ensured its ultimate victory.

The second phase of the Edwardian Reformation began with three acts of 1549-50. One was purely destructive. It ordered the suppression of all service-books other than the Prayer Book and Henry VIII's Primer, and the destruction of all remaining religious statues, and paintings. 'All books called antiphoners, missals, scrayles, processionals, manuals, legends, pyes, portuyses, primers in Latin or English, cowchers, journals,' so ran the catalogue of these fine flowers of medieval faith and medieval art which were to be 'abolished, extinguished and forbidden for ever' in favour of the austerity of the printed Book of Common Prayer. And in the frenzy of destruction which followed there perished much more than was warranted even by this comprehensive schedule. At Oxford the vice-chancellor, Richard Cox, earned the sobriquet of the 'cancellor' for his zeal in proscribing, with the condemned liturgies, priceless books and manuscripts whose only taint of 'superstition' was their red-lettered or geometrical embellishments. Of the other two acts of this session the first, which provided for the reform of the canon law, came to nothing, chiefly because of the jealousy with which laymen, especially lawyers, viewed the prospect of a more efficient and therefore more dangerous rival to secular law. But the second produced the Ordinal, the new code governing the structure and functions of the hierarchy. In place of the eight orders of the medieval church, the present threefold division into bishops, priests, and deacons was adopted. The same simplifying tendency was apparent in the abolition of much of the ceremonial surrounding the ordination of priests and the consecration of bishops. But the most significant change was the transformation of the priest endowed by divine grace with the power to offer sacrifice into the minister appointed to preach, teach and conduct worship. This was, of course, the counterpart of the conversion of the Mass into the Communion. There were some who would have gone further and, by stripping ordination of its sacramental character, have denied the priest any power of conveying grace to others. Cranmer himself leaned in this direction, and the retention in the Ordinal of the 'power of order' is thus another example of his readiness to compromise in the interest of unity.

The decision was of more than theological significance. Once it was conceded that ordination was a mere man-made ceremony whose omission was no bar to the exercise of the ministry, the clergy would have become indistinguishable from those who served the state in secular offices, it would have become a sort of civil service for religious matters. Alike in theory and practice the crux of the question was the position of the bishop. No one of responsibility had yet thought of abolishing the episcopate, but the changes of the last generation had seriously weakened both its formal authority and its actual power. The bishops were given their orders by the Crown and if they refused to obey were reprimanded, imprisoned, and in the last resort dismissed. Such treatment was fatal to their prestige and authority, and they were constantly complaining of the disrepute into which they and their office were brought. And with their power went their property. Both Henry VIII and Somerset had helped themselves to episcopal lands, but it was left to Northumberland to despoil the bishops on a scale approaching the spoliation of the monasteries. When its bishop, Tunstall, was deprived in 1551 the immense lands

of Durham were largely applied to supporting Northumberland's ducal dignity. New sees like Gloucester and
Westminster were suppressed, the lands of others taken over
in exchange for annuities.

The Edwardian Reformation culminated in the revised
Prayer Book and the Forty-Two Articles of Religion. The
first completed the reform of the Anglican liturgy, the
second gave the Church of England its first creed. The
Prayer Book which had goaded the South-West into
rebellion was still too conservative for many in the South-
East. Hooper, a royal chaplain and soon a bishop, poured
out a ceaseless flow of criticism; the foreign theologians,
Bucer, Dryander, Fagius and the rest, joined in; and from
his watch-tower at Geneva Calvin urged Edward VI and
Cranmer to uproot the 'relics of popery'. But it was the new
Bishop of London, Ridley, who, exchanging counsel for
action, forced the government's hand. In May 1550
Ridley began a great mopping-up operation in his diocese.
It included a campaign against altars. Convinced that so
long as they remained they would keep alive the notion of
sacrifice, Ridley ordered their removal and replacement
by a simple table in the chancel or choir. During Whit-
week 1550 the altars disappeared from all the London
churches. Ridley's temerity – for he was acting upon his
own authority – carried the day. In November the Council
instructed all bishops to follow his example. After that
a revision of the Prayer Book was only a matter of time.
But in this, as in so many things, action had to await the
outcome of the duel between Somerset and Northumberland. Somerset's fall was followed by the issue of a commission for the purpose. Convocation, which met in
January 1552, may have been given the opportunity of
discussing the revision which had been denied it in the
case of the original, and the new Book had an easier passage

through Parliament. The most important changes were again those concerning the Eucharist. No longer was it possible for conservative minds to give the communion service that Catholic interpretation which had reconciled Gardiner and others to it in 1549. Communion was now to be celebrated at a table, not at an altar; ordinary bread was to be used, and any left over was to be consumed by the curate; the celebrant could no longer wear special vestments nor make devotional gestures; and the order of the service was changed so as to block the last loophole through which anyone might glimpse the forbidden vision of sacrifice.

The Second Act of Uniformity was passed on 14 April 1552 and came into force in the following November. Like its predecessor it penalized the holding of or attending any other form of worship than that authorized. But it also sanctioned ecclesiastical punishment, including excommunication, for laymen who failed to attend common prayer on Sundays and festivals. This was a significant addition. For the enforcement of a national minimum of church-going, besides being the simplest test of conformity in doctrine, could also be the first step in that programme of moral regeneration to which the best among the Reformers had dedicated themselves. No one could deny that something of the kind was urgently necessary. One of the new things on which enlightened opinion, of whatever political or religious persuasion, was agreed was the lamentable state of the nation's morals and manners. Whether we regard this as a legacy of the past which Reform had arisen to combat, or as the first-fruits of Reform itself, will perhaps depend largely upon our own religious allegiance. But the facts themselves are indisputable. Wherever we look, from the royal court and the circles of government down to the village and parish, and whatever type of evidence we choose, from Latimer's sweeping denunciations to the detailed facts and figures yielded by the records of royal and diocesan visitations, we are confronted by the same black picture of irreligion, irreverence and immorality on a truly terrifying scale.

Deplorable as were his own example and influence in this sphere, Northumberland could not but welcome a movement which might help to bind his crumbling régime with the cement of religious discipline. From early 1552 Edward's health, never robust, began to give grounds for alarm, and from early 1553 for despair. Northumberland knew that his days of power, if not of life, were numbered if the King were to die and be succeeded, as his father's will and an act of parliament required, by his half-sister Mary. For Mary had shown the stuff that was in her and it was not such stuff as Northumberland's dreams were made on. We do not know how early he conceived the scheme which, instead of the intractable Mary, should give Edward a successor as docile as himself, but before the end of 1552 it was common talk that he was tampering with the succession. The scheme itself was worthy of the clever, crooked mind which had begotten it. Northumberland had one unmarried son, Lord Guildford Dudley. This youth was to marry one of the four grand-daughters of Mary, younger sister of Henry VIII, and the dying King was then to make the bride a wedding-present of his crown. Of the four potential queens Northumberland eventually chose Jane, eldest daughter of Henry Grey, Duke of Suffolk, and the marriage took place on Whitsunday, 21 May 1553. Edward had then only six weeks to live, and it called for some quick thinking, helped by what looks like an act of forgery, to get the King's bequest into the right shape in time. Then the judges had to be terrorized into embodying it in an instrument which over one hundred notabilities, from archbishops to aldermen, were persuaded to sign. But by 21 June 1553 all this was done, and nothing remained but for Northumberland to seize the Princess whose heritage he had wallowed in illegality to filch from her.

Had Northumberland managed to do so, the great conspiracy might have succeeded, at least for a time. But when on 4 July she was summoned to Edward's death-bed Mary fled instead to Framlingham in Suffolk, where her reception encouraged her to stand her ground with an order to the Council to proclaim her Queen. The Council, which had already proclaimed Jane and denounced Mary's refusal to submit, replied by raising troops which Northumberland led out of London against her. It was more than fifty years since England had seen an armed contest for the throne, close on one hundred since the first battle of the Wars of the Roses. But this time there was not even a battle. Northumberland's puny force was no match for the thousands who, in the greatest mass-demonstration of loyalty ever accorded to a Tudor, flocked to Mary's camp, and he fell back before them to Cambridge. There he received the crushing news that London, too, had declared against him and that the Council had proclaimed Mary. His own last act of state was to do the same. Within a week he had rejoined his son and daughter-in-law in the Tower, where all three awaited their trial for treason. The arch-conspirator was quickly dealt with. On 18 August he, his eldest son Warwick, and his confederate Northampton were convicted, and on the 22nd he was executed. His last-minute reconversion to Catholicism, gratifying as it was to Queen and government, did not save his life. But for the time being Mary was content with similar convictions against Lady Jane and her husband, the remaining Dudleys, and Cranmer, who were then sent back to the Tower. With offenders of less eminence or culpability she was still more lenient. She lost no time, however, in removing from office most of the men who had helped Northumberland to mis-govern the country, and in promoting those distinguished by their loyalty to her person or faith. Gardiner was the man of the hour. He exchanged a hard and solitary bench in the Tower for the soft and thronged seat of the Chan-cellor, and came near to deserving the title of 'prime minister' given him by foreign diplomats. The Catholic bishops who had shared his deprival and imprisonment were restored, and their places in the Tower were soon taken by their Protestant successors.

Her enemies overthrown and her government purged, Mary set herself to fulfil what she had long known to be her life's mission, the shepherding of her people back to Rome. At first sight her reign appears to provide the most con-vincing proof that the fate of religion in Tudor England was the sport of chance, the chance which governed the succession to the throne and which had now placed upon it the most ardent Catholic in the country. Within six months of her accession England was again a Catholic kingdom, within eighteen the prodigal had returned penitent to the welcoming arms of the Holy Father in Rome. And this dramatic counter-revolution had taken place solely because one monarch had died and another reigned in his stead. Even its speed and its air of inevitability were only a measure of the monarch's singleness and strength of mind. For Mary threw herself into her task with a vigour and an imperiousness which were wholly Tudor, and without her insistent pressure it would not have been achieved. Even so, no degree of determination in its royal driver would have sufficed to hurtle the coach of national religion back along the road by which it had come if the passengers – or may we call them the 'fellow travellers'? – had not acquiesced so readily in the change of destination. The government's early encouragement of priests to revive Catholic rites provoked one or two scenes, especially in London, but soon the Mass was being celebrated in London churches 'not by commandment, but of the people's devotion,' and news was coming in of its unopposed revival throughout the country. The 'hard core' of resistance the government sought to liquidate by encouraging irreconcilables to remove themselves beyond its jurisdiction. The foreign Protestant congregations, and the refugee divines, were soon packed off to the Continent, and native sympathizers were given ample time to follow. It was to Gardiner's regret, although to their own credit, that such outstanding figures as Cranmer, Hooper and Latimer scorned to escape. But many lesser folk chose to go. Their movement overseas and settlement in the Protestant strongholds of Frankfurt, Strasbourg, Basle and Geneva form a unique chapter in the history of English religion. It was no disorderly flight, but a highly successful experiment in religious migration, designed to protect and fortify English Protestantism against the day of liberation.

As the first of the emigrants were betaking themselves abroad, parliament was beginning to demolish the temple which they had helped to build. Unlike Northumberland, who had interfered considerably with elections, Mary at first made no attempt to pack the House of Commons, and her first Parliament contained some scores of Protestants. Yet up to a point it proved amenable enough. The divorce of Queen Catherine was annulled and Mary's legitimacy established. All recent treason laws were repealed. Then at one sweep all the religious legislation of the last six years – the two Acts of Uniformity and those concerning the election of bishops, the marriage of priests, the removal of images and the keeping of festivals – was swept away.

It was no small achievement to have destroyed the Edwardian Reformation, and knocked one or two holes in the Henrician, within a single session. But it was less than Mary had hoped for, and it had been accompanied by more than one rebuff. With two of the Queen's major projects, the revival of Papal power and the restoration of Church lands, this Parliament had shown that it would have nothing to do. It had declined to gratify her longing to dispense with her title of Supreme Head, thus driving her into the subterfuge (afterwards copied by Elizabeth) of replacing it by the non-committal 'etc.'. It had also refused to attach any penalty to non-attendance at Mass. And beyond these obstacles to the complete restoration of the old order there loomed a last and insurmountable barrier. Even though a regenerate parliament might be induced to undo everything which its misguided predecessors had done, the old order, thus become the new, would have acquired in the process the taint of secular sanction. If the Mass was now legally restored, it was because parliament had restored it; and if Mary were now accounted legitimate, it was because parliament had declared her to be so. What a statute had taken away, only a statute could restore; and what one statute had restored, another statute could rescind. In grounding his Reformation upon parliamentary authority Henry VIII had invested parliament with a competence in matters spiritual which not even the most Catholic of his successors could take away.

Before Mary's first Parliament ended it was moved to counsel the Queen against a project of a different kind. This was her proposed marriage to Philip of Spain. The rooted prejudice against women rulers was inevitable in a society where women were legally and conventionally subject to men and where therefore the marriage of a queen regnant presented an almost insoluble problem. For a

queen to take unto herself a lord and master meant conferring the kingship either upon a native inferior or upon a
foreign equal. To do the first was to compromise internal
peace, to do the second was to jeopardize national independence. Elizabeth would evade the dilemma by remaining single. But Mary was not free to do so. Her father's
need for an heir had driven him to make the Reformation;
if Mary were to unmake the Reformation she, too, must
have an heir of her body. For otherwise the crown would
pass, and with it the religious destiny of the realm, into
the hands of the princess whose birth had occasioned the
breach with Rome and whose very right to succeed involved
a repudiation of papal authority. There were, to be sure,
other possible ways of impeding Elizabeth's succession,
and they would be much canvassed during Mary's reign;
but the only method which was both impeccable and
infallible was to produce an heir to supplant her. When it
came to the choice of a husband, one royal house seemed
pre-eminently suited to Mary's purpose, the house of
Habsburg. Headed by the most powerful of living rulers,
the Emperor Charles V, the Habsburg dynasty sprawled
mammoth-like across the European scene. Its prestige and
resources were immense, its loyalty to the Catholic faith
unquestioned. The regal pride which forbade Mary to wed
a subject would be gratified by a connexion with the
greatest of reigning houses; the filial piety which likewise
strove against an English marriage such as had ruined her
mother's life and embittered her own welcomed a union
with her injured mother's family; and the plain middle-
aged woman whose life had been pathetically barren of
love or friendship was easily captivated by the youthful
vigour of the Habsburg claimant to her hand. Philip of
Spain was no Prince Charming, but he was much more
eligible than either of the Englishmen who had been

mentioned, the fifty-year-old Cardinal Pole and the foolish Edward Courtenay, Earl of Devon.

The considerations which moved the Queen were not calculated to weigh with her subjects, and she came to her decision against the almost unanimous advice of her counsellors, the remonstrance of her parliament and the unconcealed hostility of her people. Hatred of the foreigner was rampant in Tudor England. Henry VIII had both exploited and mightily fostered it in his conflict with Pope and Emperor. In his day the national xenophobia had vented itself chiefly upon Frenchmen, the traditional enemies in war, and on Germans, Netherlanders and Italians, the chief rivals in business; Spaniards, being less familiar, were less unpopular. None the less it was a bad moment to introduce a Spanish consort. Although Tudors and Habsburgs had long been allies, the real tie which bound them was economic, and it passed through the Netherlands. So long as the Low Countries remained at once the fountainhead of Burgundian-Spanish finance and the cynosure of English commerce, the Anglo-Spanish entente was strong enough to survive dynastic and religious estrangements. But by 1553 the economic bond was being fatally weakened. The collapse of the Antwerp market in 1550 was already sending Englishmen in quest of new markets in more distant lands, and it would soon lead them to challenge the Spanish-Portuguese monopoly of the Southern Hemisphere. At the same time the possession of that monopoly was progressively distorting Spain's outlook and encouraging her to sacrifice the welfare of Antwerp to a programme of political domination and religious bigotry sanctioned by the illusory wealth of the Indies. It was upon this sinking foundation of common interest that there was now to be erected the intimate alliance resulting from the marriage. Under the strain the foundation would crack and break and the whole edifice of Anglo-Spanish accord collapse in ruin.

The marriage-treaty concluded in the first days of 1554 was on paper very favourable to England. Philip was to be styled king and was to assist in the government, but Mary alone was to bestow, and Englishmen alone to fill, offices in Church and State. The treaty was not to affect England's foreign commitments nor involve the country in war. Of the clauses governing the succession to the various thrones concerned only one was destined to become operative, the one which terminated Philip's regal status in England in the event of Mary's dying childless. But it is interesting to reflect that a child of the marriage would have been Philip's heir in Burgundy and the Netherlands as well as Mary's in England. Neither these contingent provisions (which to contemporaries were not the mere 'might have been' that they are to us) nor the immediate concessions did much to reconcile English opinion, and there were many 'looking daily for worse matters to grow shortly after'. They did not have to look for long. Even while the treaty was under negotiation the Council was arresting potential rebels, and within a fortnight of its signature the Tudor monarchy was facing the third, and in one sense the greatest, of its crises, the rebellion of Sir Thomas Wyatt.

What made Wyatt's rebellion momentarily so serious was its location. The risings of 1536 and 1549 had broken out – and the same would be true of the rebellion of 1569 – too far from London to bring effective pressure to bear on the national nerve-centre. (The same factor was to tell against attempts at 'direct action' later in English history, and it may be that we have here one of the clues to our boasted immunity from revolution.) Of the series of risings planned in 1554, all misfired except the rising in Kent. Its leader, Sir Thomas Wyatt, was a man whose proven military qualities fitted him ill for the humdrum of civil life. For religion he cared little, and although he might pose as the champion of the Prayer Book, what had stung him into rebellion was not the return of the Roman faith but the advent of a Spanish king. It was that, too, which brought him most of the four thousand followers who thronged his camp at Rochester in the last days of January 1554. A force of Londoners led against him by the Duke of Norfolk went over to him in a body. But when he reached Southwark it was to find London Bridge defended against him. Mary had shown herself a Tudor in her courage and her capacity to evoke loyalty, and the citizens had rallied to her cause. Baffled by their resistance, Wyatt carried out, on the night of 6–7 February, a swift flanking movement which took him over the Thames at Kingston and thence towards London from the west. History has often been made on the square mile of ground about Charing Cross, but seldom so dramatically as during the brief daylight of that February afternoon. Brushing aside the royal troops under Pembroke, Wyatt pushed through Fleet Street to the city wall at Ludgate only to find it, like the Bridge four days earlier, held against him. The Queen was still in the city. Had she taken Gardiner's advice and fled, she might have lost both city and kingdom. As it was, London held firm, and Wyatt, the cup of victory snatched from his lip, turned back to find Pembroke hemming him in at Temple Bar. As darkness fell, he surrendered. He and his lieutenants were taken to the Tower, his followers rounded up and herded into the city prisons and churches. They had come nearer to unseating a Tudor sovereign than any others before or after them. But in failing to pass the gates of London they had also failed to breach the rampart of loyalty which ringed the Tudor throne.

The first to suffer for the rebellion were two who had no share in it. Five days after Wyatt entered the Tower, Lady Jane Grey and her husband were brought forth to their execution. That these two young lives, which had for months lain forfeit to one man's ambition, should have been doomed by another's recklessness, adds the final poignancy to the most pathetic page of Tudor history. Few lovelier heads have worn a crown, and no purer a spirit ever inhabited a royal person, than Jane Grey's; and if she lacked the divinity which hedges kings, she had more than a touch of the sanctity which hallows saints. The 'traitor-heroine of the Reformation' was followed to the block by her father Suffolk and her uncle Thomas Grey, and by Wyatt himself. Others escaped with their lives, among them Sir Nicholas Throckmorton, whose acquittal by a London jury, amid the applause of the populace, showed that the same public opinion which had ensured the rebels' failure would have them spared its penalty. But the man in the street was seldom much affected by the sight of noble and gentle heads being struck off for real or imagined threats to those in power; it was one of the dangers of being a gentleman which, like the compensating privileges, lay outside the range of his experience. What was more disturbing was the score of gallows at the city gates and in its thoroughfares, each bearing the rotting remains of a simple fellow man. About a hundred of Wyatt's rank and file were hanged, some in London, the rest in their native Kent. If at the time their fate may have been adjudged a 'cruel necessity', it was otherwise when they were followed by the three hundred men and women, like them chiefly common folk, whom the same government was to send to the stake for their religion. Then it was easy to think of those who had hung with Wyatt because they could not stomach the marriage with Spain and those who burned with Cranmer

because they could not abide the reunion with Rome as
fellow-victims of a single system of frightfulness.

Had Wyatt succeeded, Mary's reign would have gone
down to history, like that of the only previous woman ruler
in England, as a time of anarchy and civil war. His failure
spared the country this ordeal, but at the cost of hardening
the Queen's determination to go through with her programme. A month after Wyatt had vainly tried to stop her,
Mary was married by proxy to Philip. She had to wait
another five before they could be wedded in person in
Winchester Cathedral. That was in July. Four months
more, and the Queen touched a summit of ambition and
achievement. On 24 November the long-awaited papal
legate arrived in London. On the 29th both Houses of
Parliament petitioned for reunion with Rome, and on the
following day, after the King and Queen had interceded
for their realm, the legate pronounced its absolution
from schism. It was just twenty years since the passing of the
Act of Supremacy. The new King was a foreigner, but the
new Legate was a descendant of English kings. Reginald
Pole's unswerving loyalty to his Church had brought his
mother and brother to the block and earned him an
attainder for treason and twenty years' exile from his
native land. In 1549 he had narrowly missed being elected
Pope. But Mary's accession had opened to him the prospect
of realizing a more cherished ambition, that of reconciling
his country with Rome. The Emperor would not let Pole
leave for England until after Philip had established himself there, and even then there were certain obstacles to
be overcome. In law Pole was a traitor, and until Parliament had removed this disability he could not enter
the country. Mary did her best to secure the return of
men of the 'wise, grave, and catholic sort' to the Parliament
which met in November 1554, and it was to prove the least

intractable of her reign. But although, unlike its predecessor, this Parliament consented to reunion with Rome, it too set its face resolutely against any restoration of Church lands. Only after they had been reassured on this point did Lords and Commons proceed to the reversal of Pole's attainder and so make possible his reception. It was a sore trial to one who bore the priceless gift of absolution to see that gift dishonoured by such shameless bargaining. But the choice between accepting or refusing it was parliament's, and parliament was the landowners'. A statute safeguarded the holders of Church lands against papal afterthoughts or canonical subtleties. All that Pole could do was to appeal to conscience, and there were few consciences which responded. One of the few was the Queen's, who went out of her way to restore the lands which had remained with the Crown. Thus Mary's attempt to undo what her father had done only upset still further the balance between the landed wealth of the monarchy and that of its subjects.

The Parliament which was so determined to keep the Church out of its lands was perhaps for that reason the more willing to give it a free hand in matters of faith and discipline. The heresy laws were revived, the limitations on ecclesiastical jurisdiction abolished, and thus the way made plain for the great persecution. The first martyr, John Rogers, was burnt at Smithfield on 4 February 1555, and before Mary's death brought the persecution to an end some three hundred persons had suffered this horrible death. About one-third of them were clergymen, and among the lay victims were sixty women. Varied as was this heroic company, it was not a wholly representative section of the English people. London and six home counties supplied more than two-thirds of the total, while the whole of the North saw only one burning, as did the region south-west of Salisbury. Differences in persecuting zeal may have accentuated this geographical contrast, but the main reason for it is clear: the South-East was the stronghold of Protestantism. A social and occupational analysis of the martyrs reveals a similar limitation. The few men of gentle birth who went to the stake were clerics, the lay victims without exception common folk. In this respect the Marian martyrs offer a striking contrast to the Marian exiles. It may be that some of the gentlefolk who had gone abroad might, if called upon, have remained faithful unto death; but the fact that no single layman of birth or breeding appears on that roll of honour suggests that the English upper class contained little of the stuff of martyrs. The same might be said of the rural population generally, for most of the martyrs dwelt in the towns or the industrialized countryside, and the proportion of artisans among them was high. England was no exception to the rule by which Protestantism took root most easily in urban and industrial communities.

By Continental standards the number of English martyrs was small. But this is not how their fellow-countrymen measured the death-roll. Their yardstick was the national history and their own experience, and in neither did they find anything to approach it. The century and a quarter preceding 1529 had seen perhaps a hundred Lollard martyrs, and during the first twenty years of the Reformation some sixty individuals had been executed for religion.* And even if we regard the two hundred Catholic victims of Elizabeth's reign as martyrs to their faith rather than as traitors to their realm, their death-rate of eight a year does not compare with the Marian figure of nearly ninety. Mary's persecution is thus something unique in English

---

* This figure includes both Catholic and Protestant martyrs, but not those executed for treason in the form of rebellion on religious grounds.

history. The Queen and her abettors could, indeed, be pardoned for not foreseeing the lengths to which they would be carried. At the first examination of the first martyr one of the judges had sneered: 'Thou will not burn in this gear, when it cometh to the purpose; I know well that.' But John Rogers had belied the prophecy and had set a standard of courage which was well maintained. The belief that an example or two would be sufficient proved equally false. Every fresh martyr became an inspiration rather than a deterrent, and it was only when some influential figure flinched from its horror, as did Sir John Cheke in 1556, that the ranks broke behind him. What was the supreme test for the martyr was also a test of his persecutors. Gardiner soon sickened of the work, and before his death in November 1555 he could see its futility. But among his brother-bishops there were enough who neither saw nor felt with him to ensure that it went on, and Pole, Cranmer's successor as Archbishop of Canterbury, was to rank second only to the implacable Bonner in the number of his diocesan victims. To say that the Queen herself bears the heaviest responsibility is as much a tribute to her sincerity as a reflection on her statesmanship. For Mary was far from being the inhuman creature which her unenviable epithet suggests. Where her own safety and authority were at stake she showed herself the most merciful of her line, and her clemency to traitors more than once bordered on folly. But with heresy it was different. There conscience, not inclination, was her guide, and the fierce glare of religious passion blinded her to the softer lights of humanity and good sense.

So there was played out the drama which, for good or ill, was to remain one of the most vivid in the collective memory of the English people. Latimer's exhortation to Ridley as the fire licked around them was indeed prophetic, and the flame of remembrance which was lit at Oxford and Smithfield, at Norwich and Chichester, is not yet out. But there is no light without shadow, and the bright candle which has illuminated many a pilgrim's way has also darkened many a page of the national story. For the burnings did more than anything else to generate that 'unthinking, ferocious, and almost indelible' hatred which generations of otherwise tolerant and short-memoried Englishmen were to nourish towards Rome. Not for nothing was Foxe's *Book of Martyrs* to become the most widely read and possessed of English classics, nor a score of memorials to testify to Protestantism's fiery Confirmation. During her brief reign Mary Tudor was her Church's greatest asset in England; since the day of her death her memory has always been its greatest liability.

What Mary's devotion to her Faith did for its future in England, her devotion to her husband did for the future of English relations with Spain. During his eighteen months in England Philip behaved much better than might have been expected, and although Parliament could not be induced to allow his coronation it so far relaxed its earlier hostility as to give him the protection of the treason laws and the regency of any child whom Mary might leave at her death. But with the best will in the world Philip could not have avoided mistrust, and he would have been more or less than human if he had not sought to turn his wife's affection to his own ends. He had married her solely to bring England into the Habsburg combine, and although in theory England preserved her liberty of action the marriage had none the less aligned her with the Imperialist bloc and against its enemy, France. The French King thus became the natural ally of all opponents of the Marian-Philippine régime and his hand was seen in every rebellion and plot against it. When in January 1557 a brief truce between France and the Habsburgs dissolved into a fresh war, only a determined effort of self-abnegation on Philip's part, and of self-assertion on Mary's, could have kept England at peace. Since leaving England Philip's conduct had been such as to convince all but his doting wife that he no longer felt a shred of conjugal duty. But the marriage, loveless and sterile as it was, remained his strongest political asset, and in the spring of 1557 he came over to claim the dividend. Mary, who still clung desperately to the hope of a child, was overjoyed, and in his presence her doubts and scruples melted away. When her counsellors obstinately opposed the war, she summoned them individually to her room and threatened them, 'some with death, some with the loss of their goods and estates, if they did not consent to the will of her husband'. It was Tudor language, but put to such a use as no other Tudor would have dreamt of. And it might have failed of its purpose if a hare-brained adventurer, Thomas Stafford, had not chosen this moment to resurrect the distant claim to the throne which had brought his grandfather, Buckingham, to the block in 1521, and if the King of France had not chosen to support his enterprise. This display of French arrogance destroyed the Council's will to resist their imperious Queen, and in June 1557 war was declared.

The waging of war, even on the modest scale of the age, was an undertaking which strained to the utmost the resources of the sixteenth-century state, and every campaign brought its tale of financial shifts, administrative breakdowns, and civil and military disorders. But the war of 1557 was certainly more difficult than most. The government's forced loan met with unusual opposition; in some areas martial law was needed to suppress popular agitation; and the armed forces themselves were deplorably lacking in morale. Even Philip's early success at St Quentin proved a misfortune, for it induced the false sense of security which was partly to blame for the fall of Calais (8 January 1558). The loss of Calais has been called one of the enduring benefits which Mary gave to her country. The town was both expensive and burdensome. Its possession was a perpetual incitement to attacks on France, and for her part France had never ceased, and would never cease, to covet it. As a trading centre, too, Calais had lost its former importance. The wool-trade was in its death-throes, and attempts to erect Calais into a cloth-mart had broken down in face of the superior attraction of Antwerp. If England had men and money to spare for overseas possessions, it was far better that these should be sited with an eye to the new world-strategy than to the old limited strategy of North-West Europe. Englishmen are quick to make a virtue out of necessity, and they were soon using such arguments to reconcile themselves to the loss. But they could not excuse the disgraceful way in which England parted with Calais or the failure to attempt its recapture, and Mary admitted as much with the remark for which, after her persecuting zeal, the ordinary Englishman alone remembers her.

'Sterility,' so runs Pollard's famous epigram, 'was the conclusive note of Mary's reign.' Frustrated in all her hopes and aims, the Queen herself sank into a melancholia bordering on insanity. Her marriage had brought her, instead of marital affection and the joy of motherhood, the lonely bitterness of desertion and the dread realization that she would never bear a child. From the reconciliation with Rome, instead of the exaltation of high spiritual achievement, she had reaped the groans of a nation whose stubborn lesion of heresy she strove vainly to cauterize. Emotionally deranged and mentally exhausted, this least Tudorlike of Tudor sovereigns could neither depend on herself nor find anyone on whom to lean. Gardiner, her ablest minister, was dead; Pole, once the channel of papal benediction, was now in disgrace at Rome and, like his Queen, was carrying his grey hairs in sorrow to the grave. Within the Council all was jealousy and faction, every man working for himself and no man for the state. And since, alike in theory and practice, Tudor government knew no other initiative than that of the Crown and its advisers, the entire realm, thus deprived of its accustomed leadership, drifted purposelessly through the last empty years of the reign. Parliament could obstruct, but obstruction was no substitute for direction. The restored Church was too much engrossed in restoring its monopoly to undertake the immense and urgent task of spiritual reawakening. Men of property were immersed in the rewarding task of modernizing estates and businesses, and the mass of the people had enough to do to wring a livelihood out of a world in which everything grew steadily dearer. Politically bankrupt, spiritually impoverished, economically anarchic, and intellectually enervated, Marian England awaited the day of its deliverance.

VI

THE RANKS REFORMED

In our own time November brings two anniversaries, falling on its fifth and eleventh days. But for close on two centuries our ancestors observed another November day, the seventeenth. It was the anniversary of the accession of Queen Elizabeth. Originating in the outburst of relief which followed the Northern Rebellion of 1569, the celebration was also a measure of the growing conviction that the English had been blessed among nations when on 17 November 1558 the Lady Elizabeth had become their Queen.

Elizabeth's fame rests upon three things, her longevity, her long-preserved virginity, and her political genius. Together they made possible the Elizabethan Age. Yet no one could have prophesied when she came to the throne that she would see the dawn of a new century, die a spinster or live so glorious in the national memory. Of the Tudor royal line only two men and one woman had passed the age of fifty, two women had died in middle life, and two* youths at sixteen. It was not a good heredity. True, Elizabeth had reached twenty-five without serious malady and she had all the signs of good health and something of her father's passion for physical exercise. But the preacher's warning that 'in the midst of life we are in death' applied with great force to the sixteenth century, with its virulent disease and vicious doctoring. Within four years Elizabeth was nearly dead of small-pox (October 1562). It was the one grave illness of a remarkably healthy life, but it showed

* Or, if we include the illegitimate Richmond, three.

by how slender a thread the tranquillity of the realm was upheld.

For there can, and could, be little doubt that if Elizabeth had died before the age of fifty-five – and only one Tudor had lived so long – there would have been civil war in England. The reason was fatally simple: she had no generally acceptable successor. Elizabeth was the last of Henry VIII's children. If she herself left no child, the throne would in law pass to a descendant of one of the old King's sisters. Henry had given priority to his younger sister Mary, Duchess of Suffolk. Of Mary's three grand-daughters the eldest, Lady Jane Grey, had paid with her life for her nearness to the throne, and it was the second, Catherine, who now bore the claim. Henry's other sister Margaret had married James IV of Scotland, and her only living descendant by that marriage was Mary Stuart, Queen of Scots since she was a week old. Both potential successors were open to grave objections. Catherine was a subject at whose elevation faction would infallibly raise its head, Mary an alien with only one English grandparent. More serious still were the complications introduced by international politics and religion. We have seen that for fifty years European politics had been dominated by the struggle between the Habsburgs of Spain and the Empire and the Valois who ruled France. England's alignment was normally with the Habsburgs, and the French kings countered by allying with Scotland. This 'back door' of the Scottish Border Henry VIII and Somerset had striven to close by uniting the two crowns, but when that project foundered both countries returned to their traditional roles. In 1554 Mary Tudor had married Philip of Spain, in 1558 Mary Stuart was married to Francis, the Dauphin of France. Thenceforward Mary Queen of Scots personified the Franco-Scottish alliance, and her claim to the English succession became a bid to convert it into a triple one by absorbing England. To Philip II of Spain the prospect of seeing his late kingdom thus annexed by his enemies was one not to be borne. His own offer of marriage to Elizabeth was certainly reluctant and perhaps only half-serious. But he was intensely interested in the future of Catherine Grey, and there were various projects for marrying her to a Habsburg.

But more was at stake than the succession. Was Elizabeth herself rightfully seated on the throne? Her father's will and an act of one of his parliaments said so, and doubtless for the vast majority of Englishmen these were title enough. But what of those who did not admit the competence of kings or parliaments to turn black into white merely by calling it so, making and unmaking marriages and legitimizing or bastardizing their offspring as seemed good to them? In Catholic eyes Elizabeth, child of an unlawful union, could not be a legitimate sovereign, and her throne ought to pass without delay to the person next in line whose legitimacy was beyond dispute. Such at least was the letter of the canon law. Whether or when it would be applied depended, however, less on spiritual than on secular considerations. The Catholic Prince who was most doctrinaire on the subject was Henry II of France. For in his daughter-in-law Henry had the obvious Catholic claimant to the English throne. He had thought of asserting Mary Stuart's claim even against Mary Tudor. On her death he did not hesitate. He had Mary Stuart proclaimed Queen of England and the arms of England quartered on her shield. But his action stung his fellow-Catholic Philip II into a vigorous defence of Elizabeth's right to her throne. At Rome, while the French ambassador urged the Pope to denounce the English Queen, Spanish influence was exerted to protect her.

The inveterate hostility of France and Spain was Elizabeth's greatest initial asset. To the game of playing one off against the other she brought both supreme natural aptitude and the experience of having long played it on a smaller field, and she needed no further lessons. But there were signs that this reassuring state of affairs might not last. For France and Spain were making peace. Both were bankrupt, both needed to put their houses in order. In particular, both kings were alarmed at the spread of heresy among their subjects and longed to get to grips with it. The outlook for liberty has always seemed blackest when the two greatest powers have come together to settle affairs between them. Just as in 1807 the Treaty of Tilsit, or in 1939 the Moscow Pact, appeared for a time to portend a universal condominium, so in 1559 the Peace of Cateau-Cambrésis was big with menace to political and religious unorthodoxy. None could doubt that it would go hard with heresy in Paris and in Antwerp. But would the two crusaders stop at their own frontiers? Germany was safe, for Catholics and Protestants had fought each other to a standstill there and the Settlement of Augsburg (1555) would give them half a century of uneasy peace. Yet more than one country might be confirmed in or reclaimed for the Faith if France and Spain were to support a great Catholic drive. Already the Church was regaining its lost leadership and in the Society of Jesus it had a magnificent weapon. Before this formidable array of spiritual and secular power the ranks of Western Protestantism might break and scatter.

It was with the knowledge that every move she made would affect this great balance of contingencies that Elizabeth began her reign. While in one sense the problem which faced her was bewilderingly complex, in another it was starkly simple. Could the country be preserved from the twin catastrophes of internal anarchy and foreign domination? That was the question, and the answer to it would depend upon the answers to a number of others. First, and fundamental to all the rest, was the question whether a young princess whom a hitherto unkind fate had robbed alike of an unchallengeable right to rule and of all formal education in the art of ruling could restore to the throne the strength and the prestige with which her great forbears had invested it. Hers was the kingdom, would hers be the power and the glory? Could she tame the unruly and factious spirits who would see in her advent fresh opportunity for self-assertion and mischief-making? Would her ministers be her servants, not her masters? Could she lean on her parliaments and yet secure that they did her bidding? And what of the great national issues – religion, the succession, defence, economic reconstruction, overseas expansion? Could she frame policies and see them, if not fully carried out – that would be Utopian – at least not openly challenged or ignored? And while she strove to do these things, could she hold at arm's length those sinister figures from abroad who would press in upon her with their whispers, their threats, their blows? The first year was to answer some of these questions, the next twelve would answer them all. Elizabeth had not been a month on the throne before the Spanish ambassador was reporting that she seemed incomparably more feared than her sister, and that she gave her orders and had her way as absolutely as her father did. That was, of course, the first of her secrets. Riding through London in her coronation procession she smiled in gratification when an onlooker was moved to call out, 'Remember old King Henry the Eighth.' To those who could recall Henry in his splendid youth the resemblance must have been striking – the tall, athletic figure, the golden hair, the fine skin, the flashing eye. He lived on, too, in her physical awareness and vanity. From the thirty-year old Elizabeth forcing an embarrassed young Scots envoy into a comparison of her charms with those of his own Queen the mind leaps back to the twenty-four-year old Henry baring his leg to the French ambassador and demanding whether his King could show such a calf. Again like her father, and again largely owing to him, Elizabeth was both well-educated and had a genuine love of learning. Roger Ascham, who had succeeded Grindal as her tutor in 1548, was still reading Greek and Latin with her every day when she had been four years a queen. But her forte was modern languages: she spoke and wrote French, Italian, and German. Her written style was too laborious for our taste, but she always spoke well and, as her most famous speeches prove, she could on occasion use the language of Shakespeare with an eloquence which her predecessors emulate only in his pages.

Elizabeth's fulfilment of the first duty which fell to every sovereign, the selection of councillors and office-bearers, was not unindicative of the shape of things to come. When complete her Privy Council consisted of eleven men who had served under Mary and seven new ones. But whereas Mary had favoured ecclesiastics as councillors, Elizabeth began with only one, who soon dropped out, and then for many years kept the council an exclusively lay body. Of her new appointments none represented greater continuity than the most important of all, that of Sir William Cecil as Secretary. Since he first came to the fore under Somerset, Cecil had survived two crises which would have cut short the career, if not the life, of a less dexterous or less useful minister, and through eleven turbulent years he had never been far from the seat of power. Lawyer-trained, he had already been Secretary, had sat in every parliament since 1547, had been on missions abroad, and at thirty-eight was master of his trade. His religion would never have stood in the way of his duty to his sovereign or to himself, but what there was of it was Protestant. He had forty years of life and service left in him, and he gave them all, without stint, to his mistress. 'This judgement I have of you,' she said at his appointment, 'that you will not be corrupted with any manner of gifts, and that you will be faithful to the state'. She never made a sounder judgement, or a better appointment.

Their first great task was to settle religion. Elizabeth was wholly lacking in the conviction which had both compelled and enabled her sister to carry through her great reversal of policy. Reared in her father's Catholicism she had adapted herself with little difficulty first to the Protestantism of her brother's mentors and afterwards to her sister's orthodoxy. Thereafter expediency dictated that she should keep her real opinions to herself, and apart from the frank impatience with theological hair-splittings which she shared with most Englishmen and the instinctive repugnance for clerical marriage which she shared with her father they have remained largely a matter for speculation. But was not a ruler whose only real belief was belief in herself, and whose only real devotion was devotion to her people, the ideal restorative for a country which had just undergone the drastic purge of the Marian Persecution? Undoubtedly it was, and therein lies the master-clue to the success of the Elizabethan Settlement. Yet, as the greatest of modern English historians has reminded us, when we look back at the circumstances in which that settlement took shape, we cannot be certain that the path which Elizabeth chose was, or could have appeared, the safer of the two which lay before her. For there were two paths, and only two. Within the last generation the country had tried in turn three. It had followed Henry VIII along one which, when three centuries later it reappeared, would be labelled Anglo-

Catholicism. But that path had been petering out even before 1547. It had served only so long as most Englishmen, the King included, hated the Pope but still adored the Mass. Since those days much water had flowed under many bridges – in Rome, in Trent and Bologna, in Geneva, in London. The Papacy, after being thrust this way and that and all but thrown, was getting firmly seated again, and the great campaign to transfer supreme power in the Church from a Single Head to an Assembly was on the point of ending in complete failure. Looking at either France or Spain, Elizabeth might indeed have wondered whether she too could not remain orthodox and yet keep the Pope almost as powerless as her father had made him. But that could have succeeded only if there had been more Englishmen devoted to the old Catholicism which was dying at Trent and fewer to the new Protestantism which was being born at Geneva.

Elizabeth had to choose, then, between 'Catholicism with its Pope and the creed for which Cranmer and Ridley died'. She was well aware of the benefits which would flow from a decision for Catholicism. At home, everything and everybody could be left practically undisturbed; the burnings would have to stop, but that would gratify all but a few bigoted bishops. Abroad, she would be free to make her peace with the Pope (and doubtless have the little matter of her legitimacy set right), to bind Philip of Spain firmly to her cause, and to extort a favourable peace from Henry II – might she not even recover Calais? – as the price of Mary Stuart's succession. It was a prospect with which a Catholic Queen might hope to seduce all but the staunchest Protestant. The loss of Calais, it was said, had emptied English churches; a diplomatic triumph on this scale would help to refill them. Why did Elizabeth turn away from these tempting vistas? We know, of course, that she did her shameless best not to lose sight of them altogether. But she had to choose, and she chose against Rome. Elizabeth always hated medicine of any kind, and Papal Supremacy, however diluted, would have been a bitter draught, too bitter, perhaps, for this daughter of Henry VIII and Anne Boleyn, to swallow. The doctrinal issue was less clear-cut. But there a staunch heart might have overborne a neutral conscience. For Elizabeth, too, had suffered under Mary. She had been the Protestants' hope then, and some of them were dangerously near to making her their idol now. She could not desert them. Pride and loyalty, two fundamentals of Elizabeth's nature, were thus engaged, and both fought against Catholicism. So did a third – courage. For the choice which their ruler had to make for the English people in 1559 was no other than the choice which their elected rulers had to make nearly four hundred years later: it was the choice between appeasement and defiance. To conciliate the Catholic Powers might have seemed then, as to conciliate the Axis was to seem later, the way to pluck the flower safety from the nettle danger. But what would this safety cost, and what would it be worth? The road which led to Rome was certainly broad and in some respects inviting, but so too, the Queen's Bible told her, was the road which led to destruction. Her decision to take the other, whose perils, if greater, were less insidious, was thus after all an act of faith, of faith in herself to lead, and in her people, united behind her, to follow, past all perils and through all ordeals. The Elizabethan Settlement was to be the fitting prologue to the Elizabethan Age.

The Settlement was hammered out in Elizabeth's first Parliament, which sat from January to April 1559. It was not easy work. The House of Commons was hardly content to follow the government's lead, the House of Lords much less so. The bishops stuck manfully to the principles in which they had been reared and preferred. In the Lords they voted solidly against every government proposal; in Convocation they reaffirmed the old doctrines and the Papal Supremacy and vetoed Parliamentary meddling with them. In the Commons, by contrast, it was the Protestant radicals who made the running: the minimal changes with which, so it seems, the Queen would have contented herself left them unsatisfied. At Easter the battle shifted momentarily from the Palace of Westminster to the Abbey, where a public disputation – one of those colloquies so much in vogue – took place between champions of either party. But this soon broke up in disorder, and its only result was to translate two obstreperous bishops to the Tower. This strenuous opposition, if it did not make the government change its mind, did cause it to moderate its language. A bill giving the Queen the Supreme Headship had already passed both Houses. But at the last moment it was abandoned and after a ten-day adjournment Parliament was set to work upon two new bills. The first declared Elizabeth the 'Supreme Governor' of the realm in matters spiritual. The new formula was meant to placate both those who objected to the Headship altogether and those who objected to conferring it on a woman. To us it is a distinction without a difference, and new 'Governor' is but old 'Head' writ large. But it mollified both Philip II and zealous Calvinists, it eased all doubtful minds, and it passed both Houses. The second bill proposed to restore, with a few modifications, the Prayer Book of 1552 as the only authorized liturgy. If safety had been the prime consideration Elizabeth might have borrowed the Lutheran worship now legalized in Germany. But her settlement was nothing if not indigenous, and the Prayer Book already shone with the lustre of its martyred authors. Both

Houses now adopted it with alacrity. The Uniformity Bill was through by 28 April, the Supremacy Bill by the 29th. The Church of England was by law established.

The great battle which had been won and lost at Westminster had then to be refought in innumerable little engagements all over the country. To enforce its measures the government sent commissioners, organized in six circuits, to visit every diocese and parish. With one dishonourable exception the bishops refused to take the Oath of Supremacy and were deprived of their sees. How the clergy responded it is not so easy to decide. There were about 8,000 beneficed clergy in England. Estimates of the number who refused to conform and lost their livings range from a near-contemporary figure of 177 to a modern Catholic one of 2,000, and the student is free to place his guess at any point in between, at 200 with Maitland, at 300 with Powicke, at 1,000 with Pollard. The commissioners did not go out of their way to make recusants, rather they tempered the Protestant wind to the hesitant shepherd Again, whereas under Mary deprival had sometimes beeι. the prelude to martyrdom, under Elizabeth it was seldom followed by further penalty. The bishops were put under custody, but despite a Protestant howl for vengeance not one was executed. Of the deprived clergy some went into exile and were heard of again, but the great majority were reabsorbed into that vast and (outside the parish register and the muster roll) nameless body of Englishmen who lived and died in an obscurity which no historian can penetrate. If their numbers approached the higher estimates, the Elizabethan Church must have begun its career with an acute labour shortage. There were, of course, the returning exiles, who, as soon as the new régime showed its hand, came flocking back full of expectations. But the exiles could not have made good so large a defection, and they presented a problem in themselves, with their advanced notions and, in many cases, their dubious clerical status. It was, however, mainly from their ranks that Elizabeth replenished the bench of bishops, now all but empty. Her first Primate, Matthew Parker, was not an exile, but a retiring scholar who had gone 'underground' during the persecution. Devout, moderate, and passionately loyal, Parker has been called the ecclesiastical counterpart of Cecil, and in her satisfaction with him Elizabeth could overlook, as her father had overlooked in Cranmer, his one drawback in her eyes – his wife.

At home the Settlement gave promise of fulfilling its primary purpose, the union of all moderate-minded men behind the throne. Abroad, it was soon making its contribution to an immense strengthening of England's position. In April 1559 England and Spain made their peace with France at Cateau-Cambrésis. Elizabeth had to renounce all but the slenderest hope of recovering Calais; it was inevitable, it was galling, it was a blessing in disguise. Far more disturbing was the projected marriage between Philip II and the French King's daughter which formed part of the bargain between them. For marriage was the chosen instrument of Habsburg diplomacy, and this one boded no good to the Queen who had first rejected Philip's hand and since clouded their friendship by her patronage of heresy. But kings do not only marry, they also die. Within eighteen months two kings of France were dead, Henry II through an accident at a tourney (July 1559) and his son Francis II of an infected mastoid (December 1560). At the time English brows were furrowed and English heads shaken at what these royal demises might portend. The first placed the Queen of Scots on the French throne and her relatives the Guises round its steps; the second made a child King of France and Mary a childless dowager, and supplanted the power of Guise by that of the great rival house of Bourbon. France was, in fact, standing in 1560 where England had stood in 1547, on the threshold of a royal minority which would unleash the three monsters of political faction, religious frenzy and social ferment. But before Francis died French power was still formidable, and it was during his brief reign that Elizabeth had to brave the Gallic wrath. The campaign against the French Huguenots which followed the peace with Spain also extended to the growing Calvinist movement in France's province of Scotland. The reaction was swift and violent. In May 1559 the greatest of Scottish Calvinists, John Knox, arrived from Geneva white-hot with zeal and indignation. His coming set Scotland aflame. The Protestant nobles, the Lords of the Congregation, called out their feudal hosts. The government drew up its French troops. A religious revolt was fast developing into a bid for national independence. But it also became clear that without foreign aid that bid would fail. The Scots had long been accustomed to look to France to help them preserve their independence against the English. But the former protector had turned tyrant. Might not the former enemy turn friend? In the summer of 1559 the Lords addressed themselves to Elizabeth.

Only a government which is itself revolutionary can wholeheartedly welcome revolution in a neighbour state, and the sentiment of monarchical solidarity weighed heavily against support of the Scottish rebels. So did other things. These rebels were also heretics. In succouring them Elizabeth would be helping to disperse the smoke-screen of doubt with which she had veiled from foreign, and especially Habsburg eyes, the realities of her religious policy. By their fruits, it was written, ye shall know them, and the first-fruits of the Elizabethan Settlement would be a hand stretched forth to drag Scotland down the path to perdition. Again, Elizabeth had just brought to an end a war which had all but bankrupted the country, exposed its military incompetence, and lost it Calais. Was this the moment to risk renewing the disastrous conflict, with no ally save a gang of feudal-minded nobles and fanatical pastors? Here were cogent, all but compelling arguments for keeping clear of the Northern tangle. They were cogent enough to make Elizabeth's intervention in it cautious in character, limited in amount, and, as long as that remained possible, unofficial in form. But they did not prevent her from intervening any more than similar arguments had prevented her from deciding for Protestantism in her own country. Indeed, her choice then really left her no choice now. For if, lacking her support, the Scottish rebellion were to fail, and France and Rome to tighten their hold beyond the border, Elizabeth would be brought face to face with the nemesis of her earlier decision, a Franco-Scottish-Papal threat to her throne. Like Bassanio in his schooldays, Elizabeth had loosed one shaft into the void of fortune and now stood in danger of forfeiting it unless she dispatched 'his fellow of the self-same flight, the self-same way', to rescue both again.

Cecil, himself the champion of intervention, correctly forecast its three stages: the Scots would be helped 'first with promises, next with money, and last with arms'. The promises flowed north during the summer of 1559, money and munitions followed in the autumn. But the early winter found the position worsening, with the government back in Edinburgh and an expedition ready to leave France. Then the tempo quickened, the blurred lines grew sharper, the doubts were thrust behind. In December the French troops sailed, to be drowned or dispersed by a Protestant gale. In January an English squadron appeared in the Forth, its commander, Winter, empowered to damage the

French in any way which did not provoke a declaration of war. February saw a military alliance with the Lords, and March an English army passing the Border. That army was to add no name to the roll of English battle-honours in Scotland; it probably did less towards the common victory than either Cecil's diplomacy or Winter's sea power. But it embodied the welcome novelty of England's goodwill, and it made the Treaty of Edinburgh, by which the French withdrew from Scotland, a landmark in Anglo-Scottish relations. To have John Knox praying that England and Scotland might never again go to war was a surer way of fastening the 'back door' than a Flodden or a Pinkie. And even though that prayer was not wholly to be granted – one thinks of Cromwell

> When up the armed mountains of Dunbar
> He marched, and through deep Severn, ending war

– the two countries were standing in 1560 on the threshold of the longest peace that they had ever known, a peace during which they would journey far towards the union which would one day make Knox's dream come true. It was England's timely action which alone made these things possible, and for that reason the Treaty of Edinburgh must rank among the major triumphs of Elizabethan statesmanship.

Elizabeth had fought her first war largely on credit; that was unavoidable. For close on twenty years her predecessors had lived beyond their means, but Mary had broken all records in overspending and had left a debt of nearly a quarter of a million. The Scottish adventure doubled this, and to Winchester, now in his eleventh year as Treasurer, the picture must have seemed all too familiar. Where public finance was concerned, however, it was not Henry VIII's daughter but Henry VII's grand-daughter who now sat on

the throne. The first Tudor's close-fistedness had yielded
the greatest of royal fortunes, the last's would do no more
than keep her solvent; but in her day and generation that
was enough. As a princess Elizabeth had begun, and as a
Queen she remained, short of money. During her first
twelve years on the throne her annual income was only
about £200,000, and out of this she had to meet all the
ordinary expenses of government. The rise in prices not-
withstanding, she was soon managing to put by about a
quarter of this towards debt-reduction. Extraordinary expenditure such as that on war and national defence could
be met, at least in theory, out of taxation. But the country
had had its fill of taxation, and Elizabeth kept her demands
down rigorously, raising on the average little more than
£50,000 a year in this way. She did so only at the cost of
frequent dippings into capital, and here at least her
stewardship could not match Henry VII's. Her father's disposal of his own vast augmentation of the Crown estates
proved to be only the beginning of their steady diminution
over a century or more. Elizabeth's sales averaged £20,000
a year, against James I's £35,000 and Charles I's £65,000;
but neither James nor Charles knew the value of money,
whereas Elizabeth did. She chose, perhaps, what seemed
the less of two evils, loss of popularity through increased
taxation and the slow undermining of royal power through
its avoidance.

But the chaotic state of public finance was only one of the
economic problems which faced Elizabeth. An unstable
currency and an inflated price-level, a disorganized food-
market, and widespread unemployment, poverty and vagabondage fed by agrarian and industrial change, these were
some of the others, and they called for equally vigorous
handling if they were not to prejudice her régime. An unknown member of the Parliament of 1559 put his finger on

the point when he wrote, in support of a suggested labour-code, that 'by the looseness of the times no other remedy is left but by awe of law to acquaint men with virtue again, whereby the reformation of religion may be brought in credit, with the amendment of manners, the want whereof hath been imputed as a thing grown by the liberty of the gospel'. A measure of economic and social discipline was necessary, not merely for its own sake, but as a buttress to the political and religious settlements. It was not until 1563 that the government had opportunity to legislate on these matters, but in the interval Cecil had pushed ahead with the most urgent tasks. No minister was less likely to neglect the economic side of politics, and his early association with the 'commonwealth' group made it both natural and appropriate that his first achievement should be the reform of the coinage. Carried through between September 1560 and September 1561 this operation was a brilliant success. The existing currency, which included coins of all degrees of debasement and mutilation, was called in and a new one issued of the old 'sterling' standard of purity and at a face-value corresponding to its intrinsic worth. The task was greatly eased by the rate at which silver was pouring into Europe from the New World, and characteristically the government made a profit of £14,000 on the operation. Its result was to stabilize money at its current value, and it had little effect upon prices. But monetary chaos gave way to order, the counterfeiter was held in check, and public confidence was restored.

Preoccupied as it was with the great issues of the Queen's marriage and the succession, the Parliament of 1563 achieved a greater output of economic legislation than had ever been passed in a single session, and one which bears comparison with those of our own day. Its fourteen statutes illustrate many aspects of the new government's programme.

Husbandry was encouraged and enclosure frowned upon by the repeal of Northumberland's act and the revival of the earlier ones. An act concerning paupers and vagabonds was notable for its introduction of the compulsory principle into the collection of poor relief. The sonorously entitled 'Politic Constitutions for the maintenance of the Navy' combined the pre-1547 policy of direct encouragement to native shipping with the post-1547 device of compulsory fish-days, the so-called 'political Lent', in aid of the fisheries, then as now one of the chief reservoirs of men and ships for the navy. Two acts discouraged or prohibited the import of many articles of apparel, ornaments and weapons. Both were in keeping with the prevalent hostility to imported luxuries, and the second has some claim to mark the beginning of modern protectionist legislation in England. Another, by making provision for the licensing of 'badgers of corn' and 'drovers of cattle', tacitly admitted that these middlemen were essential to the efficient organization of the country's food supply.

But the session's crowning achievement was the act known to us (although not to contemporaries) as the Statute of Artificers. To the twentieth-century reader the Statute of Artificers may perhaps best be described as the National Service Act of the sixteenth. Starting from the principle of the universal obligation to work, the act sets out to mobilize the entire labour resources of the nation. Its programme of 'full employment' involves the direction of labour into appropriate callings, and this in turn makes necessary the grading of these callings in a system of 'priorities'. First comes agriculture, then the simple crafts auxiliary to agriculture, then cloth-making, and finally the 'higher' trades and professions. That was the order in which they stood in official favour, the husbandman being accounted the most, and the merchant or lawyer the least, socially useful citizen.

Ideally, therefore, there should be as many in the first, and as few in the last, category as possible. But the ordinary man showed an obstinate tendency to reverse the order. He preferred the less arduous work and the greater rewards of industry, trade and the professions to the service of the soil, and his persistent urge towards ascent in the occupational and social scale continually increased the pressure to enter them. The planned recruitment of labour thus meant relieving this pressure by means of a set of property and residence qualifications. The highest qualifications were required for the commercial and professional occupations of the last category; entry became progressively easier to the intermediate ones, while agriculture was not only to absorb all those excluded from the other categories, but whenever necessary – at harvest time, for example – was to enjoy absolute priority. Labour direction was reinforced by regulations to stabilize employment and check mobility. The seven years' apprenticeship already enforced in many trades by their guilds was now to be universal and statutory. No employee was to be engaged for less than a prescribed term – in most cases a year – and anyone entitled to offer his services was to be given a certificate to this effect. A notable exception was made in favour of London. In allowing the Custom of London, by which a person who became 'free' of one trade was at liberty to follow any other, the Statute recognized the need of the capital for a high degree of mobility and ample scope for individual enterprise.

The legislators of 1563 realized the futility of trying to regulate the flow of labour without securing its reasonable remuneration, and the second part of the Statute therefore dealt with wages. The system of wage-regulation by Justices of the Peace was a product of the dislocation of the labour-market by the great pestilences of the fourteenth century. During the fifteenth it fell into disuse, and when a statute of Henry VIII exempted employers from compliance with the Justices' assessments it practically came to an end. The rise of prices which set in after 1540 made a fresh start necessary. Cecil had already got the J.P.s to work on the problem before 1563, and the Statute of Artificers generalized their experiments into a new system. That system was 'new' only in the vigour and relative efficiency with which it was applied. In making a yearly local wage-assessment, graded for different occupations and based upon the cost of living, Elizabeth's Justices were only doing what Edward III's had done two centuries earlier. Moreover, the rates which they fixed were, as such rates always had been, maximum, not minimum, rates; it was an offence to offer or receive more, not to give or receive less, than the Justices laid down.

One lesson which Englishmen had learned from the painful experience of the last generation was that although planning, like charity, might begin at home, it could not halt there. It was natural, therefore, that the government which framed the Statute of Artificers should also strive to fit the country's overseas trade into the general pattern, and equally natural that the Netherlands trade should claim its chief attention. For Antwerp was still England's greatest overseas market and source of supply, as well as her chief banker. But the Antwerp trade was beset by growing difficulties. Security and confidence wilted under commercial and financial crises, under political and religious upheavals, and, from 1567, under the tyranny of the Spanish governor Alva. Twice during the decade – in 1564–6 and 1568–71 – there were trade embargoes. The English government and the Merchant Adventurers grappled as best they could with these disorders. In 1561 the reform of the coinage had put an end to the worst of the exchange difficulties, and in 1564 their new charter tightened the Adventurers' grip on the Netherlands trade and the Crown's grip on them. Even so, the government was far from satisfied. 'It were better for this realm for many considerations', wrote Cecil in 1564, 'that the commodities of the same were issued out to sundry places, than to one, and specially to such as the lord thereof, is of so great power, as he may therewith annoy this realm.' It was not a new idea, this uneasiness at England's over-dependence upon Antwerp, but recent developments had given it added weight. Every fresh trouble in the Netherlands meant trouble in the English cloth-making districts, and it was well known that 'the people that depend upon making of cloth are of worse condition to be quietly governed than the husband men'. Moreover, dependence upon Antwerp meant dependence upon Spain, and Spain was already on the way to becoming the national enemy. To a government whose watchwords were stability and security there was everything to be said for reducing this unhealthy concentration of the country's industrial and commercial energies and encouraging them to spread more widely, more remuneratively, more safely. The change had begun under Northumberland and Mary; it was continued under Elizabeth and integrated into her New Order.

In her first five years Elizabeth had done great things. Cecil, preparing perhaps for the Parliament of 1563, tabulated the main achievements. '1559 The religion of Christ restored. Foreign authority rejected ... 1560 The French at the request of the Scots ... sent back to France and Scotland set free from the servitude of the Pope. 1561 The debased copper and brass coinage replaced by brass and silver ... 1562 The tottering Church of Christ in France succoured ...' A few months later he would have been forced to strike out the last item – it referred to the ill-starred attempt to do for the French Huguenots what the exploit of 1560 had done for the Scottish Calvinists – but in its place he might have written: '1563 Many good laws made for the commonweal. Labourers, etc.' Elizabeth had given her country many blessings. She had not given it that without which all the rest might be turned into a mockery. There was as yet no hint of an orderly succession.

Everyone took it for granted that Elizabeth would marry. Her grandfather, father and sister had all done so within a year of their accession. But in March 1563, after four-and-a-half years on the throne, Elizabeth bade farewell to her twenties still unmarried. Seldom outside fable had a princess been so sought after. A reigning king had offered himself, another his eldest son, an emperor his younger ones, and before the end the tale would be doubled. None of these foreigners had any real chance with her. The time was not yet when the consort of an English queen could, like Victoria's, be rendered politically negligible even if he were not, like Anne's, entirely negligible already. Queen Elizabeth's husband would have expected – and have been expected – to be more than Queen Elizabeth's husband. What such expectations might mean both Queen and country knew only too well. For Elizabeth her sister's example was probably decisive; she would not commit her own happiness and her country's welfare to any foreigner. But it did not pay her to say so; on the contrary, to keep the possibility open would greatly strengthen her hand with the Continental dynasties. So for twenty years she toyed with these foreigners in turn, while in herself she dwelt apart.

An Englishman, then, or – somewhere between the two – a Scot, was there not one man in Britain who would do? Names were mentioned, chuckled over, wagered on, forgotten. But there was another name, a name of doom, the name of Dudley. Grandson of Henry VII's hated minister, son of the would-be kingmaker Northumberland, Lord Robert Dudley at twenty-seven was all but kingly in his looks and bearing, in his pride and ambition, and he was to come nearer than any other of his time to wearing the crown so costly of his family's blood. For two years and more Elizabeth and Dudley shared in a romance which bred wild rumours, ugly suspicions, nightmarish fears. Halfway through it Dudley's wife, Amy Robsart, broke her neck down the stairs of their house at Cumnor. The jury found that death was accidental; posterity is disposed to call it suicide, provoked by neglect and shame; contemporaries whispered that it was murder, procured by an adulterous-minded husband. If Elizabeth had married the widowed Dudley, she would have risked her throne. But the idea was abandoned, the emotion itself came to be recollected in a mood approaching tranquillity, and Dudley's strivings throneward were to carry him no higher than the earldom of Leicester and the governor-generalship of the United Netherlands. Whether, or how, the affair influenced the prospect of Elizabeth's marriage to another are questions easy to speculate on, impossible to answer. There seems less reason to doubt that she could have borne a child than that she could have known or aroused the desire which would give her one. It may be that Dudley embodied the best, if not the only, chance of these things, that Elizabeth came to realize this, and that her decision not to marry him was thus in effect a decision against marriage. But this is delicate ground, indeed doubly delicate, for the difficulty of the subject is matched by the fragility of the evidence, and the traveller who wants to get on with the journey will be content with the solid and unequivocal fact that, alone among thirty-six English sovereigns since William Rufus whose span of life allowed, Elizabeth did not marry.

While rumour yet had it that the Queen had secretly married a Dudley, the heir-presumptive had secretly married a Seymour. One version of the marriage of Catherine Grey to the Earl of Hertford, son of the Protector Somerset, depicted it as the outcome of a conspiracy among leading councillors to set Catherine up as queen if Elizabeth married Dudley. There is doubtless exaggeration here, and in any case Elizabeth was not going to marry Dudley. But it is all too reminiscent of 1553 to be treated as a fairy-tale, and it helps us to glimpse the depths across which England was making her way to safety. When Catherine's condition led to disclosure, Elizabeth had the marriage declared void and sent both parties to the Tower, where first one and then a second son were born.* Her disgrace virtually cut Catherine Grey out of the legal succession, leaving only Mary Queen of Scots. But Mary's antics during the next few years were to prove almost as fatal to her claim as Catherine's marriage had been to hers. Returning to her native kingdom in 1561 Mary made almost every blunder possible. She never regarded her sojourn there as other than a wearisome interlude between the France of her memories and the England of her dreams. A vain, artful, bewitching creature, she played at being queen as she played at nearly everything. Even her steadfastness in her faith appears to those who do not share it as but the obverse of her political ineptitude. But it was men who were Mary's undoing. Her second husband, Lord Darnley, had nothing to commend him save his looks, his lineage, and his ability to get her with child. From this graceful but vicious puppy she turned for diversion to the Italian lap-dog Rizzio, only to have him torn

---

* An old friend of the Seymours, John Hales, made his last appearance on the stage of national history by publishing a defence of the marriage and of the Suffolk claim to the throne which earned him six months in the Fleet Prison.

from her skirts and done to death by her jealous husband.
The birth of her son in June 1566 momentarily satisfied
and steadied Mary. But within a few months she had surrendered to the fatal fascinations of the Earl of Bothwell
and Darnley had expiated the murder of Rizzio amid the
blown-up ruins of Kirk o' Field. Politically it mattered less
whether Mary was an accessory before the fact than how
she behaved after it. Mary's conduct was damning. She
let the man whom everybody called a murderer and whose
Church pronounced him an adulterer first abduct and
then, as soon as he was divorced, marry her. The Lords
rose up against the guilty pair, drove Bothwell into exile
and forced Mary to abdicate in favour of her son. The
next year she made another bid for power, was quickly
defeated, and escaped recapture and a speedy death by
crossing the Border to Carlisle.

Mary's arrival set Elizabeth a problem which was only
to be solved nineteen years later by her execution. There
were really two Mary Stuarts to be dealt with. One was
the sister sovereign in exile, who merited honourable
asylum and perhaps assistance to regain her throne. The
other was the Catholic claimant to the English succession,
if not to the English throne, the woman who would be
under Elizabeth – only much more actively and dangerously – what Elizabeth had been under Mary Tudor,
and Mary Tudor under Somerset and Northumberland,
the magnet drawing together scattered elements of religious
and political discontent. How powerful a magnet Mary was
her first eighteen months in England amply demonstrated.
They saw the first of the reign's conspiracies and its only
serious rebellion. Hitherto Elizabeth had kept England
immune from such things, and the decade which saw the
Scottish Reformation and the casting out of Mary, the
opening of the French Religious Wars, and the

preliminaries of the Revolt of the Netherlands had seen no blood spilt upon an English battlefield, no head fall for treason or religion on an English scaffold, and no burning at Smithfield save of rood-screens and effigies. It had not, of course, been all harmony, but only once had Elizabeth provoked real opposition – by her affair with Dudley – and the questions of marriage and the succession which remained the chief matters of contention between her and her parliaments sprang from satisfaction, not dissatisfaction, with her rule, from the fear, not the hope, that it would early give place to another's. Yet there were many Englishmen for whom that prospect held no terrors, and some who looked forward to it. This cleavage in national opinion was largely, although not wholly, a matter of geography. If civil war had come to England in the fifteen-sixties it would have been fought, as it was to be fought in the sixteen-forties, by the North and West against the South and East. For it was in that 'natural refuge for lost causes' which lay beyond the Trent that the lost causes of Tudor England, the cause of feudalism, the cause of Rome, held out most stubbornly. There a neighbouring Percy or Neville counted for more than a distant Tudor; there, amid the continuing turbulence of private feud and border warfare, the retinue rather than the rent-roll was the measure of power; there the Mass defied the visitations and the deprivals. True, there was a new North Country springing to life, a country of coal-mines and alum-plants, of cotton firms and mineral-workings; of business magnates and industrial workers who would think better of the new morality than of the old; of landlords who read Tusser's *Hundred Good Points of Husbandry* and enclosed their farms. The North had not risen since 1536, the North might not have risen again if Mary Stuart had not been at hand, the delusively pathetic figurehead of a pathetic fallacy.

It was Mary, too, who brought another pustule of discontent in the country to a head. This was also an affair of great men who wanted to be greater, or feared to become less, but unlike the movement in the North it had no popular backing. What these men aimed at was the overthrow of Cecil and the other upstarts who were elbowing them out of place and power, and the bridling, if not the breaking, of Elizabeth herself; and these things they hoped to accomplish by asserting the right of Mary Stuart, 'naturalized' by a suitable English marriage, to succeed, or if need be, to supplant, their present Queen. The central figure of the plot, and the man chosen to be Mary's fourth husband, was the Duke of Norfolk. Norfolk was not a Catholic (perhaps John Foxe, who had once tutored him, had seen to that), but he was second cousin to Elizabeth, he was England's only duke, and he symbolized that conception of nobility which the Tudors had laboured to destroy. His name, it was hoped, would rally conservative opinion to the programme, while Mary's won the support of Catholics and the Catholic Powers. But Norfolk brought little to the plot save his name, and that was not enough. He gave Elizabeth and Cecil ample time to make their dispositions, and when fate knocked at his door bearing a royal summons he crumpled up. He was sent to the Tower (October 1569). The weakness which led him there also doomed his Northern allies. In September the Earls of Northumberland and Westmorland had awaited his signal; it did not come, and they went home. But a month later they, too, were summoned to court, and fearing for their lives, they rose. Some who might have joined them earlier held aloof, and the hoped-for aid from Scotland and the Continent did not appear. But several thousand peasants marched, as their forbears had marched in 1536, in a mass-denunciation of the new way of life and the new technique of government. In Durham Cathedral they tore up the bibles and prayer-books and celebrated Mass. Then they moved south, towards York and Mary. But their cause was already hopeless, and before the large government forces could get at them they retreated and dispersed. A crazy little revolt by Leonard Dacre in Westmorland three months later was beaten in one engagement, and soon the gallows in every Northern village were once more proclaiming the futility of rebellion against a Tudor.

Rebellion may have been futile, but the rebellion of 1569 might have failed less dismally if the rebels had been assured of their Church's blessing. As it was, they rose in defiance of pastoral opinion that only a ruler who had been excommunicated was a legitimate target of rebellion. Three months later Pope Pius V removed this handicap to their beaten cause. By the Bull *Regnans in Excelsis* of February 1570 he pronounced Elizabeth's excommunication and deposition, and absolved her subjects from their allegiance. Sooner or later Elizabeth was bound to incur Rome's denunciation. But to be more than an empty manifesto the denunciation of 1570 came either too soon or too late. It was too soon by fifteen years to enlist the cooperation of Catholic Europe, too late by eleven to win the effective support of Catholic England. In Pius V's view the black record of Elizabeth's wickedness during those eleven years spoke for itself; as he saw it, the Church had given her plenty of rope, and spiritually and morally she had hanged herself. But Englishmen, even Catholic Englishmen, saw it otherwise. Instead of a heretic unfit to reign, they saw a daughter of the Tudors manifestly born to rule; instead of a realm groaning under a conscienceless tyranny, they saw a government which secured every man's life and property, which was cheap, capable and constructive, which believed in letting religious nonconformity off with the mildest of penalties, and which, as the late rebellion showed, had won the overwhelming loyalty and confidence of the nation. Such a ruler and such a realm had not much to fear from the fulminations of Rome; and the Bull which was to mark the beginning of the end of Elizabethan England in truth marked only the end of its beginning.

VII

PARLIAMENTS, PURITANS AND PAPISTS

THE first-fruit of the Bull of 1570 was the Ridolfi Plot. Roberto Ridolfi was a Florentine merchant-banker settled in London who sought to apply the technique of international finance to international conspiracy. His project was the supersession of Elizabeth by Mary Stuart and of the Anglican Church by a restored Catholicism; his prospectus was headed by the names of Mary herself, who from her honourable confinement at Chatsworth gave it her ready approval, and of the Duke of Norfolk, who let himself be talked into this abusal of Elizabeth's clemency towards him after the Northern Rebellion; and the shareholders were to be recruited from the thousands of English Catholics who on Ridolfi's showing were prepared to stake their all on such an enterprise. By March 1571 Ridolfi had the whole scheme worked out on paper, with copious supporting documents and figures, and he spent the next four months endeavouring to 'sell' it to the authorities at Brussels, Rome and Madrid. The Papacy hailed it with enthusiasm as a means of executing the Bull, but Philip II was hesitant and the Duke of Alva, to whom Ridolfi looked for armed support of the rising, avowedly hostile. The Italian had made no real progress when, in the autumn of 1571, the English government, which had for some months been on the track of the conspirators, arrested Norfolk and his chief associates. Norfolk had sealed his own fate, and in January 1572 he was sentenced to death by his peers. Only the Queen's reluctance to carry out the sentence postponed its execution until June, when Parliament, which clamoured for his death as well as Mary's, was given the ducal head to save the royal one. Norfolk was, perhaps not unjustly, the only one of the conspirators to die. Ridolfi himself suffered nothing worse than the loss of his London establishment and retired to Italy, where he died, a Florentine senator, in 1612, the last survivor but one* of all the actors in the affair.

The two main results of the plot, the destruction of Norfolk and the disgrace of Mary, were both linked with a third, the summoning of the Parliament of 1572. When in 1566 Elizabeth told the French ambassador that the three parliaments she had already held were enough for any reign and that she would summon no more, she may have had her tongue in her cheek and in any case she would soon swallow her words. But they serve to remind us that what we know as Parliament, an assembly required by law to meet every year and by practical necessity to remain in session for three-quarters of it, was undreamt-of in the sixteenth century. Instead of a virtually continuous Parliament there were separate parliaments, summoned and either prorogued or dissolved at the royal pleasure, at intervals ranging from six months to as many years, and seldom sitting for more than two months at a time. It is true that in the frequency, if not the duration, of parliamentary sessions, as in much else pertaining to the institution, Henry VIII's great Reformation Parliament had heralded a notable change. The forty-four years of Tudor rule which preceded its opening had seen twenty sessions of parliament amounting to 125 weeks; in the twenty-nine years which followed there were thirty sessions totalling 223 weeks. But the forty-four years of Elizabeth's reign,

* Charles Bailly or Baillie, a member of Mary Stuart's household arrested while carrying letters from Ridolfi. He died in 1625.

with their thirteen sessions and 140 weeks, would mark a return to the pre-Reformation level of parliamentary activity, and her albeit empty threat of 1566 is oddly reminiscent of the ambition attributed to her grandfather in 1498 of dispensing with parliament and ruling 'in the French fashion'. From any such danger of extinction parliament was protected under Elizabeth, as under those who went before and came after her, by the persistence of two royal needs, the need for money and the need for cooperation. If Elizabeth's financial prudence made the first of these needs less pressing, the need for cooperation remained, and under a sovereign so sensible of it as Elizabeth this alone would have ensured the periodic summoning of parliament.

The handful of members of Henry VIII's parliaments who were still sitting in the seventies and eighties would doubtless have seen no essential difference between the parliaments of their youth and of their old age. And they would have been right, there was no essential difference. But there were changes taking place, both on and below the surface, and those changes were symptoms of a gradual transformation of profound significance. There was, for instance, a steady shifting of the centre of gravity in Parliament from the House of Lords to the House of Commons. Since Henry VIII had so drastically altered its composition, the Upper House had become a predominantly lay assembly, with nearly twice as many temporal as spiritual peers. The House was still important by reason of its great landed wealth – although before the century was out one bold spirit was to advocate its abolition on the ground that in wealth it was far outstripped by the Commons – but as it came to consist more and more of lay peers of recent creation and spiritual ones who were royal nominees it shrank in independent importance. The peers wielded their parliamentary influence increasingly outside their own Chamber, by controlling constituencies represented in the Commons. It was noticeable, too, that while some royal officials received writs of summons to the House of Lords, the privy councillors were usually to be found sitting as elected members in the House of Commons.

The only official change in the composition of that House was its increase in size. The traditional basis of representation – two members for every county and two for every city and borough – remained the rule, but the units so represented grew rapidly in number. The incorporation of Wales into the English representative system had added twelve counties and eleven boroughs, each returning one member, as well as the new English counties of Monmouthshire and Cheshire, which, with their county-towns, each returned two. Thenceforward, with only one 'county', the Palatinate of Durham, unrepresented (Durham had to wait until 1660), the number of county members became fixed at ninety. But the number of borough members went on growing. The Crown could confer the privilege, or lay the duty, of representation upon any urban community, and every Tudor in turn used this power. Henry VIII added fourteen borough seats (besides the Welsh ones), Edward VI's advisers 34, Mary 25 and Elizabeth 62. Thus the 224 borough members of Henry VIII's first parliament became the 308 of Elizabeth's first and the 372 of her last, and by the close of the century the House was half as large again as it had been at the beginning. This multiplication of seats was once regarded as a Tudor device for securing the return of members of the right complexion, and the view gains some colour from the geographical distribution of the new constituencies. When Northumberland wielded the creative power he awarded twelve new seats to the royal duchy of Cornwall. By contrast, Mary, in what looks like an appeal to the old world to redress the balance of the new, gave ten to conservative Yorkshire. Elizabeth repeated Northumberland's gift to Cornwall and was even more lavish in Protestant Hampshire, where she added sixteen seats. But to see in any of these actions an attempt to 'pack' parliament would be to ignore the realities both of the electoral system and of the relationship between Crown and Commons.

If the statutes governing elections had been observed an Elizabethan House of Commons would have consisted of ninety knights of the shire, or landed gentlemen, and upwards of three hundred burgesses, or middle-class townsmen. In practice, the figures were not far from being reversed. The landed gentry had 'captured' the boroughs and with them the House of Commons. They had done so by a process of infiltration, not by any *coup de main*; but it was the thirty years between 1540 and 1570 which had clinched their victory. A Venetian ambassador had noted, if he also exaggerated and telescoped, the change in connexion with one of Mary's parliaments, and it was these years which saw the only other section of the community which might have made a bid for parliamentary power, the industrial and commercial capitalists, elbowed out by their social betters. The business magnates, especially the clothiers, were themselves largely to blame. When the cloth industry forsook the towns for the countryside, it not only forfeited its own chance of becoming a power in the House of Commons, it presented the landed interest with an opportunity which was not missed. Two conditions made it possible for gentlemen to replace townsmen as M.P.s for the boroughs, the acquiescence of the boroughs in their election and the impotence of the Crown to prevent it. In most boroughs the franchise had come to be restricted to a small group of burgesses, and Tudor grants of representation were in line with this oligarchic tendency. To secure election for a borough thus meant gaining the support of this group, or, if there were a contest, of a majority within it, and that in turn usually meant being recommended to the town by the nobleman or gentleman whose lead it followed in such matters. There were few towns which did not owe allegiance to a great man or house, or which, when the control of seats in the Commons became one of the chief tests of rival greatnesses, were not prepared to place at least one seat at their patron's disposal. The town doing so gained in more than one way. If it returned two of its own burgesses it would probably have to pay their parliamentary wages, and that at a time when parliaments were becoming longer, if not more frequent, while municipal purses were often becoming shorter. A gentleman would either give his services or be satisfied with something less than the statutory two shillings a day. Moreover, his services would probably be worth more to the town; certainly those of his patron would be. Tudor towns, like individuals, lived in perpetual need of favours. There were municipal privileges to win or keep, interests to guard, rivals to thwart. It is little wonder if town oligarchs rated powerful patronage higher than parliamentary independence. True, electing a gentleman generally meant breaking the law which required that M.P.s should be resident within their constituencies. But that could be done with impunity. The government was well aware that a large proportion of every House of Commons was technically disqualified, and from time to time it reminded Members of the fact. But non-residence was one of those manifestations of economic and social change, like enclosures, usury, and middlemen, which laughed at prohibition, and, although an attempt in 1571 to legalize it failed, the statutes on the subject remained a dead letter.

In creating new parliamentary seats the Crown was therefore serving political interests other than its own. While here and there a town may have sought representation, in the majority of cases the real pressure doubtless came from local magnates seeking to augment their patronage and prestige. The Crown was, in fact, being pressed to multiply petty monopolies in politics, just as it would be pressed to multiply petty and great monopolies in trade and industry, by those who stood to gain; and in the one case as in the other it yielded gradually to the pressure. If in addition it cherished any hopes of providing seats for 'yes-men', the results must have been disappointing, for some of its doughtiest parliamentary opponents, among them the irrepressible Peter Wentworth, were to reach Westminster by way of new constituencies. The Crown had, indeed, almost as little control of the new seats as of the old, and that was little enough. In the democratic creed any tampering with the freedom and fairness of elections is one of the seven deadly sins, and a government which stoops to it stands condemned and excommunicated. Tudor monarchs and their ministers were in the habit of doing things at election time which would not be tolerated today outside totalitarian states. Sometimes they let it be known what sort of persons would be acceptable as M.P.s, as when in 1555 Mary asked for men 'of the wise, grave and Catholic sort'. They also made recurrent attempts to secure the return of particular individuals. But only under Thomas Cromwell and Northumberland did this otherwise spasmodic interference threaten to become a system, and neither was a good advertisement for its wisdom or efficacy. Crown interference, too, normally stopped short of being a command, and those who did not comply seldom suffered, a fact which doubtless helps to explain its lack of success but its chief extenuation, if not defence, lies in its motive.

No Tudor sovereign, with the possible exception of Mary, interfered in order to convert a potentially hostile House of Commons into a friendly one. No Tudor sovereign, again with the same proviso, needed to do so. But if the electoral machinery could be allowed to run itself with a minimum of attention, the same was not true of the assemblies which it produced. Left to itself, a collection of four hundred squires, lawyers and business men would doubtless have argued, grumbled, quarrelled with vigour and not without eloquence; it would hardly have made an end, at least not a legislative end, of the matters in hand. Yet the House of Commons was the Tudors' chosen instrument for translating the national will into legislation of unprecedented importance, volume, and complexity. The House was able to play the part assigned to it only because the Tudors at the same time planted and fostered within it a group of trained and tried statesmen who gave its deliberations coherence and direction and preserved the harmony indispensable to efficiency and dispatch. The need grew rather than lessened as the century advanced and as the House itself grew larger, less wieldy and more vocal. When, therefore, we find Elizabeth or Cecil engineering the return of particular individuals to the House of Commons, we may envisage their intended role as something more than that of mute, inglorious back-benchers obedient to the crack of the whip. They were more likely destined for membership of that group upon which devolved the management of the House.

The central figure of that group was the Speaker. Formally elected by the House itself, the Speaker was in fact chosen by the Crown, and he was its chief agent in keeping parliamentary activity along the lines and within the bounds indicated. Next in importance came the privy councillors. Under Elizabeth the Privy Council remained what it had been under her predecessors, the supreme organ of government. Reduced from the unwieldy size favoured by Mary to a maximum of twenty members, the council met as a body for its administrative work but did its advisory work in committees and groups. That work comprised all matters remitted to it by the sovereign, and in practice covered the whole range of governmental activity. The business which is now divided by a dozen departments of state – the preservation of law and order, including the handling of political and religious disaffections, the upkeep of the armed forces, the conduct of foreign relations, the control of agriculture, industry and trade – together with a mass of miscellaneous items, many of them small to the point of triviality, passed through the experienced, devoted and grossly overworked hands of this little band of public servants, the men who, under their sovereign, really mattered in Tudor England. Like the modern cabinet, the Privy Council consisted for the most part of ministers who filled the leading government offices – the Treasurer, Secretary, Chancellor or Lord Keeper, Chamberlain, Admiral, and so forth – but, unlike the Cabinet, it was solely responsible to the Crown, and its members came and went at the royal bidding. During the brief and infrequent periods when Parliament was in session, the privy councillors played a part not essentially different from ministers today. It was they who drafted all important legislation and piloted it through the Houses, and who, with the Speaker, sought to keep debate within the bounds of political decorum and practical desirability, and to send Members home at the end of the session satisfied with what had been said and done and disposed to administer the laws which they themselves had made. For every Elizabethan Parliament contained a high proportion of J.P.s, without whose cooperation Queen, Councillors and Commons would have laboured in vain.

In the view of the Tudor sovereigns – and Elizabeth held it to the end – parliaments were summoned to do three things, and three things only: to vote such taxes as were required, to legislate on topics submitted to them, and to give advice on policy when asked. Elizabeth's parliaments certainly fulfilled these functions. Each session was called with some principal object in view – in 1559 it was to settle religion, in 1571–2 to augment the security of the realm, in 1581 to hammer the Catholics, in 1586 to dispose of Mary Stuart – and, that object gained, Parliament was dispensed with for a season. But each session bore other fruit than the royal gardener expected. For it was during these sessions that the House of Commons began to grope towards another, and rival, conception of its functions, and in the process to join issue with the Crown. That issue is epitomized in the immortal words 'freedom of speech'. Today parliamentary freedom of speech means a member's freedom to voice any opinion upon any subject provided he does not transgress the rules laid down by the House itself. To its champions in the Elizabethan House of Commons freedom of speech meant something less than that, yet – despite their own assertions to the contrary – something more than it had ever meant before. The freedom of speech for which, together with freedom from arrest and freedom of access to the sovereign, the Speaker petitioned the Crown at the opening of each parliament, was the freedom of every member, as More had expressed it when Speaker in 1523, 'to discharge his conscience, and boldly in everything incident among us to declare his advice,' without fear of penalty. Such freedom the Tudor monarchs could, and did, grant without hesitation, 'God forbid,' declared Elizabeth in her reply to the Speaker's petition in 1593, 'that any man should be restrained or afraid to answer according to his best liking, with some short declaration of his reason therein,' when invited to say yea or nay to bill or resolution. Members were certainly at liberty to speak their minds upon any subject propounded to them. But who was to propound the subjects, Parliament itself or the Crown which called it into existence? The Crown wanted certain matters discussed and certain things done in each parliament, and these were clearly legitimate topics of debate for the time being. But did they remain so thereafter? During the thirty years following 1529 there was little that Parliament, with royal permission or encouragement, had not touched in debate or legislation. Who should be king, what style he should bear and what powers wield, how Englishmen should worship, if not what they should believe, such were the questions which M.P.s had helped to answer. Why should they not reopen them? An act of parliament had settled the succession to Henry VIII, should not another settle the succession to Elizabeth? If an Act of Six Articles in 1539, why not an Act of Thirty-Nine Articles in 1566? If one Prayer Book in 1549, and another in 1552 and 1559, why not a third in 1571?

Elizabeth's answer, when Members began to argue along these lines, was that such questions as religion and the succession were 'matters of state' which it lay with her to handle and which Parliament could discuss only at her invitation. There was a wide range of other topics, the so-called 'matters of commonwealth', which, since they did not directly involve the royal authority or high policy, Members could raise of their own volition and without the prior consent of the Crown. But 'matters of state' could come up only on the royal initiative. Unfortunately, the two questions which touched Members most keenly, and which they were most anxious to ventilate, were by this definition 'matters of state'. The first was the great question of the succession, with which were bound up the question of Elizabeth's marriage and, from 1571, the fate of Mary Stuart. No power on earth could have stopped any gathering of Englishmen from talking about something which, as Wentworth said, 'importeth more than all the members' heads and ten thousand more be worth,' and every parliament between 1559 and 1593 had a go at it. In 1571, under the stress of rebellion and plot, the Commons went so far as to add to a government treasons bill a clause which would have made it treason to deny Parliament's right to determine the succession. That time discretion was swamped by desperation. But succeeding parliaments went on urging the Queen to ease her subjects' minds by marrying or naming a successor, or at least disposing of the claim and person of Mary Stuart. It was a persistent encroachment upon a 'matter of state', but it sprang from loyal, if lugubrious, hearts, and Elizabeth bore it with as good a grace as the House accorded her continued refusals to accede.

Much more fundamental in character and dangerous in consequence was the conflict between them over religion. Again, from Elizabeth's standpoint, the position was perfectly clear. In 1559 Parliament had declared that she possessed supreme authority in matters ecclesiastical. Within the framework of the Settlement then made – and it was only a framework and a loose and untidy one at that – she was therefore free to govern the Church as she pleased. She was not bound to consult Parliament, the less so since in Convocation the Church possessed its own law-making body and in the ecclesiastical courts the machinery for administering the law so made. It was Convocation which in 1563 gave the Anglican Church its creed, the Thirty-Nine Articles, and in 1571 its new canons, or ecclesiastical laws, which the Queen, while withholding her formal assent, allowed the bishops to enforce among the clergy. In neither case did Parliament have any real say in the matter. Indeed, when the parliament of 1571 embodied the Thirty-Nine Articles in a bill, Elizabeth quashed it, declaring that she intended to have the Articles in virtue of her own Supremacy, not in virtue of a statute. In short, it appeared that after thirty years' almost uninterrupted grazing in ecclesiastical pastures the old parliamentary war-horse was to be shut out of them by an enclosing landlord.

How the House of Commons would react to the new situation would largely depend upon how its Members regarded the Church which was arising behind the royal hedge. The broader based an institution, the less deep its foundations will, or will need to, go. The Elizabethan Church was designed to appeal to the lukewarm multitude, and it enlisted their lukewarm support. To most Members of Parliament, as to most Englishmen, its chief merits were negative. It had no Pope, it had no Mass, it made no windows into men's souls, it lit no fires to consume men's bodies. The fact that it also kindled no flame in men's hearts, if hardly a merit, was less of a defect in that most men's hearts were not inflammable. But the new Church had by no means rid itself of all the features which had excited the ordinary man's hatred in the old. It had banished the Pope, but it still kept two dozen 'petty popes' in its bishops; it had abolished the Mass, but not ignorance and inefficiency among its ministers; it made no windows into souls, but it still made holes in pockets. It abounded with pluralities, sinecures, licences, dispensations, officials, fees. Its courts were riddled with abuses, especially that 'petty little stinking ditch' the Commissary's Court. Episcopal jurisdiction was probably as hateful to the ordinary Englishman as papal jurisdiction had been to his kings.

As slow to make firm friends as the men and women whom it enfolded, the Elizabethan Church was soon to turn some of them into enemies. Within ten years of its foundation a new force was at work in English life and a new word had been added to the English language. While the origins of Puritanism are to be sought in earlier decades, if not centuries, it was the fifteen-fifties which saw the birth of the Puritan movement. It was born on the Continent, among those English men and women who had gone into exile to preserve their faith from a Catholic sovereign. The five years of their exile were to leave an indelible mark on them. Beyond the reach of king, parliament and bishops, breathing an unaccustomed air and exposed to alien influences and associations, they made proof of more than their zeal in the godly cause. Some, in a revolt which was also a prophecy, renounced the Prayer Book which they had brought with them and with it the authority which had made the English Reformation; all returned burning to share in that salvation of their country which had been the aim of their exile. The name 'puritan' was applied in the late sixteenth century, like the name 'communist' in the early twentieth, to much that formed no part of the orthodox movement, and to attempt to describe Puritanism briefly is to risk endowing it with a coherence of theory and practice greater than it possessed. The whole-hogging Puritan certainly saw all things in heaven and earth with marvellous clarity. And with good reason, since his eyes had been opened, under God, by the magical genius of John Calvin. To the two basic tenets of Protestantism – the unique and exclusive authority of the Scriptures and the sanctity of the human conscience in their interpretation – Calvin had welded a third, the doctrine of predestination. While the Catholic held that any man might be saved by faith and conduct, and the

Lutheran that he could be saved by faith alone, the Calvinist knew that God has predestined every human being either to salvation or to damnation, and that no intensity of faith or integrity of conduct could alter that divine foreordinance. Considered objectively, a doctrine which makes mankind the helpless victim of an arbitrary Will must seem abhorrent in its cruelty and injustice. But since that doctrine was the monopoly of those who, with only occasional lapses into agonizing doubt, dwelt in the serene certainty that they were numbered among the 'elect', its fatalism was invariably optimistic, and it generated in its holders a depth of conviction and a height of exaltation known to few who did not share its secret.

The Puritan, then, had a world of his own, a world of literal truth and unqualified error, of absolute good and absolute evil, of white and black. It might be thought that his spiritual isolationism would have impelled him to cut himself off from the unregenerate and irredeemable multitude, to withdraw into his inviolable inner life, and to let the world go to the devil its own way. This was, as we shall see, one of the impulses towards Separatism. But for the majority of Puritans the Separatist solution was psychologically as well as practically impossible. The same urge which turned other deeply religious men into missionaries for their faiths turned the Puritans into policemen for theirs. Granted that most of their fellow-beings were lost eternally, they must none the less be persuaded, or compelled, to conduct themselves so as not to give scandal to God and to his Elect. Moreover, although Calvinism was international, the Puritans were Englishmen, and they thought instinctively in national terms. Calvin's model Church had been erected within the narrow confines of a Swiss city-state. But there could not be an English Geneva, there could only be a Genevan England. French Huguenots and Scottish Presbyterians were hard at work creating National Reformed Churches. England had a National Church which was but half-Reformed. The Church of England must be Puritanized.

There was a good deal of Calvinism or near-Calvinism in the early Elizabethan Church. A number of its clergy, including several bishops, were of that persuasion, and the leaven of their enthusiasm soon began to work. Had all of them been as successful as some in reaching a working compromise between public duty and private conviction it might have gone on working quietly until it had leavened most of the lump. But the call of conscience was too insistent to be smothered and the royal ear too sensitive to miss its jarring note. The trouble began with clerical vestments and liturgical ceremonies. In the Convocation of 1563 the Puritans only just failed to carry a series of Articles wholly at variance with what had been laid down in the Ornaments Rubric of 1559, and two years later a survey made by Parker in consequence of a peremptory letter from the Queen revealed the utmost diversity of practice. Two former exiles, now highly placed at Oxford, Humphrey, President of Magdalen, and Sampson, Dean of Christ Church, were ordered to conform. Both refused. Sampson was deprived, and Humphrey, although he kept his post, remained for some years under a cloud. Parker then set about stimulating the bishops into some activity in the matter, and from 1566 the drive against recalcitrant clergy gathered momentum. But the Vestiarian Controversy was only the prelude to widening and deepening conflict. By 1573 Hutton, the Dean of York, could write: 'At the beginning it was but a cap, a surplice, and a tippet; now, it is grown to bishops, archbishops, and cathedral churches, to the overthrow of the established order, and to the Queen's authority in causes ecclesiastical.' Hutton's rhetoric may have been alarmist, but it was not exaggerated. For the progression was a continuous, not to say an inevitable, one. From refusing to wear a surplice it was not far to denying the power of a bishop to enforce such a thing, and from that to denying his authority altogether; and to deny the authority of a bishop was really to deny the authority of the Crown which appointed him and gave him his orders. Those who take the power must also take the blame for its alleged misuse, and as Supreme Governor of the Church Elizabeth was ultimately responsible for the things of which her Puritan subjects complained.

The second stage of the conflict opened in 1570 with another academic dismissal, that of Thomas Cartwright from a Chair of Divinity at Cambridge. Cartwright had survived his part in the Vestiarian Controversy, but upon his appointment as professor he delivered some lectures so critical of the Established Church that Cecil, who was Chancellor of the University, agreed first to his suspension and then to his dismissal from his post. This was the signal for the first great literary engagement between Anglicanism and Puritanism. In 1571 and 1573 there were published the two Puritan *Admonitions to the Parliament*. In 1572 the first of them was answered by Whitgift, Dean of Lincoln and future Archbishop. Since Whitgift, as Vice-Chancellor of Cambridge, had been mainly responsible for Cartwright's expulsion, it was natural that Cartwright should join in, which he did in 1573 with his *Reply* to Whitgift's *Answer*. Whitgift's *Defence of the Answer* of 1574, and Cartwright's *Second Reply* of 1575-7, completed the series. In their contributions to it the Puritan authors set out to do two things: to describe, and in describing to condemn, the Church of England as it was, and to show what it ought to be. They developed their charges under three main heads. They attacked first the ignorance and inefficiency of the clergy, and above all their inability to preach. From the outset the Puritans attached the greatest importance to preaching, and their own high standard in it was one of their major sources of strength. Their remedies for its neglect were clear and to the point. 'Appoint to every congregation a learned and diligent preacher. Remove homilies, articles, injunctions, a prescript order of service made out of the Mass book. Take away the Lordship, the loitering, the pomp, the idleness, the livings of Bishops, but yet employ them to such ends as they were in the old church appointed for... So God shall be glorified, your consciences discharged and the flock of Christ ... edified.' Next, the Puritans demanded further changes in doctrine. The Prayer Book was 'an unperfect book, culled and picked out of that popish dunghill, the Mass book full of all abominations.' (A Book containing prayers that all men might be saved could hardly satisfy those who knew that most men were damned.) The sacraments were administered with unlawful ceremonies. But it was in the spheres of discipline and organization that the Puritans made their most trenchant criticisms and most radical proposals. They could not abide bishops. 'Instead of an Archbishop or Lord bishop, you must make equality of ministers.' Episcopal authority should be replaced by the discipline exercised by ministers, elders and deacons, and the existing system of ordination and presentation by 'that old and true election, which was accustomed to be made by the congregation.' What the Puritans wanted was the presbyterian system which they saw already established in Scotland.

Clearly a Puritanized Church of England would be a very different institution from the Church established in 1559. It could not fail to be, since it was designed to serve a quite different end. To the Puritan, just as religion was the be-all and end-all of a man's life, so the Church was either the agency for sanctifying the national life, or it was nothing worth. Here was the real issue between Puritanism and Anglicanism, to which all else – sermons, sacraments, bishops, presbyters – was subordinate. The Church of Puritan dreams would serve but one end, the greater glory of God, and live by one rule, the rule of the Scriptures. The Established Church appeared less concerned with seeking the Kingdom of God than with supporting the Kingdom of England. It set uniformity before truth and conformity before conscience, and the peace which it ensued was not the peace which passeth all understanding but the peace which the Tudors understood so well. Yet if religion had become largely a matter of politics, it was, as Pollard reminds us, some compensation that politics became largely a matter of religion. It was to Parliament that the authors of the two *Admonitions* addressed them, and it was in Parliament that Puritan discontent found its most important outlet. Between Puritanism and Parliamentarism there was, of course, a fundamental incompatibility which would one day stand revealed. Puritanism was the creed of the elect, Parliament the council of the elected. Puritanism glimpsed a theocracy in which the saints should rule the sinners, Parliament was the preserve of a ruling class which, if God had called its members to their station in life and their seats in St Stephen's Chapel, he had chosen on a different principle from that which would govern the seating in Heaven. But if they were unlikely to thrill to the Puritan vision of a 'godly Utopia', the noblemen and gentlemen who made up three-quarters of an Elizabethan Parliament often showed much sympathy with Puritanism's more limited aims. In particular, the influence of the universities, the stronghold of Puritanism, quickly transmitted itself to the House of Commons, where the proportion of university-trained men was both substantial and increasing. It was naturally the Puritan members who took the lead in Parliamentary efforts to reform the Church, and who bore the brunt of the resultant royal displeasure. In 1571 Walter Strickland, member of a well-known North Country family, introduced a bill to reform the Prayer Book. He was suspended from Parliament and summoned before the Council. The House, which had realized Strickland's error and tried to redeem it by asking the Queen's leave to discuss his bill, was none the less indignant at his removal. When Sir Francis Knollys, one of the 'managerial' group and himself something of a Puritan, spoke in its defence, he was answered by Yelverton, who came of a family of judges, that 'the precedent was perilous', and that 'since the Queen could not of her self make laws, neither might she by the same reason break laws.' This plain speaking had its effect, and Strickland reappeared on the morrow. There was a similar passage in 1572, when the Queen impounded two bills touching religion, this time contenting herself with expressing her 'utter mislike' of the author of one of them.

But the greatest name in the parliamentary agitation over religion was that of Wentworth. The brothers Peter and Paul Wentworth came of an Oxfordshire family, although they generally sat for Cornish constituencies. Both were ardent Puritans, both were hot of temper and intemperate of speech. Peter Wentworth first earned a place in the Parliamentary Book of Quotations with his reply to Archbishop Parker's invitation to a Commons committee to accept the text of the Thirty-Nine Articles as settled by Convocation. 'No, by the faith I bear unto God,' answered Wentworth, 'we will pass nothing before we understand what it is; for that were but to make you popes. Make you

popes who list, for we will make you none.' That was spoken
in 1571. Five years later Wentworth blundered into his first
great parliamentary row. His action was precipitate, but
not unpremeditated, for the speech which he started to
deliver on 8 February 1576 had been composed two or
three years earlier. It was a bitter attack on the Queen's
prohibitions of bills about religion. Her messages, and the
hints of royal displeasure which clustered round them,
were not only 'very injurious to the freedom of speech and
consultation', they were making of the House of Commons
'a fit place to serve the Devil and his angels in, and not to
glorify God and benefit the Commonwealth.' 'God,'
declared Wentworth, 'was the last session shut out of
doors.' After some minutes of a harangue the like of which
no House had ever heard Wentworth was stopped and his
fellow members anticipated royal action by committing him
to the Tower. He was left there for a month and then, at the
Queen's own suggestion, was brought back to the House,
made humble submission, and took his place 'to the great
contentment of all that were present'. His outburst had, for
the moment at least, done his cause more harm than good.
Earlier in the session the Commons had petitioned the Queen
to give legislative sanction to the scheme put forward in
Walter Travers' *Book of Discipline* of 1574 for ecclesiastical
self-government on a voluntary basis. Wentworth destroyed
any possibility of their following up this move. He had
made his name almost enough in itself to provoke the royal
veto. When in the next session, called in 1581, his brother
persuaded the House to appoint a day of prayer and
fasting and to begin its daily labours with a sermon,
Elizabeth forbade even this godly proposal, with an
oblique denunciation of its author, and its only result was
another Commons apology. But the Wentworths were
untameable. In the Parliament of 1587 Peter Wentworth

made his second great gesture in the cause of free speech. When the two documents known to posterity as Cope's Bill and Book – the first sweeping away all existing ecclesiastical legislation, the second replacing it by the Genevan Prayer Book and Discipline – were withdrawn from the Commons by Royal command, Wentworth addressed to the Speaker a series of leading questions on the privileges thereby infringed. He was removed to the Tower, where he was quickly joined by the offending Sir Anthony Cope and three of his associates.

Wentworth was eventually to die in the Tower, after a final challenge and incarceration, a martyr to the cause of free speech. He had come nearer than any of his contemporaries to seeing that freedom of speech was the first of freedoms and the greatest of causes, and he rendered it notable service. But if the road to hell is paved with good intentions, the road to liberty has been laid upon many illiberal ones. Wentworth fought for freedom of speech, not for its own sake, but as a means to an end, and had he achieved that end, the result would have been, not more freedom, but less. For the Puritans whose cause he championed were no more the standard-bearers of liberty than the Fascists who in our own day revile a democracy which curtails their freedom to propagate their particular brand of tyranny. How little of tolerance there was in their make-up appears from their attitude towards their fellow-dissenters, the Catholics. To the Puritan Rome was anti-Christ, and its adherents little better than infidels. 'Such be the humours of the commons house,' said Cecil of the parliament of 1563, 'as they think nothing sharp enough against the Papists', and throughout the reign it was the Puritan element in the House which took the lead in devising ever sterner measures of repression.

During the first ten years of the reign the English

Catholics had enjoyed a large measure of practical toleration. Confident of their loyalty, the government had shown itself content with a minimum standard of outward conformity, and, at least after the first crucial months, had shut its eyes to what went on in certain country houses and in the embassy chapels of Catholic Powers. The Catholics were not ostracized. As the Catholic author of *Leicester's Commonwealth* was to write later: 'There was no mention then of factions in religion, neither was any man much noted or rejected for that cause; so otherwise his conversations were civil and courteous.' The arrival of Mary Queen of Scots, the Northern Rebellion, the Bull of Excommunication, and the Ridolfi Plot were the first four nails hammered into the coffin of that comfortable compromise. Pius V compelled English Catholics to choose between loyalty to their Faith and loyalty to their Queen; Mary, the Northern Earls, Norfolk and the Ridolfi plotters sharpened the horns of the dilemma. With its former test of loyalty, the Oath of Allegiance, vitiated by the papal absolution, the government sought new means of identifying and penalizing its potential enemies. Parliament, when it met in 1571, had its own answer to the problem: compulsory church-going should be reinforced by compulsory partaking of the communion. The member for Warwick, Edward Aglionby, condemned this inroad upon the sanctuary of the conscience. 'The conscience of man,' he declared in the unforced yet forceful language which adorns many an Elizabethan debate, 'is eternal, invisible, and not in the power of the greatest monarchy in the world, in any limits to be straitened, in any bounds to be contained, nor with any policy of man, if once decayed, to be again raised.' But the Puritan Strickland found scriptural authority for forcing man's consciences; Thomas Norton, whose literary labours had included a translation of Calvin's *Institutes*, said that it had been done under Mary; and the bill 'for coming to church and receiving the communion' passed both Houses.

Elizabeth vetoed the bill. It was a gage of her resolve not to be diverted by the clamour from her declared policy. Within two months of the Northern Rebellion her government had drawn up a *Declaration of the Queen's Proceedings in Church and State* which reiterated the earlier assurances that all who obeyed the law would 'certainly and quietly have and enjoy the fruits of our former accustomed favour, lenity and grace in all causes requisite, without any molestation to them by any person by way of examination or inquisition of their secret opinions in their consciences, for matters of faith.' The government's refusal to trample on peaceful Catholicism did not mean its abandonment of the ideal of religious unity. Elizabeth and Cecil hoped that Catholicism, deprived of its priests, banned from schools and universities, and sundered from its continental headquarters, would become moribund and perhaps in time die out altogether. The government's hope was the Catholic's fear, and it was to cast out that fear and to prepare for a brighter future, that a group of Catholics resolved to emulate the Marian exiles by giving English Catholicism a Continental base. In 1568 William Allen, once the Principal of an Oxford Hall, established an English College under the aegis of the newly-founded University of Douai in the Netherlands. The primary aim of the College was to train missionaries for the English field. After ten years at Douai it was shifted to Rheims in France, and in 1579 the Pope himself founded a second College in Rome. There were already many English Catholics on the Continent, and others followed in a steady trickle. It was always an offence under the Tudors to leave the country without licence, and in 1571 all Catholics were ordered to return within a year under penalty of forfeiting their property. But the Englishmen who came home from the seminaries did so at the bidding of a higher Power. In 1574 the first three missionaries arrived from Douai, pioneers of an heroic enterprise. By 1578 their number had risen to fifty, and by 1580 to over a hundred. They were soon breathing into English Catholicism something of the restless vitality of the Counter-Reformation. 'These priests,' wrote the Spanish ambassador, 'go about disguised as laymen, and although' – should he not have written 'because'? – 'they are young, their good life, fervency, and zeal in the work are admirable.' But the labours which revivified the Faith in England did so at the cost of giving it an exotic flavour, and the national prejudice against everything foreign found an obvious target in a religion which, once the chief bond between England and Europe, had since been redefined by a Council of foreigners, was expounded in foreign seminaries, and was identified with hated foreign potentates. Even Catholic Englishmen were not immune from this prejudice, besides appreciating its baneful hold over their non-Catholic countrymen, and it helped to inspire their own revolt against their Jesuit leaders towards the close of the century. The same resentment operated, although not to the same extent, against the Geneva-inspired creed of the Puritan, and the ill wind of nationalist prejudice which hindered both forms of dissent blew fair for the 'mere English' Church which had taken its stand between them.

Coinciding as it did with the rise of militant Puritanism, the Catholic revival constituted the most searching test of the Elizabethan essay in religious toleration. In 1571, while rejecting Parliament's programme against the ordinary recusant, the government had joined with it in increasing the penalties for Catholic activism. To introduce the Bull of 1570, or to do any of the things which that document encouraged English Catholics to do, was made treason. Less patently necessary to national security were the provisions against reconciling individuals to Rome and possessing 'papal objects'. It was under the shadow of these laws that the first wave of missionaries broke upon the English scene. The government soon laid hands upon several of them, but for three years it did not go beyond imprisonment. Then in 1577 Cuthbert Mayne was executed for treason under the act of 1571. The verdict was not irreproachable, for there was less evidence that Mayne had acted treasonably than presumption that he would do so if the situation demanded. But the Council chose to connect his activities in Cornwall with Spanish dealings there, and he was adjudged too dangerous to live. Early in the following year two other ex-students of Douai suffered under the same act. If the small number of such tragedies in the ten years following the Bull is first of all a measure of that document's futility, it is also a tribute to the government's restraint in applying its counter-measures. While the lot of the 'passive' Catholics had so far undergone little deterioration, few 'active' Catholics had suffered the extreme penalty provided for them.

With the advent of the eighties the situation took a decided turn for the worse. The mounting total and expanding activity of the seminarists would sooner or later have had this effect, but what stung the government into action was the arrival in England, in the summer of 1580, of the Jesuit mission headed by Edmund Campion and Robert Parsons. The Jesuits had already secured control of the English College in Rome, and they were now to take over the leadership of the movement in England. The aims of the mission were set forth in the declaration which came to be known as 'Campion's Brag'. 'My charge,' wrote its author, 'is of free cost to preach the Gospel, to minister the Sacraments, to instruct the simple, to reform sinners, to confute errors – in brief, to cry alarm spiritual against foul vice and proud ignorance, wherewith many my dear Countrymen are abused.' The words might have been written by any Puritan. There followed an emphatic disclaimer of any political purpose, 'from which I do gladly restrain and sequester my thoughts', a request for facilities to dispute the questions at issue with representative Anglicans, and a promise to undergo cheerfully the more rigorous ordeal which was doubtless in store. The writer concluded by recommending both standpoints to Almighty God, 'to the end we may at last be friends in heaven, when all injuries shall be forgotten'. It was a noble manifesto, and in Campion's case there is no reason to doubt either the sincerity of the undertakings or the faithfulness of their performance. For Campion shared in abundant measure that integrity of mind and spirit which, enlisted under hostile banners, was to war so tragically with itself. His comrade Parsons was a man of different stamp, 'a politician in a priest's disguise'. Devoted to the same end, he could not resist the temptation to achieve it by other means than those included in his mandate; and when he escaped from England he left behind an added weight of prejudice against his undeserving colleague.

The government opened its counter-attack by securing greatly increased powers of repression. The Parliament of 1581 furnished these powers willingly. The Act 'to retain the Queen's majesty's subjects in their due obedience' not only rounded off the earlier treason legislation, with an eye to the Jesuit and seminarist, but enormously increased the penalties on ordinary recusancy. Saying Mass was to cost 200 marks and a year in prison, hearing it 100 marks and the same imprisonment, recusancy unaggravated by these offences £20 a month, and the employment of a recusant schoolmaster £10 a month. The Act spelled gaol for every priest and beggary for every layman, and Catholic England was in despair. Compared with the twelvepence of 1559, this was a price revolution indeed. And although the campaign against Catholicism was to fall far short of the war of extermination legalized by these provisions, the drive against the limited objective formed by the missionary priests was pushed home with growing vigour and diminishing scruple. From 1581 the executions multiplied. Campion himself was captured in June 1581 after twelve months of tireless and triumphal labours. The proceedings against him illustrate the strength and weakness of the government's position. He was first summoned before the Council and offered, not merely safety, but the prospect of speedy preferment, if he would abjure the Pope. Neither a Church whose first generation of ministers had for the most part made this abjuration, nor a State which reckoned obedience to be nine points of the law, was likely to neglect the chance of winning over such a recruit. But Campion was not for sale. He was next subjected to a different ordeal, the torture of the rack. The extortion of evidence by the infliction of intolerable pain is a barbarism whose recrudescence in our own day has not rendered it less revolting to humane minds, and all who touch it are defiled. But in so far as judicial torture has become a thing of the past, it has done so less because men have come to think it wrong than because they have come to find it unnecessary. The doubtful and fragmentary evidence once elicited by torture has been superseded by the fuller and more trustworthy evidence collected by the police. Tudor England had no police force. It had its informers and its spies, and during the plot-ridden eighties these multiplied and developed into something approaching a system. But the same conditions intensified the need to secure all possible information by all possible means, and a man like Campion knew too much to be spared the most brutal of them. A few names of confederates were forced out of him, but he wrote afterwards that he had revealed 'no things of secret', a phrase which was to go against him at his trial. He was next given the opportunity, asked for in his 'Brag', of defending his standpoint in public disputation. Weak from imprisonment and torture he none the less acquitted himself so ably that the government decided to transfer the contest from the debating-room to the law-court, where the issue would be less in doubt. Campion and a number of other priests were put on trial for treason. They were arraigned, not under any recent act, but under the historic statute of 1352, a decision which, designed to convince contemporary opinion of the legality of the proceedings, has helped to compromise them in the eyes of posterity. The trial was, however, conducted no more unfairly, and a good deal more humanely, than most treason trials in that age of professional witnesses and faked testimony, of prosecuting counsel who were allowed to do almost as they liked and defendants who were allowed no counsel at all. The result was a foregone conclusion, and Campion and two others were executed at Tyburn on 1 December 1581.

On the scaffold Campion reaffirmed what he had urged repeatedly during his imprisonment and trial. 'If you esteem my religion treason,' he declared, 'then am I guilty; as for other treason, I never committed any, God is my judge,' and he wished the Queen 'a long quiet reign with all prosperity'. It was magnificent, but it was also war. It was war between a spiritual power which, let the duty weigh never so lightly with unpolitical minds like

Campion's, enjoined the duty of deposing a reigning sovereign, and the temporal power thus attacked whose duties as certainly comprehended the duty of self-preservation. So long as heads of churches claimed this power over heads of states, so long would it be possible for one honest man to call treason what another called religion. But it was also a war between religion and irreligion. The deeds and words for which the government indicted Campion were themselves an indictment of the government. He and his fellow-workers were labouring and suffering to recover England for a faith which, once enthroned, would have done again what it had done under Mary, have burnt dissenters as heretics. Elizabeth burnt only four persons for heresy, and none was a Catholic. On the contrary, she never tired of proclaiming that she had punished, and would continue to punish, only those whose actions threatened the State. This was, as Allen pointed out, for the government to admit either that 'our religion is true', or else that 'they care not for it nor what we believe, no further than toucheth their prince and temporal weal.' Since the first alternative was out of the question, there remained only the second. And that was indeed the right one.

The decade which saw the Catholic assault at its height, and the government's defence at its fiercest, also saw the citadel of the Elizabethan settlement threatened from within. Balked of their hope of achieving reform in Parliament, the Puritans turned increasingly to 'direct action' to gain their ends. They had first attempted, during the 1570s, to use the weekly or fortnightly 'prophesyings' – clerical discussion-groups to which the laity were admitted – which had come into vogue in the south-eastern dioceses as platforms for the dissemination of their views. The prominence given on these occasions to the exposition of Scriptural texts made them peculiarly appropriate to the Puritans' purpose, and there can be little doubt that, used as the Puritans meant to use them, they constituted a serious potential threat to that measure of discipline which Elizabeth had been struggling to establish over her Church. So, at least, the Queen herself thought, and in 1577 she ordered Archbishop Grindal, Parker's successor, to put a stop to them. Grindal, a reformer and something of a Puritan, who favoured the 'prophesyings' as a means of educating the clergy, refused. Elizabeth suspended him for five years from his office, and on his death in 1583 she chose in his place the most ardent anti-Puritan among her bishops, and the champion of the Church against Cartwright, John Whitgift. It was a declaration of war, and Whitgift went into action immediately. He drew up a set of Articles demanding unqualified subscription from the clergy to the Royal Supremacy, the Prayer Book and Ordinal, and the Thirty-Nine Articles. Armed with this weapon, and using the inquisitorial procedure of the High Commission, the ecclesiastical counterpart of the Star Chamber, he pursued the enemy with relentless zeal.

The enemy were already taking up new positions. The Puritan challenge of the eighties took two opposing forms. The 'classical' movement was an attempt to presbyterianize the Church from within. It takes its name from the 'classis' or local synod of Puritan clergy which did everything in its power to give the constitution of the Church a presbyterian content and meaning. Candidates for the ministry were put forward for consecration after being elected by congregations, the Prayer Book was judiciously emended in use, the Scriptures expounded in a Puritan sense. These local efforts were supplemented and coordinated by those of district conferences and even by national conferences held in London. It was the same pyramidal structure which the Puritans had seen arise in Huguenot France and

Presbyterian Scotland. The Presbyterians accepted the connexion between Church and State and were only concerned to make the Church pull the State instead of the State's pulling the Church. The 'separatist' movement determined to cut the connexion altogether. To the Separatist the only true Church was the congregation of believers, the 'two or three gathered together' in God's name and neither owing allegiance to, nor deriving authority from, any other power. Where the Presbyterian laboured to convert the magistrate, the Separatist founded his Church without tarrying for the magistrate. Ritual, ceremony, theological learning, these were but dross to men who more than made up for their lack of them by their emotional power and inspirational fervour. The Separatists were few but formidable.

The Presbyterians strove to undermine episcopacy, the Separatists treated it as though it did not exist. But Martin Marprelate threatened for a moment to blow it down in a gale of laughter. The Jesuits had tried to operate a secret printing-press in England in 1580. Those responsible for the production of the Martin Marprelate tracts succeeded in doing so, in 1588-9, long enough to produce a series of nine tracts in which the bishops were held up to merciless ridicule. The weapon struck deep, but it proved to be a boomerang, and it returned with dreadful violence upon the camp which had hurled it. For the nation-wide hunt for the author and the press yielded a lot of evidence about puritan ramifications, and further ferreting soon produced more. From 1589 the government struck blow after blow. Cartwright and other presbyterian leaders were gaoled and the classical organization broken up. Udall, suspected of having written the tracts, died in prison while under sentence of death. A religious maniac, Hacket, two of the Separatists, Barrow and Greenwood, and one of the marprelate conspirators, Penry, were executed. In 1593 a fierce act promised exile or death to all who refused to attend church or attended unauthorized religious gatherings.

Neither Puritanism nor Catholicism was to be destroyed in England by persecution, and the triple division of English religion into Anglican, Nonconformist and Catholic bears witness to the survival-value of the conceptions which clashed so tragically in Elizabethan England. But to the peace in which they now dwell both the Queen and her opponents can claim to have made their contribution. Elizabeth was the first English sovereign to repudiate the right, claimed by all her predecessors and by most of her fellow rulers, to penalize religious opinion. Those whom she punished, she punished not to save their souls in the next world, but to save her state in this. 'Reason of state' has covered a multitude of crimes, and it is less easy to forgive some of the things that Elizabeth did than to accept her motive for doing them. But her opponents would not have thought so. Intolerant as they were themselves, their indictment of her was not that she persecuted, but that she persecuted for the wrong reason; and had they wielded her power, there would have been much more opening of windows into souls. But no good man ever died wholly in vain, and these were good men who died doing their duty. They were the opposition, and it was their duty to oppose. By continuing to oppose they proved that the old unity was gone, never to return, and by making that plain they paved the way for the new unity in diversity. They were saving others, if themselves they could not save. For it is not only men's evil that lives after them; and great things can be achieved, as well as great crimes committed, by men who know not what they do.

In the midst of the storm and stress of religious conflict

another victim was laid upon the bloodstained altar of the State. On 8 February 1587 Mary Queen of Scots was executed at Fotheringay Castle. During her nineteen years in England Mary had repeatedly committed what in any of Elizabeth's subjects would have been high treason. She had been implicated in practically every plot against Elizabeth, and it was abundantly clear that given the opportunity she would have stopped at nothing which promised her the liberty that she had lost or the crown that she still hoped to gain. Surely she deserved the death which she had done so much to contrive for another. So thought every one of Elizabeth's parliaments, so thought all her ministers and councillors. And it was her Secretary, Walsingham, who early in 1586 set the trap which proved Mary's connivance at yet another plot; it was the parliament of 1586 which extorted from Elizabeth the death-sentence against her; and it was the privy council which in the end shouldered the responsibility of sending it off to Fotheringay. Elizabeth's long refusal to take the step which almost any of her subjects, in her place, would have taken long before was a mixture of sentiment and reason not unlike that which had earlier determined her, also in defiance of the nation's earnest wish, to refuse to marry. Her womanly tenderness fought against taking the life of a woman, her regal loyalty against taking the life of one who had been a queen. But may not her reason also have told her, as, indeed, experience had proved, that if a pretender was a magnet to disaffection, a pretender in captivity was a key to its exposure? Elizabeth never acted solely out of sentiment, and if she had earlier judged Mary's death a necessity, she would not have shrunk from its cruelty. When, at last, she yielded – although even then she left the final responsibility to others – the argument for Mary's death was overwhelmingly strong. The country was moving towards the grand climacteric of the reign, and Mary living would be infinitely more dangerous than Mary dead. Justice had long demanded that Mary should die, but it was expediency, not justice, that sent her to her death in 1587.

VIII

THE SEA AND ALL THAT THEREIN IS

THE years from 1568 to 1572, during which Elizabethan
England weathered its greatest crisis, are no less momentous by neighbouring national reckonings. In the history
of the Netherlands they mark the opening of the Eighty
Years' War for independence. The rebellion which the
first twelve years of Philip II's rule had made probable the
five years during which it was personified in Alva made
certain. The first campaigns led by the Prince of Orange
from Germany were a fiasco. But although Alva might
mark the earth with their ruin, his control stopped with the
shore, and the Dutch Republic was born, as it was to live
and thrive, not on the land but on the sea. It was the
amphibious warriors of the seaboard who showed how to
fight the monster of the land. From carrying most of their
country's overseas trade the shippers of the coastal towns
turned to destroying it. For the first few years the Sea
Beggars, as these pirate-patriots were called, disposed of
their booty and replenished their supplies principally in
English ports. English trade with the Netherlands was
suspended by the embargo of 1568, and Elizabeth looked
tolerantly on freebooters who were enemies of Spain. But
in March 1572 she gave them notice to quit. Whatever the
motive behind this sudden reversal of policy – whether it
was a gesture towards Spain or a Machiavellian thrust at
her – its effect was decisive. On 1 April 1572 – Alva himself was the victim-in-chief of that All Fools' Day – the Sea
Beggars seized the town of Brill, commanding the mouth

of the River Maas. Four days later Flushing, which similarly commanded the Scheldt, went over to them, and one by one, during the weeks that followed, the towns of Holland and Zeeland were brought over to their cause. The Revolt of the Netherlands had begun.

Meanwhile the situation in France was crystallizing into a not dissimilar pattern. The third war of religion, fought from 1568 to 1570 between the monarchy, dominated by the house of Guise, and the Calvinists, patronized by leading noblemen, went little better for the Huguenots than Orange's efforts against Alva. But it was then that the Huguenots took the capital decision to make their head-quarters at the west coast port of La Rochelle, and to intensify their hostilities at sea. Their privateers developed in and around the Bay of Biscay a campaign against 'papist' shipping identical with the one which the Sea Beggars were waging in the Narrow Seas, and the two Protestant rebellions were soon knit together in a naval war which raged incessantly along two thousand miles of coast, and, as we shall see, across the Atlantic as well. Now if ever seemed the time for the French and Spanish monarchies to draw together for mutual support, and while the Guises remained in control in France this was, indeed, the way the wind promised to blow. But with the peace of 1570 the Huguenot leader Coligny rapidly gained influence at the French Court and in him the old secular hostility to Spain was reinforced by the new spiritual one. Thus in 1571–2 France came to stand 'on the edge of one of the most momentous decisions in her history'. The choice lay between Guise and Coligny, between unbending Catholic-ism and religious compromise, between civil war and a national war, a war against Spain, a war in the Nether-lands. For more than a year a struggle went on for mastery of the feeble-minded youth who was King of France.

Twice Coligny brought Charles IX to the verge of launching the 'Flemish enterprise', twice the Queen Mother Catherine de Medici dragged him back. When, in August 1572, Coligny tried for the third time, Catherine's reply was to plot his assassination. The assassin blundered. Few blunders have been more ghastly in their consequences. For Catherine's panic-stricken effort to convince her son that Coligny was the centre of a great Huguenot design against his throne provoked that easily deluded mind, and at its instance the easily inflamed rabble of French cities, to a deed of insane ferocity. On Sunday, 24 August 1572, there began the Massacre of St Bartholomew. Within eight days some four thousand Huguenots, among them Coligny himself, were slaughtered in Paris, and within eight weeks perhaps twice that number in the provinces. France had made her choice. The sword which Coligny had pointed towards the Netherlands now dripped with French blood, and if Philip II did indeed greet the news with the only smile which ever lit that face of stone it was the Habsburg monarch as well as the Catholic bigot who rejoiced.

The Massacre had results commensurate with its scale and appropriate to its savagery. It did not exterminate French Protestantism. The surviving Huguenots rallied to the martyred cause and, sundered by its river of blood from their Catholic countrymen, fought on for a generation to achieve a settlement which in effect gave them a state within the state. They kept La Rochelle and with it their command of the sea. But France paid a heavy price in the miseries of protracted civil war, in the forfeiting of her influence in the Old World and the fading of her prospects in the New. To Protestants everywhere the Massacre came to stand for what Catholicism, given the opportunity, would do to them, and its memory must have doomed the life or liberty of many a Catholic in many a land. But nowhere did its effects strike deeper than in the Netherlands. To pursue the 'ifs' of history is as fruitless as it is fascinating. Yet we can scarcely doubt that the outcome of Coligny's projected French invasion of the Netherlands would have been very different from the outcome of the blood-bath in which it perished with its author. For one result of the Massacre was to undermine the Prince of Orange's conception of a rebellion thrusting in from the South and East, a rebellion which should be national in its politics and religion and conservative in its social philosophy, and to leave in tragically splendid isolation that other rebellion, the ruthless, ruffianly, socially uninhibited rebellion of the Sea Beggars. If the Sea Beggars were the shock troops of the Revolt, their shock was felt almost as much by their countrymen as by the Spaniards. William of Orange had the eyes to see that, with France lost, the fate of the Revolt lay in their hands, and he straightaway threw in his lot with them. But he was the only man of his standing who did so. Such was the contribution of the Massacre to the tangle of causes which, within a few years, transformed the Revolt of the Netherlands from a nation-wide and all-party protest, headed by the great ones of the land, against a centralizing, persecuting and overtaxing government, into a desperate struggle for survival by a string of seaward towns, half-inspired, half-terrorized by the minority in their midst, against the avenging arms of Spain.

It was the tragedy of sixteenth-century Spain that she had greatness thrust upon her. Where other nations – our own furnishing perhaps the best example – came to occupy great positions in the world only after they had developed powers proportionate to the task, Spain was called upon, by the accident of her absorption into the Habsburg conglomeration, to shoulder responsibilities far beyond her capacity to bear. That she did not sink sooner, or further, beneath their weight was chiefly due to the fact that two of her heaviest territorial burdens were at the same time sources of added power. These two were the Netherlands and the Empire in the New World. For the first three-quarters of the sixteenth century the Netherlands were a prime source of strength to Spain. So conscious were Spanish kings of the fact that they were to struggle for the same length of time to recover what they had lost there. The American possessions, which to many contemporaries appeared even more valuable, were in fact much less so, and they, too, were subject to what might be loosely termed a process of diminishing returns: the longer Spain held them the greater grew the strain and the less the yield of their possession. But if their real value declined they grew ever more precious to their masters, and any enemy who touched Spain there was touching her at her most sensitive, if not perhaps at her most vital, point. That was the point at which the *toreros* of Tudor England prodded the Spanish bull, and the bull reacted with noisy fury. At the moment when the English attack was developing in earnest – the year was 1580 – Philip II carried Habsburg expansionism to its farthest point by annexing Portugal and the Portuguese possessions overseas. Brazil, West Africa, Ceylon and the East Indies then joined Spanish America and the Philippines to create the first empire on which the sun never set. It was also an empire on which the sun was not to shine for long. For the accession of strength to Spain was more apparent than real, whereas the extra burden of responsibility was real enough; and during the sixty years of the union both the English and the Dutch were to begin carving new empires in the East out of Portuguese possessions which Spanish kings were powerless to defend.

It was not the English, but the French, who had first

broken in upon the Spanish preserves. The long struggle between France and Spain was fought out, not in Italy and the Netherlands alone, but on the Atlantic and in the Caribbean. French privateers preyed upon Spanish shipping and plundered Spanish settlements. As Calvinism made headway among the French seamen, they began to mark down priests and churches for destruction, and a war of trade became also a war of religion. What stayed the French onslaught was not the Peace of 1559 (on the contrary, by adopting the so-called 'Lines of Amity' beyond which infractions should not invalidate its clauses, that treaty helped to establish the famous maxim 'No peace beyond the Line'), but the growing inability of a France torn by civil war to keep it up. For ten years after the Peace the 'French Fury' continued to rage in the Caribbean, and that fact goes far towards explaining the ambiguous character of the first English expeditions to those waters. It is with these ventures that John Hawkins steps on to the spacious stage of Elizabethan history. Hawkins had begun his career as the mobile partner in a Plymouth firm which mingled trading with privateering, and it was his youthful voyages to the Canaries which first quickened his interest in the fabulous islands across the Atlantic. Behind a conventional middle-class exterior Hawkins possessed qualities of mind and personality such as only great enterprises could satisfy. The starting-point of his schemes was the provision of negro slave-labour from West Africa to the West Indies, a lucrative trade reserved to a ring of Spanish, and a few foreign, firms under licence from the Spanish government. Hawkins relied upon a mixture of personal ability, influential connexions and disciplined force to gain him admission to their charmed circle. In 1562–3 he carried across his first cargo of slaves, bartered them for pearls, hides and sugar, and came home showing a good profit for the syndicate which had financed the voyage. There had been a little trouble with the Portuguese in Africa and with Spanish officialdom in America, and two ships sent home to Seville and Lisbon had been confiscated. But to Hawkins this was evidence of misunderstanding rather than malevolence, and in October 1564 he was off on a second voyage. The commercial pattern was the same as before – it was that triangle of barter whose three sides ran from England to West Africa, where English manufactures were exchanged for negro bodies, thence to Central America, where the bodies which had survived the horrors of the 'middle passage' were exchanged for the fruits of tropical earth and sea, and so back to the West Country apex. This second voyage was, however, more than a private trading venture. Hawkins sailed with the Queen's approval, flew her standard, and took with him one of her ships, the *Jesus of Lubeck*. The ostensible, and, as his biographer believes, the genuine motive for this officializing of the expedition was to enable Hawkins to offer something which might smooth his entry into the slave-trade, the services of his squadron to clear the Caribbean of privateers. Hawkins certainly spoke of himself as 'commanded by the Queen my mistress to serve [the King of Spain] with my navy as need requireth', and even lapsed into the anachronism of calling Philip 'the King my master'. Preposterous as it would become only a year or two later, the notion that England should gain a footing in the Spanish colonial trade as the reward for acting as its policeman was not so impossible in 1564, when France had barely ceased to be, and Spain not yet become, the obvious national enemy. It was not, indeed, until Hawkins was homeward bound from this second voyage, which had passed off without serious incident, that Philip took a decision which made such an arrangement impossible. He decided to defend his American monopoly with his own naval power, and to begin by wiping out the settlement which some Huguenots had established in Florida. The French were liquidated in the autumn of 1565, and during the next two years Spanish defensive preparations were pushed ahead. The result was that Hawkins's third voyage ran a course which Tudor English, with its mastery of meiosis, labelled 'troublesome', and which we should call disastrous. He began it in October 1567 with six ships and 408 men. For four of the ships, including the old *Jesus*, and not a few of the men, the voyage ended, on 23 September 1568, in the little road-stead of San Juan de Ulua, where Hawkins was trapped, tricked and then battered by a Spanish fleet of thirteen great ships. Only two ships, the *Minion* and the *Judith*, made their escape. Hawkins, in the *Minion*, having put ashore over a hundred men who could not face the weeks of starvation which lay between them and home, sailed for Plymouth with the remaining hundred and arrived there, it is said, with fifteen. The *Judith* had come in five days before.

After San Juan de Ulua it was clear that, whatever happened in Europe, any English ships which ventured to Spanish America must be prepared for a 'troublesome' time. It followed almost inevitably that those which did so would seek a reward commensurate with the penalty of failure. Thus although illicit slave-trading went on, it was largely eclipsed by a new campaign, a campaign of unlimited reprisal for the misdeeds, actual or alleged, of the Spaniards themselves. In 1570 Hawkins himself sought permission to attack the plate-fleet as a reprisal for San Juan de Ulua. But it was the man who had brought the *Judith* out of that treacherous affair who was to be its Avenging Angel. His name was Francis Drake. 'Drake', we sing with Newbolt and Stanford, 'he was a Devon man.'

But the Western Rebellion of 1549 had driven his Protestant father from Devon when Francis was a boy, and the
sea by which he grew up was the Thames Estuary off
Chatham. He learned his seamanship in the coasting trade
and he was twenty-five when he first saw the Spanish
Main. He went there again with Hawkins in 1567-8, and
by 1570 he was an obvious choice for the command of one
of the expeditions which Winter, who had beleaguered the
French in Scotland in 1560 and was now Surveyor of the
Navy, and Hawkins, the government's adviser in these
matters, were planning to set forth. The year 1571 found
Drake reconnoitring and preparing an advanced base on
the coast of the Main. He took some prizes, but his real
prize was the information upon which he founded his first
great independent exploit, the raid on the Spanish treasure
in 1572-3. Drake's plan was to attack the stream of silver
which flowed from the mines of Peru to the treasury of
Seville, not at sea, but on land. The point he chose was
Nombre de Dios, the port on the north coast of the isthmus
of Panama whither the treasure was brought by pack-
mules from the southern, or Pacific, side. The plan involved
seizing Nombre de Dios, a fair-sized town, holding it long
enough to rifle the treasure-house, and withdrawing, all
before a counter-attack could develop. To carry it out
Drake embarked at Plymouth, in May 1572, aboard two
ships together displacing ninety-five tons, a total of seventy-
three men. Seldom in the history of warfare has so much
been expected from so few. But every detail had been
thought out and nearly every contingency provided for. If
Drake's singeing of the King of Spain's beard at Cadiz in
1587 was to serve as the model for the clipping of the
German Emperor's whiskers at Zeebrugge in the First
World War, his attack on Nombre de Dios, in 1572 was the
parent of all the Commando raids of the Second. The

original plan failed, but it failed in the hour of victory, and then only through two strokes of ill-fortune: the tropical storm which held up the attack on the treasure-house, and the leg-wound which knocked out the leader at the crisis of the operation. (We cannot, however, overlook the devastating suggestion of a modern expert that, since a plate-fleet had sailed shortly before Drake arrived, the door of the treasure-house would have given way only to reveal an interior bare of gold. Did its stout timbers safe-guard something more precious to England than all the wealth of the Indies, Drake's matchless reputation and unrivalled ascendency over his men?) After six months of enforced delay, while the rains halted the movement of the next load of treasure, Drake laid an ambush on the other side of the isthmus, near Panama. But again a mis-chance, this time a premature movement by one of the ambuscaders, warned the Spaniards and robbed Drake of his prize. The third attempt, an ambush laid outside Nombre de Dios with the aid of a French Huguenot party, redeemed the earlier failures and, in Drake's own word, 'made' the voyage. The attackers surprised so much treasure that they could not carry it all away. But the English share of it was worth about £20,000. Drake got back to Plymouth, with thirty survivors of the original company, on Sunday 7 August 1573, and it is recorded that hardly anyone remained in church to hear the sermon.

Drake brought back a ship laden with precious metals and a mind stored with potent memories. He remembered above all that February day when, from the bellevue of a great tree on the isthmus watershed, he had, like Cortez fifty years before, stared with eagle eyes at the Pacific, and had asked God's leave to sail it. But to do that he needed the Queen's leave as well, and it was not at once forth-coming. On the contrary, he returned to find the government negotiating a settlement of outstanding grievances with Spain, and he was warned to lie low unless he wanted his £20,000 worth of plunder brought into the reckoning. So Drake 'disappeared' for two years, and 1575 found him wasting his great talents in an ill-managed scheme of colonization in Ulster. But in 1577 he was given the command of the expedition which was both to answer his prayer and to win him undying fame.

The eighty years since Columbus had landed in the Antilles had left nothing of his claim to have reached the Orient save the habit of calling his islands Indies. It had long been clear that between Europe and Asia by the western route there lay a vast land-mass, or rather two great land-masses linked by a narrow isthmus. With the outline of South, Central and southern North America the seamen, and following them, the geographers of all the maritime nations were fairly familiar. They also knew that beyond America there lay the ocean which Magellan had named 'Pacific'. But that ocean had so far yielded up few of its secrets, and fancy was still free to wander almost untrammelled by fact across its evident immensity. English speculation on the subject was largely a matter of wishful thinking. It focused upon two questions: how to reach the Pacific by an all-water route, and once there what to look for. The Portuguese and Magellan had between them given an answer to the first question which only the opening of the Panama Canal in 1914 would render incomplete: the Pacific could be reached either by the South-East Passage round the Cape of Good Hope or by the South-West Passage round (strictly speaking, through the strait which passed inside) Cape Horn. But Englishmen clung to the belief, fostered by the preconception that a world which was spherical in shape must also be symmetrical of feature, that there were corresponding North-East and North-

West Passages. They were still clinging to it when, in the fifteen-seventies, their urge to reach the Pacific was intensified by what seemed the imminence of a tremendous discovery there. Belief in the existence of a Southern Continent, 'terra australis', a region abounding in all manner of riches, was as old as the Ancients, and the Renaissance had made available the writings, including a mistranscription of Marco Polo, relating to it. For sixteenth-century map- and globe-makers it was fatally easy to insert this unknown continent in the great void between the East Indies and the Straits of Magellan. Ortelius' world-map of 1570, the last word on the subject for Englishmen, showed its coastline as extending from Magellan's Tierra del Fuego right across the South Pacific to the neighbourhood of New Guinea. Nothing remained but for someone to find it, and when, in 1567, the Spaniard Mendaña, sailing west from Peru, reached the Solomon Islands – the name reflects his conviction that they were the biblical Land of Ophir – he believed himself on the verge of the long-awaited discovery. Englishmen who read of his exploit were disposed to agree, but with this difference, that they hoped to make the last step an English, not a Spanish achievement, and its outcome an English, not an extension of the Spanish, Empire.

It was this vision which, at least initially, inspired the two major English enterprises of the seventies, the Cathay and South Seas Projects. In both cases, it is true, the vision quickly faded under the fierce light of practical exigency. The Cathay Company, a private venture identified with the names of Frobisher and Lock, was bound up with the chimera of the North-West Passage, and foundered after three voyages in search of it and of non-existent gold deposits (1576–8). The South Seas Project, for all its official character, strayed not less far from its original objective, a five months' reconnaissance of the non-existent Southern continent. How far, and by whom, Drake was authorized to transform the expedition of 1577 into what it became, a voyage of circumnavigation which included a vicious side-thrust at the Spanish position, remains a matter of conjecture; probably Drake sailed with sufficient encouragement to indulge his appetite for gold and glory, but in a form which left no one but himself to blame if it led him into trouble. After a false start which ended in a gale and a return to refit, the expedition left Plymouth on 13 December 1577. It consisted of five ships, the largest, the *Pelican*, of about 120 tons, the smallest a 15-ton pinnace, and a total complement of 160 men and boys. Twelve months later Drake was alone in the *Pelican*, renamed the *Golden Hind*, off the Chilean coast. During those twelve months much had happened, nearly all of it adverse. The voyage to the Straits had been beset by difficulties, which one of the ships' officers, Thomas Doughty, had used to foment trouble, especially among the 'gentlemen' who had accompanied the expedition in a dangerously ambiguous capacity, half as passengers, half as working members. During a two months' stay at Port St Julian, just short of the Straits, Drake had felt compelled to reassert his authority by trying and hanging Doughty, dismissing and reinstating all his other officers, and making it clear that for the rest of the voyage the gentlemen would 'haul and draw' with the mariners. Drake could tame men, but he could not master the elements. His squadron, reduced to the three fighting ships, had barely passed the Straits when it ran into a prolonged north-westerly gale, in which first the *Marigold* was sunk and then the *Elizabeth* parted company, eventually to make her way back to England. Alone in the South Sea, Drake had first discovered Cape Horn and satisfied himself that Magellan's

Tierra del Fuego was no portion of a Southern Continent, but an island beyond which Atlantic and Pacific met in wide, open water. Then he headed north along the Chilean coast.

It was the next four months which 'made' the voyage. The Spanish Empire might have suffered more from three ships, it could hardly have suffered more from one. The *Golden Hind* played havoc with the ports and shipping of the Peruvian coast, and when in April she drew away northwards she was a golden ship indeed. The next few weeks Drake spent cruising along the coast of California. If, as is most likely, he was seeking the western outlet of the surmised North-West Passage, he did not find it, and what he found could not have tallied with arm-chair versions of that unexplored coast. In June he came to anchor in a 'fair and good' bay and spent nearly two months refitting. The native inhabitants came in crowds to watch the white men and their strange doings, and Drake thought it worth while to annex the country, christening it 'New Albion' and setting up a brass plate as a record. Two centuries later the Spaniards planted a settlement and the Franciscans a mission-post in the neighbourhood; and in the year 1934 there was picked up on the outskirts of San Francisco a brass plate which may, or may not, be Drake's visiting-card.

A three months' voyage westwards brought Drake to his third continent and his second objective, the Moluccas or Spice Islands, whose clove trees were the King of Portugal's mines of Peru. At one of the group, Ternate, Drake concluded a treaty with the Sultan giving Englishmen the exclusive right to buy its produce, and took on board six tons of cloves as a first instalment. Then, after a further scraping and refitting, the *Golden Hind* set course for the Indian Ocean, the Cape and home. On 10 January 1580,

in the maze of islands and reefs of the East Indian Archipelago, she survived the last and greatest peril of the voyage.
For twenty hours she lay on a shoal from which, with both
wind and tide unfavourable, there seemed little hope of
shifting her. The chaplain, Francis Fletcher, who saw in
her plight divine retribution for the killing of Doughty,
celebrated communion and preached a gloomy sermon.
But the theocratic principle had even less future upon that
fragment of England, the deck of the *Golden Hind*, than in
the country of her origin, and Drake, whose robust Puritanism, like Oliver Cromwell's, set much store by the gospel
of self-help, gave the order to lighten ship. Eight guns, half
the cloves, and some stores had gone overboard when, with
the wind easing, she slid undamaged off the shoal. The
authority which Drake had invoked to execute Doughty
he now stretched to excommunicate Fletcher, and the
seamanship which had taken the *Golden Hind* across one
hemisphere sufficed to bring her home across the other.
Eight and a half months later, and thirty-four and a half
after his departure, Drake brought his ship into Plymouth.
He had heard nothing of England, nor England of him,
since he had slipped away from Spanish American waters,
and his first question was whether the Queen was alive and
well.

The Queen was. She was also mightily pleased with
Drake. She summoned him to Court, spent hours listening
to his stories of the voyage, and after he had brought his
ship round to Deptford was his guest at a magnificent
banquet on board which ended in his receiving a knighthood. In honouring Drake Elizabeth was expressing the
popular mood, for his latest exploit had fired the country's
imagination and he had become a national hero. But she
was also identifying herself with his hostility towards
Spain, and in the winter of 1580–1 that appeared to many

thinking minds a piece of egregious folly. For the international situation looked threatening, more threatening, perhaps, than at any time since the beginning of the reign. Everywhere the forces of Catholicism seemed to be gathering strength and those of Protestantism to be on the decline. And there could be no doubt that the reconquest of England held a leading place among the aims of the Counter-Reformation. The reissue of the Bull of 1570, the advent of the Jesuit mission, the outbreak of a Papal-inspired revolt in Ireland, the determined attempt to seduce Scotland from the English alliance, all these pointed to a major offensive against the Elizabethan régime. It was equally clear that this offensive would gain immensely in weight if it were to enlist the active support of Philip II. The menace of Spain, which the events of the seventies had somewhat diminished, those of the early eighties caused to loom larger than ever. Overshadowing all else was the Spanish annexation of Portugal, the last and greatest step in Habsburg aggrandizement, which threatened to upset the whole balance of power in Europe and to give Spain the resources for the most grandiose plans of aggression and conquest. In the Low Countries, too, the brief revival, under the so-called Pacification of Ghent of 1576, of William the Silent's conception of a national war of liberation, had quickly spent itself, and the arrival of the Duke of Parma as Governor heralded an almost unbroken series of triumphs for Spanish arms and Spanish diplomacy. This was surely not the time – so argued the older and more prudent of Elizabeth's advisers, led by William Cecil, now Lord Burghley – to yield to the young hotheads who, reared during the Twenty Years Peace, were eager for the glory and adventure which might accrue from a war with Spain.

The Queen's patronage of Drake did not in fact betoken

any significant change in her attitude towards Philip II. Recognizing as she did that the power of the Spanish Crown had increased, was increasing, and ought to be diminished, she continued to display a rooted aversion to taking the lead in the diminishing process. That, she held, should be the task of Spain's great Continental rival, France, and she would cheerfully have fought Spain to the last drop of French blood. For about eighteen months in 1581–3 it seemed that Elizabeth might succeed in this Machiavellian strategy of warfare at one remove. In 1581 a French army entered the Netherlands to the help of the hard-pressed rebels, in 1582 a French expedition sailed to the Azores in support of the claimant to the throne of Portugal. But in both spheres French intervention proved a fiasco. The Portuguese expedition was destroyed by a Spanish fleet, and the army in the Netherlands crowned an ignominious record of failure against Parma by turning against the cities it was meant to save. By the end of 1583 France had shot her futile bolt. There followed the two crowded years 1584 and 1585 which for England marked the real dividing-line between the years of peace and the years of war. In January 1584 the Spanish ambassador in London was expelled for complicity in the Throckmorton plot. He left muttering that Don Bernardino de Mendoza was born not to disturb countries but to conquer them, and he was to have no successor until his sovereign had attempted, and failed, to conquer the country which had insulted him. A few months later that master-player, Death, took a hand in the game. His summons, in May 1584, to the Duke of Anjou, the heir to the throne of France, destroyed what little hope remained of rallying French resistance to Spain. For with Anjou died the last hope of a Valois succession, and the fact that the next prince in line was the Huguenot Henry of Navarre made inevitable a succession-struggle which would cripple France for a decade. Anjou was followed a month later to an honoured grave by William of Orange, the most illustrious victim of that campaign of legalized murder by which the Counter-Reformation sought to eliminate key-opponents. During his closing years William the Silent, the statesman who was no soldier, had been fighting a losing battle against Parma, the soldier who was also a statesman. But his death was none the less a staggering blow to the rebels' cause, and in their plight they turned this way and that for succour. France, the France of the pious nincompoop Henry III, would have none of them, and so they turned to England, the England of the unfathomable and incalculable, but at the same time the resolute and resourceful, Elizabeth.

For Elizabeth the signing of the treaty of August 1585 with the United Netherlands was the parting of the ways. Thus far, although she had connived at the furnishing of help to the rebel provinces, she had given them scarcely any official countenance or backing. So long as she could persuade herself that their recovery by Spain would not compromise her own safety she had worked for their re-submission on reasonable terms. Later, when Philip's bigotry and Parma's victories dispelled her faith in such an outcome, she had encouraged France to intervene on their behalf. But the comi-tragedy of French intervention, the assassination of Orange, and the alarmingly rapid progress of Parma brought the Queen face to face with the choice which she had laboured so long and skilfully to evade, the choice between leaving the rebels to their fate and giving them the overt and substantial support which would assist them to survive. To do the first would probably mean purchasing a brief respite in which to prepare for the wrath to come, to do the second would mean calling down that wrath at once but with the prospect of braving it in the defiant company of those who had long lived under its shadow. Elizabeth was as incapable of preferring the first of these alternatives as she was of adopting the second without profuse misgivings, hesitations and backslidings. She refused the sovereignty which the Netherlands offered her, but chose as her commander and representative the nobleman who had come nearest to sharing her own throne; and when Leicester accepted a title from her protégés which implied her assumption of political authority over them it needed Burghley's threat of resignation to dissuade her from throwing all into confusion by recalling him. She undertook to maintain an expeditionary force in the Netherlands as long as the war lasted, but she was soon complaining bitterly – and, to do her justice, with good reason – at the speed with which it swallowed her money. She even tried to delude herself that she had not broken with Spain, but merely put herself in a stronger position from which to bargain with Philip. Yet we can no more doubt that, through the fog of suspicion and recrimination, Elizabeth kept faith with the Netherlanders, than that in giving and keeping her pledges to them she threw down a challenge which Philip II could not fail to take up. For, whereas the largely unprovoked aggressions of Drake and his fellows in the years before 1585 had produced little or no retaliation, the news that England was preparing to intervene in the Netherlands had prompt and far-reaching consequences. In May 1585 English ships were included in the seizure of hostile vessels in Spain's Atlantic ports, and within a month the Spanish ambassador in Rome was laying before the Pope the first sketch of the great enterprise which is known in English history as the Spanish Armada.

The Elizabethan war with Spain was the first war in which England owed her survival to her navy. It was, indeed, England's first great naval war. 'Of all others,' wrote Sir Julian Corbett, 'the year 1545 best marks the birth of the English naval power.' The reign of Henry VIII had indeed been the period of gestation, but it was Henry's last war, in other respects so disastrous to the nation, which had bequeathed it, as some compensation, the navy which was to be its first line of defence in the perilous years ahead. The bequest could scarcely have been worse treated. No service decays more rapidly under neglect than a navy, and it took only eleven years after Henry's death to reduce the English navy to the state of helplessness which cost the country Calais. Those eleven years have been rightly called 'the blackest period in the history of the Tudor Navy'. Somerset entrusted the Admiralty to his worthless brother. Northumberland, who had held the office under Henry, gave the navy a new dockyard at Chatham but tainted it with the corruption and degradation which were the marks of his régime. Mary's pattern of national salvation did not include salvation through sea power, and her husband, while ready enough to use the English navy, did nothing to arrest its decay. Thus between 1547 and 1558 the navy lost nearly half its tonnage. Its showpiece, the thousand-ton *Great Harry,* was destroyed by fire in 1553 and not replaced, and a 450-tonner built in 1545 was disposed of ten years later for the ridiculous sum of £35. Only during the closing months of Mary's reign did the loss of Calais shock her government into planning a replacement programme, and of the twenty-two ships which Elizabeth inherited many were unseaworthy.

The first twenty years of Elizabeth's reign saw little or no increase in the size of the fleet. But they did see a welcome improvement in its quality. Worn-out ships were replaced, the dockyards put into better shape. The result was a small but serviceable fleet which did what was required of it. But it was also a fleet conceived and created on traditional lines. The men who administered and commanded the navy of the sixties and seventies regarded it as a maritime extension of the country's home defence system, and a warship as primarily a military strongpoint stationed off the coast. They therefore favoured the short, high-charged ship in which impregnability counted for more than manoeuvrability or speed and which, crammed with fighting-men, was tied to the ports whence came its supplies. Very different was the conception of the proper form and function of a warship which was developing outside the royal navy. While the Queen's squadrons went on solving the old problems in the old way, Hawkins and Drake were finding answers to new problems which also applied to the old. Out of their experiences there rose the vision of a new royal navy, a navy which should defend the country not by patrolling its coasts but by sailing the seven seas and delivering its heaviest blows far from home. To Hawkins fell the duty and honour of clothing this vision in the timber and the gunmetal, the flesh and the blood, the leadership and the discipline which went to the making of the Elizabethan navy. During the seventies Hawkins rose to be the government's chief naval adviser, and in 1578 he was appointed Treasurer of the Navy. In this office he laboured for ten years to give the country the navy of his dreams. The difficulties were formidable. His colleagues of the Navy Board, all men of the old régime, fought him every step of the way. He had, indeed, begun by exposing the scandals of their administration. Of the money grudgingly allotted to the navy by a tight-fisted government a disturbingly large proportion was finding its way into official pockets, while ships and seamen alike went short. Hawkins undertook the ordinary upkeep of the navy for £4,000 a year less than it had been costing. His opponents retaliated by accusing him of all the practices at which they were so adept. But a commission of inquiry set up in 1583 vindicated Hawkins, and two years later the government showed its faith in him by placing the entire maintenance of the navy in his hands at a contractual figure of £5,714 a year.

With Hawkins honest administration was only a means to an end, the creation of an ocean-going navy. Such a navy called for ships of a different type from that so far in favour. The new ships must be fast, manageable, and sea-worthy; that meant longer, less beamy and lower-built ships. They were to be used, not as floating fortresses, but as floating gun-platforms; that meant more and heavier guns. They must be able to keep the sea for months at a time; that meant reducing the number of mouths to feed, and seeing that every man on board earned his keep. It was from about 1570 that the influence of the new ideas began to make itself felt in warship construction. One of the first of the 'galleons', as the new ships were called, was the *Revenge,* launched in 1575. Ninety-two feet long and 32 in beam (this was the three to one ratio which Hawkins fav-oured) the *Revenge* displaced some 450 tons, carried nearly 50 guns and needed about 250 men to work and fight her. Drake considered her the perfect warship and after sixteen years of crowded life she was to achieve an almost perfect end. As soon as Hawkins got a free hand he began to multi-ply this type of ship. At first lack of money confined him to rebuilding the old ones on the new lines. But in the eighties new galleons began to come off the stocks, and by 1587 the majority of the Queen's twenty-five fighting ships had been either built or rebuilt galleon-fashion. (Galleons owned by and named after leading personages also made their appearance; such were the *Ark Raleigh* and the *Galleon Leicester.*) At the same time Hawkins's ideas on their manning began to make headway. In place of the orthodox navy ratio of one man to one and a half tons, which put a premium on dirt and disease and meant frequent revictualling, he succeeded in establishing the ratio of one man to two tons already adopted for the privateering expeditions. This twenty-five per cent reduction in personnel in turn made possible a rise in seamen's pay without increasing the total wage-bill. In 1585 the 'basic' rate was raised from 6s. 8d. to 10s. a month. It was a step towards improving the status of the naval rating and making the Queen's service less unattractive by comparison with privateering.

The royal navy was to play only a part in the defeat of the Armada. It played little or no part in the antecedent operations. There were two main reasons for this. In the first place, those operations were not recognized for what they were, the opening moves of a naval war; rather they were looked upon as a form of pressure intended to forestall that Spanish offensive which alone would mean war. In the second place, even if the English government had been less in doubt as to their issue, it would hardly have undertaken them with its own forces. Hawkins's gospel of dynamic strategy had weakened, but by no means vanquished, the old static orthodoxy. So much is clear from the ineffectual cruise of 1586, when Hawkins himself, with the strongest royal squadron which had put to sea since 1580 (yet representing only one-fifth of the strength available), was kept for three weeks on Channel patrol and only then dispatched to the coast of Spain, where he arrived too late to do anything except reconnoitre. It was to be much the same story two years later when the Armada sailed. But a prudent government saw no reason to do at its own risk and expense what could be done largely at someone else's. The two great exploits of these years, Drake's voyage to Spain and the Indies in 1585-6 and his attack on Cadiz in 1587, were organized, like Hawkins's expeditions twenty years before, as semi-official joint-stock enterprises. The Queen furnished troops, some of the ships and some of the money, and to that extent she stood to lose if things went wrong. But failure would not be catastrophic, and success, or at least the wrong kind of success, could if necessary be disavowed.

How such considerations could still apply, even after the Spanish invasion-attempt had become not merely inevitable but imminent, appears from the story of the raid on Cadiz. The fleet which Drake commanded on this famous mission comprised 23 ships, six of them belonging to the Queen, the remainder merchantmen and privateers, and carried a landing-force of royal troops. Its primary aim was to prevent the junction of the various squadrons of the Armada, and to that end Drake was empowered 'to distress the ships within the havens themselves'. Knowing the Queen's weakness for last-minute cancellations, Drake took a hurried departure on 2 April 1587 and thus missed the royal order revoking this clause, which, if received and complied with, would have hamstrung the operation. As it was, Drake translated this part of his instructions into the brilliant dash into Cadiz harbour on 19-20 April which cost Spain some thirty ships and a quarter of a million ducats, and a loss of prestige and morale not to be measured in figures. His next thrust, the storming of Sagres Castle, the fortress commanding the anchorage under the lee of Cape St Vincent, was scarcely covered even by his original instructions. But the four weeks' blockade of Lisbon which possession of this anchorage made possible was perhaps an even more effective method of fulfilling his task than the sixteen hours' destruction at Cadiz. In the final phase of the expedition, the cruise to the Azores, the profit-motive was uppermost, and it was more than satisfied by the capture of a Portuguese carrack valued at £114,000, which was twice the cost of the expedition. But since for months after Drake had returned to Plymouth (26 June) the invasion force was diverted to the protection of homeward-bound shipping, his fling at the Azores was the decisive factor in delaying the dispatch of the Armada until the following summer. Drake's brilliant feat, which lives in the national memory as the 'singeing of the King of Spain's beard' and in naval memory as a classic of preventive action, swept him on to a new pinnacle of popular fame only to cast him under the shadow of official displeasure. For a government still bent on holding the middle course between encouraging Spain by inaction and inciting her by provocation judged, and judged rightly, that in violating Spanish territory Drake had erred on the side of provocation. Elizabeth therefore disavowed the housebreaking at Sagres while pocketing her share of the proceeds – about £40,000 – of the larcenies at Cadiz and the Azores. She 'apologized for having given her enemy a hard punch instead of a warning tap'; she did not apologize for having followed up the punch by picking his pocket. But it was her refusal to accept the inevitable, reinforced by the landsmen's fear of seeing the navy renounce the security of home waters for the perils of distant seas, which prevented any repetition of the blow during the thirteen months between Drake's return and the coming of the Armada.

From 1588 to 1940 the problem of invading England was the problem of securing command of the Channel for long enough to transport the invading army from its Continental place of embarkation. What was to become the 'classic' approach to this problem envisaged its solution by the appearance of a battle-fleet in the Narrow Seas when the army was ready to cross by the shortest route available. Napoleon planned it so in 1805, Hitler in 1940. The original Spanish plan of 1586 rejected any such junction of land and sea forces in the vicinity of the objective in favour of their fusion into one gigantic force to be dispatched direct from Spain. This plan, involving 60,000 troops, 30,000 seamen, and 77,000 tons of shipping, was so vast as to be quite impracticable, and it was superseded by a more modest, although still immense, one. The number of troops was not greatly reduced – the new figure was about 50,000 – but less than half of them were to be carried from Spain; the remainder were to be supplied by Parma in the Netherlands, and they were to await on the Flemish coast near Dunkirk the arrival of the fleet which would escort them across the Narrows.

The Spanish Armada, when it sailed in June 1588, was thus neither a self-contained amphibious force nor simply a fighting fleet. That was its undoing. Had it been complete in itself, and its commander given some latitude in the choice of a landing-place, England would almost certainly have been invaded that summer, though with what result we can only guess. Alternatively, if it had been simply a battle-fleet, its chances of clearing a passage for Parma, while not brilliant, would have been a good deal brighter than those of the cumbersome monster which essayed the task. Of the Armada's 130 ships perhaps 40 could rank as men-of-war. The notion, long prevalent, that these had been designed for the old kind of sea warfare, in which two or more ships locked together became a miniature battlefield where soldiers fought a soldiers' battle and victory was the reward of carrying the enemy's position, has been shown to be an exaggeration. The Spanish guns were many and good, even if the same cannot be said of their gunners. But the Spanish galleons retained the high superstructures built to dominate such engagements, and were slower and less handy than the English ships of that name. Moreover, there were in the entire fleet only 8,000 seamen, far too few to work its clumsy ships in competition with their nimble enemies.

To oppose this floating army the defenders could count

on about the same number of men-of-war, and the much larger total of South Coast ships of all types and sizes which joined in the fighting with the same spirit as their successors, the 'little ships', were to display at another Channel crisis three centuries and a half later. The 'regular' naval forces were grouped in two fleets. To the Western Fleet, based on Plymouth, was entrusted the task of meeting the Armada as soon as it entered the Channel and of preventing any attempt at a direct landing; to the Eastern, stationed in the Downs, that of immobilizing Parma, a task ably shared by a flotilla furnished by England's allies, and Parma's enemies, the men of Holland and Zeeland. Both fleets were composite affairs, with Queen's ships and private ships, regular officers and merchant captains, naval crews and private crews serving together. It was an arrangement which, if unavoidable, might also have produced serious friction, especially at the higher levels. But the Admiral, Howard of Effingham, wielded the command of the Western Force with a modesty and tact, and his great captains, especially Drake, who had expected to be given the place, accepted it with a forbearance, which together preserved the unity, and through unity the strength, which made for victory. Englishmen were afterwards to invoke the spirit of '88 much as we invoke the spirit of '40 – and, alas, with much the same result.

Drake's game of bowls – that anecdote dates back to within a generation of the event – was probably played on 19 July 1588, the day on which the Armada came within sight of the Lizard. A magnificent and awe-inspiring sight it must have been, then and for many days afterwards as it held its course up Channel, its 130 vessels disposed arrow-headwise over several miles of sea. In the centre front sailed the main fighting force, in line abreast, under the supreme commander, the Duke of Medina Sidonia; behind it came the smaller and less defensible ships; and on each flank and somewhat to the rear moved a smaller fighting squadron. That this formation should have survived the week's fighting from Plymouth to Calais bespeaks a high standard of discipline among these captains and crews drawn from many lands and speaking many tongues. But no degree of discipline would have kept them in their stations unless the speed of the advance had been reduced to a minimum, and against the safety accruing from the closeness of their formation must therefore be set the danger inherent in its slowness. So the Armada passed steadily on, setting course from one headland to another of the country which it had been sent to subdue, but without attempting anchorage or landing along the threatened coast. The Spanish captains were nearly all for doing so. But the King's orders positively forbade it, and Medina Sidonia carried them out to the letter by making straight for his junction with Parma. Howard, for his part, was content to let the Spaniards pass to their destination, and, as he rightly believed, to their doom, while making their passage as demoralizing as possible. The story of those seven breath-taking days is thus the story of a floating army plodding on towards its imaginary goal, continually harassed, but not brought to a halt, by its nimble foes. The nearest approach to general actions took place off Portland Bill on 23 July and off the Isle of Wight two days later. Then the Armada made for the opposite coast, to cast anchor off Calais in the afternoon of the 27th. From this position Medina Sidonia sought to establish the required contact with Parma.

The initiative then passed to Howard, and the English Admiral wasted no time. When he was joined, on 28 July, by the 35 ships of the Eastern Force, he disposed of practically every ship available. At midnight he sent eight 150-ton fireships to dislodge the enemy. The Spaniards slipped or cut their cables, made sail, and stood out to sea. The night's panic cost them one great ship, which ran aground rudderless; it also cost them their formation, which vanished without trace. Dawn broke to reveal them scattered for miles along the coast. That day was fought the decisive battle of the campaign and one of the decisive battles of history. Nearly the whole English fleet went in to the attack, and before the end fifty of the Spaniards had been brought to action. For eight hours the fight went on, with the Spanish captains desperately striving to edge off the treacherous Flemish banks and the English commanders relentlessly forcing them back. When, about three in the afternoon, the wind started to blow hard from the north-west, it seemed that nothing could save the Spaniards, and the English held off. But after another night of terror the wind suddenly backed and the Spaniards were able to stand out again into the temporary safety of deep water. Several of their ships had gone down or ashore, and those that remained afloat were battle-scarred, full of sick and wounded, and short of food, water, powder and shot. Had Medina Sidonia been able to run for a friendly port or road, he might have reformed and replenished his fleet and made another attempt to fulfil his mission. But there was no such welcoming haven along these hostile coasts and nothing left but to make for home. To return through the Channel was out of the question, for within its defile the battered ships would be picked off one by one. But the 'outer' route round Scotland and Ireland remained open, and it was in this direction that the Armada fled from the scene of its last action. Howard's pursuit to the Forth was the least of the hazards yet in store. The wind which had saved the Spaniards off Gravelines now drove them headlong through mountainous seas, in which ship after ship perished as though they had never been. Others were flung on to those savage Northern coasts and their survivors massacred by the savage inhabitants. Less than half the ships, and perhaps a third of the men, got back home, many of the men only to die when they regained the land for which they had endured everything and achieved nothing.

IX

RECESSIONAL

THE defeat of the Armada, like the Battle of Britain, came at the beginning of a war, a war which would outlast Elizabeth to become the longest which England had fought since the Hundred Years War with France. Its duration was matched by its dispersal over several fronts and across half the globe. The chief theatre on land was the Netherlands. English volunteer companies had been serving there since 1572, and from the autumn of 1585, when Leicester took a royal army over with him, there were never less than 6,000 troops there, besides those in the pay of the Dutch Republic. After the initial failures, these forces rendered useful service. Under their famous captains, Willoughby, Vere, Morgan, Norris and Roger Williams, they helped the young Prince Maurice of Orange to parry Parma's final thrust in 1589, and then, with Parma diverted by Philip II into France, to begin recovering the lost towns. Maurice quickly proved himself one of the great commanders of the age, and the Low Countries became Europe's academy of war. A generation of English soldiers learned their trade there and came away to ply it in other lands, and the influence of this apprenticeship was still traceable when in 1642 Englishmen began to fight among themselves.

From the Netherlands the land-war spread to France. In 1589 the assassination of Henry III, the last of the Valois, made Henry of Navarre, the head of the house of Bourbon and leader of the Huguenots, titular King of France. Philip II promptly allied with the house of Guise

to exclude this heretic from the throne. It was clear that
he did not mean to repeat in Henry's case the mistake he
had made with Elizabeth. It was equally clear that Henry's
cause was Elizabeth's, and although she remembered
burning her fingers with it close on thirty years before she
straightway set about pulling the Huguenot chestnut out of
the Catholic fire. Between 1589 and 1595 she dispatched
five expeditions to Northern France. If they did little else,
they did hamper the Spanish bid for positions on the French
coast from which to strike at England. Even so, the Spaniards succeeded in seizing some ports and in launching a
'tip and run' raid on the Cornish coast in 1595. Henry IV's
conversion to Catholicism – the price of his acceptance in
Paris – drew indignant letters from Elizabeth but did not
make him less her ally. As soon as he was firmly seated on
his throne he formally declared war on Spain. But a France
exhausted by thirty years of anarchy, and virtually split
into two states, Catholic and Huguenot, was incapable of
waging offensive war, and in 1598 Henry made his peace
with Philip. Elizabeth, who could have done the same,
chose to stand by her Dutch ally, even though the ending of
her commitments to France coincided with the opening
of a third front, in Ireland.

To England's Continental foes Ireland has always offered
a tempting field of adventure, and it was not to be expected
that Spain would overlook the possibility of turning Ireland
into an English Netherlands. Philip II might indeed with
advantage have diverted some of the energy which he
lavished on France to the earlier support of the rebellion
which the two Ulster chieftains, Tyrone and O'Donnell,
were preparing in the early nineties. As it was, he waited
until the French game was lost before taking a hand in the
Irish one. The Ulster rebellion broke out in 1595, and in
1596 Philip got together a force of 100 ships and 10,000

men for its support. This armada achieved even less than its famous predecessor, being dispersed by a gale as soon as it set out. A second attempt in the following year fared no better, and Philip himself died in 1598 without his last great combined operation having yielded any result. But the rebellion had made progress without his aid, and in 1599 Elizabeth had to send a large army across to deal with it, whose fortunes we shall notice on a later page.

The last and widest front was the sea. It was England's sea power which had both saved her from invasion and enabled her to fight Spain in the Low Countries and France. But the sea was also the theatre of offensive warfare, of thrusts at the enemy's vitals. That had been the lesson of the eighties, and with the removal of the political and strategical restraints which had hampered the earlier operations they should, the modern critic may feel, have been followed by crippling blows. Several blows were prepared, and some delivered, in the ten years after 1588, but none was wholly successful and the majority were failures. England had yet to learn the most efficient use of sea power. The first attempt to exploit the repulse of the Armada, the Portugal expedition of 1589, certainly bore an ominous likeness to the Armada itself. A fleet of over 100 ships carried nearly 20,000 soldiers, under Sir John Norris, a veteran from the Netherlands, to the invasion and liberation of Portugal. The cost of defeating Philip II's Armada prevented Elizabeth from financing her own, and the voyage was organized on the customary joint-stock basis. Drake, who had shown in 1587 what such a venture could achieve, was again in command. But this time he was to make proof only of its limitations. After a pointless landing at Corunna, the army was put ashore again near the mouth of the Tagus and advanced on Lisbon. The fleet, which should have moved up the river, remained at its mouth; the Portuguese themselves did nothing to help; and Norris had no choice but to withdraw and re-embark his disease-ridden and demoralized army. The plan to attack the alternative target, the Azores, was abandoned in view of the rising death-roll and the dwindling stock of victuals, and the expedition straggled back to Plymouth in disorderly fashion. It had cost 8,000 men and £60,000, and had smirched a good many reputations, including its admiral's. Five years were to pass before Drake got his next, and last, active command.

Combined operations having failed, the next two years saw a half-hearted attempt to employ the navy independently. It originated in the fertile mind of John Hawkins. Hawkins wanted to maintain a continuous blockade of Spain's Atlantic ports by the alternate use of two squadrons, each consisting of six large and six small vessels and serving for four months at a time. Cruising across the track of the convoys bringing silver from America, this force was capable, so Hawkins believed, of stopping the flow of treasure and thus crippling the Spanish war-machine. Since the essence of the plan was continuity, and continuity was not realized, we cannot say whether he was right. The intermittent blockade of 1589–90 certainly disrupted the Atlantic trade, but did not prevent Spain from receiving the treasure which enabled her, in 1591, to strike back at the blockaders. The squadron with which, from May to August 1591, Lord Thomas Howard had lain in wait off the Azores was approaching the limit of endurance when it received brief warning of the approach of a greatly superior Spanish fleet. Howard got away with five of his ships, but the vice-admiral, Sir Richard Grenville, bringing up the rear in the *Revenge*, was cut off and surrounded. There followed the last fight of the *Revenge*, one of those struggles against hopeless odds which are remembered as magnificent when it is forgotten that they were not war.

The loss of the *Revenge* (the only ship lost to the enemy during the war), the revival of Spanish naval power, and the menace of the Spanish army in France, combined to limit the regular naval operations of the next few years almost entirely to home waters. The Azores station was abandoned to the privateers, who, if they could make a sensational capture like that of the *Madre de Dios* in 1592, were too few and far between to maintain a real blockade. And when Elizabeth again released some of her ships for distant service, it was not to apply the relentless pressure advocated by Hawkins but to reinforce an enterprise of the old type. True, the original aim of the expedition of 1595 was nothing less than the capture of Panama, which would have served as effectually as Hawkins's continuous blockade to cut the Spanish life-line. But before it sailed this had been superseded by another which sacrificed strategy to greed, the capture of two million ducats awaiting removal at San Juan de Puerto Rico. Even this less exalted task called for qualities which the expedition conspicuously lacked. It called, first, for unity of command. But the expedition had two commanders, Hawkins and Drake, each of whom was responsible for manning, victualling and ordering his part of the fleet. It called, too, for speed and secrecy of execution. The expedition sacrificed both by a fruitless demonstration against the Canaries. When at last it was made, the attempt on Puerto Rico was a failure. Hawkins's death on the eve of the assault, which deepened the gloom of its repulse, at least left Drake in sole command and free to redeem the fortune of the expedition by carrying out its original plan. But Drake was attacking a Spanish Main in every way better able to defend itself than when he had burst in upon it a quarter of a century before. Nombre de Dios fell to him, but the march across the isthmus failed in the face of strong opposition, and there was little momentum left in the expedition when its leader fell victim to the sickness which was ravaging its ranks. On the night of 27 January 1596 Drake died. His body was consigned to the waters where he had fought, looted and burned his way to fame and fortune. The expedition was brought home creditably by the commander of the troops, Sir Thomas Baskerville.

Drake's death was hailed with joy in Spain. Yet when, six months later, Howard, Essex and Raleigh left Cadiz a smoking ruin, the Spaniards must have imagined, as others so stricken have done since, that his defiant spirit had wafted back from whatever ghostly sea now stretched endless before it to its wonted place on quarterdeck or at council table. But the 'Drake touch' was not so easily recaptured, and with the passing of the great leaders – to Drake, Hawkins and Grenville must be added Frobisher, who died in '95 – the naval war itself seemed to go into decline. The Islands Voyage of 1597, an attempt to apply to Spain's Irish Armada the same preventive medicine as Drake had employed ten years before, produced nothing but recrimination between its commander, Essex, and its rear-admiral, Raleigh, and thereafter the demands of the Irish war prevented any further major operations being undertaken at sea. The first chapter of English naval greatness, the Age of Drake, was ended. Fifty years were to pass before a worthy successor, the Age of Blake, would begin.

It is difficult for us of the twentieth century to think of war as capable of producing any other result than national impoverishment. But in the sixteenth it was possible to argue that war, if properly conducted, could be made to show a profit, at least when the enemy was that Croesus among rulers, the King of Spain. If Drake could return from his voyage round the world with a cargo worth, it was boasted, over a million and a half sterling, or Cavendish, who repeated the exploit in 1586–8, with wealth beyond the dreams of avarice, what mountains of treasure might their Queen and countrymen not amass from an all-out onslaught on the Spanish Empire? The war, when it came, certainly made plenty of individual fortunes. All wars do. The buccaneering campaign, although its yield fell far short of expectations, put large sums into the pockets of captains and shareholders, and a good deal more into those of seamen – and those who prey on seamen – than they would otherwise have come by. Drake himself left a very considerable fortune. But as a source of personal enrichment Spanish treasure was to prove less fertile than the English Treasury. The war caused Elizabeth's government to disburse, on the average, nearly a third of a million a year, and the handling of any portion of these vast sums was the most lucrative, and the most coveted, form of national service. Military and naval contractors, treasurers, pay-masters, and the like, waxed fat on the proceeds of the hundred and one devices, ranging from ordinary sharp business practice to barefaced robbery, by which public money could be diverted into private pockets. But the war which spelled gain to the privileged few, to the unprivileged many spelled little but hardship and loss. The proportion actively engaged was, by twentieth-century standards, small enough, probably not more than one in twenty of the adult male population. (The recurring threat of invasion resulted, however, in a spate of home defence activity which must have involved many more.) But to a country which had to provide itself with most of the necessities of life, as well as with the weapons of war, the absorption of even five per cent of its able-bodied men into the forces was no negligible matter, especially as the drain of war coincided with another drain upon the nation's manpower, that of epidemic disease. Three times during the war years – in 1592, 1602 and 1603 – there were serious outbreaks of plague, notably in London and the larger provincial towns. And, alternating with plague and pestilence, there came the famine from which, with them, Elizabethan England prayed in its Litany to be preserved. Of the last seven harvests of the century five were poor, and in the resulting 'dearths' the price of corn rose to unheard-of levels. It seems likely that the English people was called upon to fight its first great modern war with numbers temporarily in decline.

If plague and famine were the two Giant Evils which stalked the England of the fifteen-nineties, there was a whole host of lesser ones. Taxation was perhaps the least of them. The war set up new records in government expenditure. Between 1588 and 1603 it accounted for over four millions sterling, about three-quarters of this going to the army and one-quarter to the navy. The four sessions of parliament during these years voted in all two millions towards this total. It was taxation upon a scale unknown for a generation, and it was far from popular. But it covered less than half the total bill. In war as in peace Elizabeth tried to minimize opposition by keeping down her demands. Of the remaining two millions of war-expenditure, slightly more than half was met out of the government's ordinary revenue, which rose from the peace-time figure of £200,000 per annum to £250,000 in 1588–9 and to over £300,000 ten years later. Much of the increase took the form of higher receipts from customs duties, and since the volume of trade was tending to shrink rather than to expand these represented heavier indirect taxation. There was also the 'concealed' taxation involved in monopolies. But there remained a sum, totalling between 1588 and 1603 nearly a million, which the government raised without calling upon the taxpayer. Two-thirds of it came from the sale of lands. The expedient of living upon capital, which Elizabeth had used on a modest scale throughout her reign, now began to assume unhealthy proportions. Another £200,000 came from the Queen's share of the spoils of war, which thus – alas! for the optimists – yielded about one-twentieth of its cost, the remainder from miscellaneous sources.

Strive as the government might to ease it, the burden of taxation weighed heavily upon a country whose taxable capacity the war was simultaneously reducing. The impact of the war was most direct and evident upon overseas trade and the industries dependent on foreign markets. The course of English foreign trade under Elizabeth falls into three well-defined periods. In the sixties and early seventies England had shaken herself free of that excessive dependence upon the Netherlands market which had earlier exposed her economy to such severe crises. Her merchants had opened up new markets, in Europe, Asia, and Africa, which they served with a wide range of goods. By about 1575 the nation began to reap the reward, and the next ten years, which saw Antwerp go down to irreparable ruin, were by contrast a boom-period for English trade and, through trade, for her industry and agriculture. A document of this time lists more than twenty regions, covering between them most of the coast of Europe from the Baltic to the Levant, as well as North Africa, the Atlantic Islands, and Central and South America, whither English goods could profitably be dispatched. Each called for particular lines and yielded its own specialities in return. But the great staples recur again and again, among the exports cloth, lead, tin, hides, and metal wares, among the imports luxury foodstuffs, fine cloth, and industrial raw materials like woad, alum, timber and marine supplies. England had long been dependent upon the foreign market for the 'vent' of her cloth. She was now developing many other industries which needed both overseas markets and sources of supply.

Unfortunately the same expansive energy which promoted this great export-drive was simultaneously blazing another and more sinister trail – the bloodstained trail of the buccaneer. Whatever their value as a school of seamanship or as a challenge to high endeavour, it is impossible to regard the exploits of Drake and his fellow gangsters as anything but a curse to the economic life of their age. At a time when the country was short of capital for peaceful enterprise, they diverted considerable quantities of capital to sterile or destructive ends. At a time when international credit was making patient headway in the face of ignorant hostility, they dealt its delicate mechanism wanton and damaging blows. And at a time when economic thought was beginning to outgrow its age-long preoccupation with the precious metals, they pandered to the fatal lure of gold and silver and gave bullionism a new lease of life. The last, and not the least serious, count in the indictment is the contribution which privateering made towards the triumph of the monopoly-principle in the sphere of foreign trade. 'The unsafety of the high seas raised freights, hindered small enterprise, necessitated Government protection, justified a system of licences, and so led on to restriction and monopoly.' It is no accident that the decade which saw the privateering campaign at its height also saw the foundation of half-a-dozen new trading companies – the Spanish, Barbary, Levant, French, and Eastland Companies all date from the years 1577–81 – less concerned with promoting the expansion of trade than with subordinating it to the control of select groups of merchants.

The opening of hostilities with Spain slammed doors which had long stood half-open. Spain and Portugal, the Spanish Netherlands and Spanish-occupied France, and large stretches of the Mediterranean coastline were all closed to English ships and goods, the routes to other markets wholly or partially blocked, and what remained of foreign trade transacted with maximum risk and difficulty. The result was a scramble by the trading community for a share of the markets still open, and by manufacturers for the patronage of the merchants who alone could reduce their mounting stocks. It is not surprising that these conditions should have given rise, on the one hand, to persistent encroachment or 'interloping' upon the company preserves by non-members, and, on the other, to stubborn defence of their vested interests by the companies themselves. The key-struggle raged round the greatest of the trading monopolies, that of the Merchant Adventurers. The Adventurers had been fighting a losing battle with the interlopers ever since they abandoned Antwerp as their mart-town, and in the semi-anarchy of the war years they lost ground heavily. When, in 1597, the Company was formally expelled from the German Empire, the interlopers rushed in to fill the vacuum, and during the closing years of the reign the Adventurers, now settled at Middelburg, were struggling to save something from the wreck of their former supremacy.

To the generally unfavourable effect of the war upon English overseas trade there was, however, one outstanding exception. Just as it was the urge to evade the Portuguese spice-monopoly, when in 1580 Portugal became a province of Spain, which had led to the development of the Levant trade, so the stimulus which the war gave to breach that monopoly prompted the resumption, in the 1590s, of the direct contact with the Far East pioneered by Drake and Cavendish a decade before. The start was inauspicious. Of the first expedition, dispatched to the East Indies via the Cape in 1591, there returned, nearly three years later, but a single ship and twenty-five men. The second venture, in 1596, was a still costlier failure. But the Dutch were being more successful, and it was largely the determination not to be outdone by these war-partners and trade-rivals which led to the foundation of the most famous of English trading corporations, the East India Company. A royal charter of 31 December 1599 granted to 218 persons, under the name of 'the Governor and Company of the Merchants of London trading into the East Indies', the right to conduct 'the whole, entire, and only trade' to and from that region, and the following spring saw the first of the Company's fleets set sail from Torbay. Thus there was planted, in the last year of the Tudor century, the seed of trade and dominion far exceeding the wildest flights of Tudor fancy; and few investments have yielded such a stupendous dividend as the £72,000 which floated the East India Company out on to the stream of history.

But foreign trade had no monopoly in monopolies. For the restrictive principle had, like some giant squid, fastened its embracing tentacles round many branches of domestic trade and manufacture, and 'in the last decade of Elizabeth's reign scarcely an article in common use – coal, soap, salt, starch, iron, leather, books, wine, fruit – was unaffected by patents of monopoly.' What privateering was to the State's prosecution of war, and the trading companies to its conduct of commercial relations, these patents were to its system of internal administration: a delegation to individuals or groups of functions and powers which it was unable or unwilling to exercise for itself. They also served certain other purposes, among them that of rewarding unpaid or underpaid officials and courtiers, and that of levying a rudimentary excise upon the articles concerned. With the exception of copyright, which stands rather apart from the rest, the only one of the several types of Elizabethan monopolies which has continued to the present day – and in the process has come to monopolize the name 'patent' – is the grant made, to use Bacon's definition of 1601, where 'any Man, out of his own Wit, Industry, or Endeavour, find out any thing Beneficial for the Commonwealth'. In the sixteenth century, however, such grants covered not only original discoveries and inventions but also, in the absence of the international agreements which exist today, the introduction of manufacturing processes from abroad; and several of the new industries of Elizabethan England – alum, glass, and paper are three cases in point – were established with their aid. As an encouragement to original or immigrant invention, and as a protection to infant industry, the granting of monopoly-rights for limited periods was eminently justifiable. But the temptation to maintain them after they had fulfilled their original purposes was often too strong to resist, and they therefore merge almost imperceptibly into a second type of monopoly, that which conferred the exclusive right of engaging in an established industry or trade. This type was, in turn, hardly separable from another, which conferred the right, not to produce or sell, but to regulate these processes in others. Both these categories of grant sought and found justification by faith, that faith in the virtue of regulation which was the first article of the Tudor economic creed. The Tudor State aspired to apply on a national scale the control of economic activity formerly exercised locally by gilds and municipalities. But, lacking the administrative resources necessary to so immense a task, the State was forced to delegate fragments of it to chartered individuals and corporations. To confer upon one of these patentees the sole right to produce a particular article was, at least in theory, to facilitate the enforcement of whatever conditions the government wished to impose upon its production. The same object might be served by investing him with powers of inspection and regulation, including the power to relax the rigidities of a uniform code by the issue of exemptions from it in appropriate cases.

But it was not by faith alone that the monopolist needed to be justified, and his works were too often the works of iniquity. Just as in the case of the trading monopolies, so with the patent system at home it was the war which was most productive both of perversion and of denunciation. That system, to be tolerable, demanded a restraint in the issue of patents and a control over their exercise such as Elizabeth's government had hardly attained to in peace and was almost to lose sight of in war. The needs of war certainly accounted for one or two of the new patents, notably that covering the manufacture of gunpowder, which Burghley more than once described 'as the greatest service that could be done for the security of the kingdom, the strength of the wars being altered from bows and arrows to ordnance.' But it was money, not munitions, which explained most of the war-time grants. A government as hard pressed as Elizabeth's was ill-placed to resist either the importunities or the inducements which those interested could bring to bear upon it. To the courtiers by whom, since they alone had the royal or ministerial ear, the petitions had to be preferred, their sponsorship was usually a mere episode in the great game of place- and fortune-hunting which swayed and swirled incessantly round the steps of the throne. There were cases, such as the great tin monopoly, which after years of high-level man-oeuvring fell to Raleigh, where the courtier was also the beneficiary. But more often it was the 'projectors', the speculation-mongers, who, eager to tap funds amassed during the prosperous years before the war narrowed the investment-field, conceived and floated the enterprises which the men of place and title were induced to take under their influential wings. It was the same hard-bitten crew which, once they had secured a patent, exploited it for all it was worth. Armed with its coercive or dispensatory powers they waged private war upon all who stood in their path. The 'saltpetre men' of the gunpowder contract 'dug in every man's house' for the nitrate-laden soil which was their raw material. The minions of the playing-card monopoly invaded shops in search of cards lacking its seal and browbeat their owners, under threat of summons to a distant court, into compounding for their offences. The search-warrant was, indeed, indispensable to the monopolist if he were to eliminate competition and leave himself free to fix the price of his wares. As to what would happen when he did so contemporaries were unanimous. A monopoly always raised prices, sometimes by as much as 300 or 400 per cent. Truth in the matter is hard to come by, for to the steady rise in prices which had been going on for half a century there was now added the further increase occasioned by the war. But no monopolist has ever set himself to lower prices, and we can scarcely doubt that it was the consumer who had to bear the large 'overhead' costs of securing, defending and enforcing an Elizabethan patent in the form of a dearer, or an inferior, article.

It was in the parliament of 1597 that the growing public hostility to monopolies first found expression in the House of Commons. That parliament had assembled in a disturbed and critical mood, and not without cause, for the country was in the grip of a depression which for combined length and severity exceeded anything known for close on half a century. Three successive harvest-failures had driven up the price of wheat from twenty to nearly sixty shillings a quarter. Starving peasants had been demonstrating against their landlords with a bitterness reminiscent of '49. Industry, especially the great cloth-industry, was stagnant, and the trade which alone could revive it was throttled by the war. The spectre of economic collapse came to haunt the parliamentary scene at a time when the bogies of religious disaffection and an uncertain succession had lost most of their terrors; and it was a sign of the times that Elizabeth's last two parliaments made themselves memorable chiefly by their activity in the economic and social sphere. In 1597 monopolies were mentioned but not enlarged upon. Their turn was to come in 1601. Instead the House of Commons followed the ministerial lead by tackling certain other pressing problems, and it was a melancholy memorial to the prevailing distress that the session's outstanding piece of legislation should have been a Poor Law. Like that other pillar of the Tudor Temple of National Welfare the Statute of Artificers, the Poor Law of 1597 was a codifying measure which contained little that had not appeared in earlier legislation on the subject. The principle of a compulsory poor-rate had been recognized in 1563 and the method of its collection settled in 1572; the provision of 'houses of correction' for those who would not work and of facilities for those who would dated from 1576; and the apprenticing of pauper children had been foreshadowed as early as 1536. The Act of 1597 also resembled the Statute of Artificers in its application upon a national scale of ideas and methods already familiar to local authorities. It was the towns of Tudor England which were of necessity the pioneers in poor law admin- istration. Confronted by a body of distress continually swollen by the drift from the countryside, the governments of London, Norwich, Coventry, York, had been compelled first to supplement and then largely to supersede those private agencies which, since the dissolution of the monas- teries, were all that remained of the medieval charity- régime. It was town councils which first transformed their communities' financial provision for luckless and handicapped members from voluntary almsgivings into compulsory assessments; London took this decisive step in 1547, Norwich in 1549. It was town officials, too, who first 'broke down' the whole complex mass of social distress into its component parts and then set about providing appropriate treatment for them – homes and schools for children, hospitals for the sick, outdoor relief for the aged and impotent, workplaces for the willing and houses of correction for the idle. The institutions founded or taken over for these purposes became objects of civic solicitude and pride. London had its Christ's Hospital for children, its St Bartholomew's and St Thomas's for the sick, its Bridewell for vagrants, its Bethlehem – in common usage Bedlam – for the insane. And lastly it was the towns which led the way in providing cheap food and fuel for their poorer inhabitants. In London the City Companies, at the instance of the Mayor and Aldermen, regularly bought and stored grain which in time of dearth was released at less than the market-price.

It was the comprehensive and practical system evolved through half a century of municipal enterprise and experiment which the central government 'nationalized' in the series of statutes culminating in the Acts of 1597 and 1601. Seen through twentieth-century spectacles the Elizabethan Poor Law doubtless displays many repellent features. It was as much the offspring of fear as of pity, of hatred as of charity. Tudor England 'lived in terror of the tramp', and this fear was not easily cast out by a society so lacking in the resources which four centuries later have domesticated him into the registered unemployed person. It was, too, a society which ranked, not cleanliness (of which it had scarcely heard), but industry, next to godliness and loyalty, and which condemned idleness as both a sin against God and a crime against the commonweal. The 'sturdy beggar' was thus doubly hateful, and his bloody back or bored ear was the forfeit which he paid to the fears and prejudices of a barbarous age. But it was also an age which was learning fast. Savagery had reached its peak before the middle of the century, and thereafter repression yielded ground steadily to reason in the handling of the problem. If the law still had no mercy on those who persisted, despite its rigours, in leading any of the ways of life which it called – and still calls – 'vagabondage', to the aged and infirm, the 'genuinely seeking work' or the derelict child it offered a measure of social security unknown either to their English forbears or to most of their European contemporaries. It was a notable beginning to a long journey; and an England which has just buried the unwept remains of the Poor Law may yet salute across the centuries that earlier England which cradled so long-lived and, for all its shortcomings, so memorable a forerunner of National Insurance.

The economic malaise which called forth the Poor Law of 1597 was a heavy price to pay for the elusive rewards of the Spanish War. But it was not the whole of the account. For the war also takes its place among the factors which were undermining the nation's political health. In this respect, indeed, the war's course could hardly have been less propitious. The exhilarating triumph over the Armada, a victory such as in other circumstances might have yielded a handsome peace, gave place instead to a long-drawn-out struggle of attrition. So deflationary a sequence would in any case have conduced to political disenchantment and ennui. But the coming of the Armada had been the climax, not merely to the two or three years of its preparation, but also to the twenty or thirty during which the dread of such an onslaught had ever lurked at the back of English minds and beneath the surface of English politics. It was the imperative need for national unity in the face of this menace which had determined the main lines of Elizabethan policy – the ignoring of politically harmless and the hammering of politically dangerous brands of dissent, the mobilizing of the national resources and the exalting of the national idea – just as it was their recognition of the need which had rallied most Englishmen to support that policy. England was living dangerously and must live in unison if she was to live at all. The danger itself seemed to mount yearly, and with it grew the tension, until both reached their peak during those ten world-shaking July days. Then the danger suddenly lifted, the tension abruptly relaxed. A nation which had long braced itself to meet this ordeal found that it had come through with hardly a scratch. The first article of the Tudor creed, that a united England was an invincible England, was triumphantly verified, and when a few years later the greatest living Englishman was to boast

> Come the three corners of the world in arms,
> And we shall shock them

he would but voice a conviction which his audiences had seen demonstrated as a fact.

Of the ebullient self-confidence of post-Armada England the very centre and symbol was the elderly spinster who wore the crown. As, indeed, she deserved to be. For she was both its architect and its incarnation. Had she not, out of the gloom of '58, allured to this brighter world and led the way, guiding her people with matchless skill and devotion? Yet the great deliverance of '88, if it served to grapple Queen and nation together with the steel hoops of tried comradeship, at the same time loosened the bands forged between them by the fears of the past. Those fears had proved to be liars, and their explosion cracked and weakened the crust of ideas and habits which had accreted round them. For thirty years the most precious national possession had been the Queen's life, which alone stood between the country and a succession-struggle whose issue no man could foretell. But the events of 1587-8 went far towards dispelling the dread obscurity which had always lain beyond the Queen's death. For Mary Stuart's only son, James VI of Scotland, coveted nothing so much as the throne which had cost his mother her life. Himself enough of a Protestant to satisfy Protestant England, this son of Mary would also be acceptable to Catholics. Parsons and his brother Jesuits might indeed canvass the Spanish Infanta and trace her descent from John of Gaunt, but to the ordinary Catholic Englishman her claim appeared scarcely less fantastic than it did to his Protestant fellows. Time and another marital mischance had also reduced the Suffolk claim to the verge of extinction. Thus, although Elizabeth persisted in her refusal to name her successor, every year made it more certain that her death would see realized, not the nightmare of a disputed succession, but the dream of a Union of the Crowns. The Queen's enemies recognized the change by abandoning the attempt to assassinate her (although as late as 1594 there was an obscure plot to that end involving her own physician), her servants by beginning to speculate on, and manoeuvre for, the changes which her death would bring.

But Death was to strike the throne only after sweeping through the ranks of those who had long served it. Leicester came home from the Netherlands to die within a month of the Armada. He was followed in 1589 by Mildmay, who had issued Elizabeth's new coinage in '61 and afterwards for twenty years had helped to husband her resources as Chancellor of the Exchequer; in 1590 by Walsingham, who as Secretary of State for seventeen had frustrated every trick of her enemies, and Croft, a link with Wyatt's Rebellion and long Controller of the Royal Household; and in 1591 by Shrewsbury, who had fought with Somerset at Pinkie and spent fifteen years as gaoler to Mary Queen of Scots. Then, after a brief respite, the Queen's aged cousins Hunsdon and Francis Knollys disappeared from the scene, and, last of all, in 1598 died the 'grand old man' Burghley. As, one after another, they were laid in their sumptuous graves the Old Guard of Elizabethan England left behind them a sovereign who, beneath her mask of perennial youthfulness and vitality, grew ever more conscious of her years and her loneliness, and a government which lost, with them, not a little of the stability which had been the fruit of their long service and ripe experience. In particular, it was the partial vacuum created by their passing which helped to raise that political whirlwind of the nineties, the career of Robert Devereux, Earl of Essex.

The hand which fate had dealt this last of the Tudors' over-mighty subjects was strong in two suits. There was that unique complex of charms – the beautiful face and body, the brilliant personality and style – which first captured the royal favour and then time and again recovered it after follies which would have doomed a less ornamental offender. Then there was the 'noble forwardness in arms' which made its possessor the darling of the 'men of action', that significant element in the nation which the war had precipitated to the surface of affairs. 'I love them,' avowed Essex of these gallants, 'for mine own sake ... for their virtues' sake ... for my country's sake ... If we may have peace, they have purchased it; if we must have war, they must manage it'; and it was to them that he looked to support his bid for power. He had himself graduated early as a 'man of action'. Succeeding, at the age of nine, to the youngest and poorest earldom in England, he had become, first Leicester's stepson, and then his General of Horse in the Netherlands. The charge at Zutfen which ended Philip Sidney's career was the first step in Essex's, and on his return he moved with swift agility up the golden ladder. At twenty he was the Queen's Master of the Horse. A few months later he wore the Garter. He saw no active service in Armada Year, the Queen keeping him down at Tilbury with Leicester and the troops. But in 1589 he played truant on the Portugal Voyage, and in 1591, after he had charmed away Elizabeth's displeasure at this escapade and at his marriage with Philip Sidney's widow (who was also Walsingham's daughter), he commanded the first of the expeditions sent to assist Henry IV. He, and it, alike failed, but, as always, he carried off the failure well, and he came home with the aureole of one who had fought for Queen and country on many a foreign field.

His sovereign's favour and his standing as a soldier, these were the foundations on which Essex now set himself to build a 'domestical greatness'. The political situation was as tempting to ambition, and as fraught with peril, as that which had lured Northumberland to destruction forty years earlier. Of the duumvirate which for a generation had partitioned prestige and power the favourite-in-chief, Leicester, was dead and the statesman-in-chief, Burghley, failing. Essex had already gone far towards succeeding the one; could he not also hope to supplant the other, and so attain a position which, with an ageing and complaisant sovereign, would be almost viceregal? Essex was, of course, no second Northumberland. Left to himself, this creature of mood and impulse would have been as incapable of conceiving as of carrying through a systematic campaign directed to that, or any other, end. But among those who early perceived its possibilities both for him and under his banner, for themselves were the brothers Anthony and Francis Bacon, two nephews of Burghley's who, when they realized that the old man was not disposed to exert himself on their behalf, transferred their allegiance to the young one. Both had heads on their shoulders, Francis indeed possessing one of the greatest minds of the age. Both looked instinctively to politics as the market for their talents. The Essex-Bacon alliance was thus a formidable combination. It was certainly more outwardly impressive than its rival, the Cecil faction. The Cecils had their succession-troubles as well as the Tudors. Burghley's first-born, Thomas, redeemed a dissolute youth by a soldierly middle-age. But he could not redeem his mediocrity of mind, and it was on the hunched back of the younger son that the mantle of state had to fall. From an early age Robert Cecil had been groomed for the Secretaryship, the office which had made his father, and which his father in turn had 'made', and it was the vacancy left by Secretary Walsingham's death in 1590 which provoked the first trial of strength between Essex and Burghley. The Queen compromised by leaving the office unfilled, with Burghley responsible for its duties. Her choice was doubtless already made, but Cecil's youth, and Essex's opposition, were to hold up the appointment until 1596. In the meantime the contest between the two had become general. Not only did they vie with each other in their own advancement, but for every other promotion or vacancy Essex had a candidate whom he canvassed with a vehemence which made each fresh appointment the occasion of jealousy and friction. When he unsuccessfully 'ran' Francis Bacon first for the attorney-generalship and then for the solicitor-generalship there were stormy scenes with the Queen, who had a grudge against Bacon and would not appoint him. Behind Essex's pertinacity in these demands there was more than the man's own temperament. For the multiplication of his own and his supporters' offices was an integral part of his political offensive. Every position thus carried would enable him to bring greater pressure to bear on those that remained, and above all on the citadel of the throne. Moreover, to increase that pressure upon others was a way of relieving pressure of a different kind upon himself – the financial strain imposed by the extravagant mode of life which was also part of his programme of self-glorification. Patronage meant perquisites, and it was from the *pourboires* of its unending stream of clients that a great household like Essex's expected to eat, drink, and be merry.

For Essex 1596 was both *annus mirabilis* and the beginning of the end. His showy part in the Cadiz raid identified him with that brilliant exception to the war's record of hopes deferred and turned him into something of a national hero. An inflated military reputation brought Essex important new offices – in 1597 he became Earl Marshal and Master of the Ordnance – and swelled his clientele – he missed no opportunity of conferring knighthoods for service under his command. But it also imposed obligations. Martial renown had to be sustained by martial action, military patronage confirmed by command in the field. It was in obedience to these dictates that Essex sought, and was given, first the command of the luckless Islands Voyage, and then, even less advisedly, the task of subjugating Ireland. Such employments meant absence from Court, and to a man in Essex's position absence from Court was a risk. Had not Robert Cecil obtained both his Council seat and his Secretary's seal while Essex was out of the country? But it was a risk which the warrior had to take. 'The Court is the centre,' wrote Essex after engaging for Ireland, 'but methinks it is the fairer choice to command armies than honours.' What he really hoped was to command both, and he had but to repeat his triumph of '96 to put himself fairly in the way of doing so.

But Ireland was to yield Essex no laurels. Vested with wider powers – which he yet consistently exceeded – and disposing of greater strength – which he yet insisted on having reinforced – than any Lord Deputy before him, he spent six months (at over £1,000 a day) in eliciting from the rebel Tyrone his terms for a settlement, which fell little short of a demand that England should abdicate. Yet, dreadful as was this failure, it was less dreadful than the dark courses into which, as its consequences were borne in upon him, Essex was drawn by outraged pride and insensate jealousy. It was not only the Irish, but also the English, political scene which he discussed with Tyrone in their half-hour parley. For by then Essex had decided on what was practically a *coup d'état*. He would return to England, in defiance of the Queen's orders, taking with him an escort of young gentlemen, most of whom he had – also against the Queen's orders – bound to his cause with knighthoods. If the old magic worked, and the Queen forgave him, he would contrive to restore his fortunes and to overthrow the Cecilians; if there was trouble in store, his young friends would stick at nothing to save him. Essex left Dublin on 24 September 1599. Four days later, after leaving his escort in London, he burst in upon an astonished Queen and Court at Nonsuch in Surrey. Elizabeth handled a situation which was momentarily dangerous and which remained delicate with the same sureness of touch as had confounded the traitor-earls of thirty years before. She did not confine Essex to a prison from which there would certainly have been a move to free him. Instead, he was committed to the custody of a friendly councillor. When in November he fell ill, she showed obvious solicitude, and in the following March she allowed him to return home. But after nine months thick with rumour and slander, Essex was brought before a special commission and sentenced to the loss of his offices and detention during the Queen's pleasure. In July 1600 his custodian was withdrawn, and in August he regained his freedom of movement, the Court alone being barred to him.

If this was clever, it was also humane, treatment. For Elizabeth had not lost all affection for this wayward creature, nor did she altogether despair of reforming him. Thus when at Michaelmas his lease of the customs on sweet wine – one of the monopolies with which, as a leading courtier, he had had much to do – came to an end, she did not grant it away, but kept it in her own hands as a prospective reward for his better behaviour. As it was, the loss of this financial prop only piled the dread of material ruin upon the load of misery under which Essex was now dragging out his days, and the implied inducement to reform can have meant nothing to a mind so consumed by hatred and self-pity. He gave way to frequent and savage outbursts of rage, during which he used violent language about the Queen. But hard words do not break thrones, and Essex was determined to break the power which had brought him so low. He had never rid himself of the treasonable thoughts which had taken possession of him in Ireland. And it was to Ireland – and Scotland – that his mind kept turning. His friend and successor as Deputy, Mountjoy, had at first toyed with his project for a march on London, and had even approached James VI with a promise of the succession. But Mountjoy, who was to redeem Essex's Irish fiasco, soon wearied of his English fantasies, and the earl was thrown back on his own resources. These consisted of a group of disgruntled men of title, and of the motley crowd which, at his invitation, thronged the great house overlooking the Thames, just outside the city wall, where the names of Essex Street and Devereux Court yet recall its vanished glory. It was to this private army of 'swordsmen, bold confident fellows, discontented persons, and such as saucily used their tongues in railing against all men', that Essex, who epitomized them all, looked to support designs which grew steadily more desperate.

Early in February 1601 his lieutenants gave the final touches to a plan for seizing the Court, the Tower, and the City as the prelude to imposing their will upon the Queen. But the government forestalled it with a timely summons to Essex to appear before the Council. He refused to go, then, knowing that the Court was proof against surprise, he attempted to raise the City, as his French counterpart Guise had raised Paris a dozen years before. On Sunday morning, 8 February, Essex House was the rendezvous of a tumultuous assembly. Four officers of state, sent to learn the reason, were seized as hostages. Then Essex, with about 200 followers, mounted and galloped into the City. Crying 'For the Queen! For the Queen! The crown of England is sold to the Spaniard! A plot is laid for my life!', he led them up Ludgate Hill and along Cheapside. But the Mayor had been warned, neither arms nor men were forthcoming, and the Londoners merely gaped at a spectacle more suited to the stage of the Globe than the streets of the capital. Speedily proclaimed a traitor, and knowing the game was up, Essex turned for home, to find, as Wyatt had found in '54, Ludgate locked and held by troops. A charge against them was repulsed, and Essex had to steal back to his house by water. He found the hostages gone and the house besieged, and when in the evening the Lord Admiral threatened to blow it up around his ears he gave in. It was the end. Within ten days his peers had condemned him for treason, within another week he was dead. It was better so for Essex than to let him linger as Norfolk had lingered, a hostage to royal indecision; it was better so for the state than to court a revival of popular sympathy for a fallen idol. The swift justice which overtook Essex was matched by the clemency shown to his associates. Five ringleaders only were executed, and of the rest only those of wealth were fined. The last armed challenge to the Tudor throne was the cheapest of them all.

It was also – with the exception perhaps of Northumberland's – the one least dignified by principle. Essex died, as he had lived, a man of one idea, the idea of his own aggrandisement. He had served no worthier cause in church or state, had identified himself with nothing of permanent importance in the national life. A fashionable partiality for puritans and poets, and an indirect share in the foundation of the Bodleian Library, are things too flimsy to veil the naked egoism which inspired this most glamorously misspent of Elizabeth's careers. Thus it came about that, widely as Essex's death was mourned, its morrow found his compatriots going about their tasks of living, working, and waging war much as a candle burns on after its victim, the wheeling moth, has fallen. And, freed from those distracting gyrations, to distinctly better purpose. For the Essex Rebellion was but the first of the notable events which combined to give the opening year of the new century its climateric quality. In the chronicle of the war 1601 is memorable for the long-awaited Spanish invasion of Ireland, an enterprise which, if its epitaph must be the mournful words 'too little and too late', was none the less Spain's last serious effort at crippling her adversary. But the 3,000 troops who landed at Kinsale in mid-September were quickly besieged by land and blockaded by sea, and when in December they failed to make junction with advancing rebel forces their position became hopeless.

They capitulated to Mountjoy in the first days of 1602, and were shipped home at the victors' cost. This resounding success, following upon Prince Maurice's triumph at Nieupoort (1600) in which English troops had fought valiantly, did much to redeem the futilities of recent years and to scotch the nascent Essex legend.

It also formed a fitting pendant to the proceedings of the parliament which, summoned in November 1601 to contribute to its cost, had also contributed handsomely to the year's tale of memorabilia. Met by a government demand for taxation at a still higher level than that which had disturbed its predecessors of 1589–97, the House of Commons was already out of hand when one of the Members rose to denounce monopolies. It was the signal for the greatest parliamentary outburst of the reign. Member after Member joined in the onslaught, while the few who, like Raleigh, held patents vainly tried to exculpate themselves. As Sir Robert Wroth was reciting a long list of grants made since the last parliament, another Member interrupted him to ask whether bread was not included, and added: 'if order be not taken for these bread will be there before the next parliament.' But to denounce monopolies was one thing, to reform or abolish them another. For the power of granting, and thus of withdrawing, patents was part of the Queen's prerogative, and that, as old parliamentary hands were well aware, Members touched at their peril. Cecil and his fellow-councillors argued, pleaded, threatened, but without making any impression upon a House bent on having its way. The constitutional clash which the Queen, by her tact and firmness, and her parliaments, by their moderation, had succeeded in staving off for a lifetime – the clash between the authority of the Crown, enshrined in the prerogative, and the power of Parliament, implicit in its privileges – appeared imminent and unavoidable.

But long practice in the art of saying 'no' had not impaired Elizabeth's gift of knowing when, or how, to say 'yes', and she did so now with a skill and an effect which were alike magical. She informed the Speaker that 'she herself would take present order of reformation', and that no monopoly would be suffered to continue which had not been vindicated in a court of law. The royal declaration soothed and gratified the angry Commons; the speedy appearance of a proclamation implementing its promises filled them with joy; and when the Queen consented to receive a deputation it was clear that there was an occasion in the making.

On 30 November 1601 one hundred and forty Members crowded the Council Chamber at Whitehall to hear the Speaker return their thanks and the sovereign accept them. Elizabeth was in the sixty-ninth year of her age and the forty-fourth of her reign. Not many present could remember the time when she had not been Queen, and those who could did not cherish the memory. But all could imagine – as she herself must have done – that she was addressing them for the last time, and even those who were already looking forward to the exciting novelty of a King could not deny the majesty of this Queen's leave-taking. It was the majesty which stoops to conquer. 'Though God hath raised me high,' they heard her say, 'yet this I count the glory of my crown, that I have reigned with your loves . . . It is not my desire to live or reign longer than my life and reign shall be for your good. And though you have had, and may have, many mightier and wiser princes sitting in this seat, yet you never had, nor shall have, any that will love you better.' It was in such golden phrases of affectionate humility that the last of the Tudors wrote her epitaph, and the epitaph of her line, that line of statesmen-monarchs than whom, indeed, no wiser or mightier ever adorned the English throne, and of whom she herself, if she yielded perhaps to her grandfather in wisdom and to her father in might, was in the fullness of her genius the superb and matchless flower.

EPILOGUE: 1603

LIKE another great and long-lived Queen, Elizabeth did not long survive the century to which she belonged. In September 1602 she entered her seventieth year, and in November the forty-fifth of her reign. Her health and physical vigour remained the wonder of all who knew her; she continued to ride and hunt, walk and dance, without showing fatigue or taking harm. But life, that long-lasting fire before which she had warmed her splendid hands, was sinking, and she made ready to depart. She brooded on the past, and above all on that cruel tragedy which had robbed her Essex of his life, and her life of him. In June 1602 she told the French ambassador that there was nothing which could give her any enjoyment, and when, six months later, her godson Harington came to Court he was moved to grief by her 'show of human infirmity'. By then, indeed, the end was near.

It came at Richmond in Surrey in the bleak and windy March of 1603. The death of yet another close friend, the Countess of Nottingham, induced a fit of melancholy which in turn brought on serious illness. Unable to eat or sleep, the Queen refused either to take physic or to go to bed. For a fortnight she lay huddled on her cushions in silent misery. Within her chamber all was deathly silence. But without all was bustle and activity. Sir Robert Cecil was putting the finishing touches to his plans for bringing in her successor, Sir Robert Carey posting horses all along the route to Holyrood to speed himself North with the tidings. At Richmond there still stands the gate – spared by the

German bomb which damaged the courtyard within – where in the early hours of that twenty-fourth of March Carey waited for the signal which should send him galloping away. Between two and three o'clock a light appeared, a door was opened, whispered words were spoken. Then Carey mounted and was gone; and the hoofbeats which told his departure were the knell of Tudor England.

A Note on Further Reading

THE reader who desires a fuller treatment of Tudor history than has been compressed into this volume may pursue his chosen subject through the vast literature devoted to this, the most discussed century of English history. Of its two standard bibliographies the more comprehensive is the *Bibliography of British History, Tudor Period*, edited by C. Read (2nd edn., 1959) and the more helpfully annotated *Tudor England*, edited by M. Levine (1968). The following selection concentrates upon the work of recent years.

The best one-volume survey is G. R. Elton's *England under the Tudors* (1955), while C. Russell, *The Crisis of Parliaments, 1509-1660* (1971) and D. M. Loades, *Politics and the Nation, 1450-1660* (1974) set the period in a longer perspective. Studies of different portions of it include G. R. Elton, *Reform and Reformation, 1509-1558* (1977), W. K. Jordan, *Edward VI* (2 vols., 1968, 1970), W. MacCaffrey, *The Shaping of the Elizabethan Regime* (1968), and A. L. Rowse's trilogy *The England of Elizabeth* (1964), *The Expansion of Elizabethan England* (1955) and *The Elizabethan Renaissance* (2 vols., 1971, 1972). Three leading students of the period have published collected essays, the late Sir John Neale in *Essays in Elizabethan History* (1958), G. R. Elton in *Studies in Tudor and Stuart Politics and Government* (2 vols., 1974) and J. Hurstfield in *Freedom, Corruption and Government in Elizabethan England* (1973). A generous selection of original documents is presented in *English Historical Documents, 1485-1558*, edited by C. H. Williams (1967).

Constitutional history in general is best represented by the documents and commentary in G. R. Elton's *The Tudor Constitution* (1960); Professor Elton has also written *The Tudor Revolution in Government* (1953), *Policy and Police* (1972) and *Reform and Renewal* (1973), as well as the numerous articles reprinted in the collection mentioned above. Parliament under Henry VIII is treated by S. E. Lehmberg in *The Reformation Parliament* (1970) and *The Later Parliaments of Henry VIII* (1977), and under Elizabeth by Sir John Neale in *The Elizabethan House of Commons* (1949) and *Elizabeth and her Parliaments* (2 vols., 1953, 1957). By far the best survey of religious change is A. G. Dickens' *The English Reformation* (1964). The three volumes of P. Hughes' *The Reformation in England* (1950–54) give a challenging Roman Catholic interpretation, and David Knowles' *The Religious Orders in England: The Tudor Age* (1959) supersedes all earlier accounts of the dissolution of the monasteries. The early cleavage in doctrine is studied in W. A. Clebsch, *England's Earliest Protestants* (1964) and J. K. McConica, *English Humanists and Reformation Politics* (1965). The Elizabethan Settlement is analysed in Claire Cross, *The Royal Supremacy in the Elizabethan Church* (1969) and its opponents in P. Collinson's *The Elizabethan Puritan Movement* (1966) and A. Morey, *The Catholic Subjects of Elizabeth I* (1978). Two outstanding books in their fields are K. Thomas, *Religion and the Decline of Magic* (1971; Penguin Books, 1973) and W. K. Jordan, *Philanthropy in England, 1480–1660* (1959).

In economic history the pioneer work of W. Cunningham, G. Unwin and R. H. Tawney has generated intensive study, especially of the century 1540 to 1640. Some of this awaits synthesis, but agriculture is comprehensively treated in *The Agrarian History of England*, edited by Joan Thirsk, vol. IV 1500–1640 (1967), and foreign trade surveyed in G. D. Ramsay, *English Overseas Trade during the Centuries of Emergence* (1957). The stresses in the economy are diagnosed in P. Ramsey, *Tudor Economic Problems* (1963), the topical subject of inflation viewed from various standpoints in *The Price Revolution in Sixteenth-Century England*, edited by P. Ramsey (1971), and the role of money examined by J. D. Gould in *The Great Debasement* (1970). The three volumes of *Tudor Economic Documents* edited by R. H. Tawney and Eileen Power (1924) remain valuable. The social scene is well sketched in P. Williams, *Life in Tudor England* (1964) and A. H. Dodd, *Life in Elizabethan England* (1961). L. Stone deals exhaustively with the topmost layer of society in *The Crisis of the Aristocracy, 1558–1641* (1965); there is no equivalent book on the much-discussed gentry, but J. T. Cliffe's *The Yorkshire Gentry from the Reformation to the Civil War* (1969) performs the task for England's largest county. The vigorous cultivation of local and regional history may also be exemplified by W. G. Hoskins' *Essays in Leicestershire History* (1950), A. L. Rowse's *Tudor Cornwall* (1941), A. H. Smith's *County and Court: Government and Politics in Norfolk* (1974), W. MacCaffrey's *Exeter, 1540–1650* (1958), J. W. F. Hill, *Tudor and Stuart Lincoln* (1956) and M. A. James, *Change and Continuity in the Tudor North* (1965).

Foreign relations are well surveyed in R. B. Wernham, *Before the Armada* (1966). Military affairs are now best represented by J. R. Hale's *The Art of War and Renaissance England* (1961) and C. G. Cruickshank's *Elizabeth's Army* (2nd edn., 1966), while the works of J. A. Williamson, notably *The Ocean in English History* (1941), remain essential reading on naval history. G. Mattingly's *The Defeat of the Spanish Armada* (1959) is a classic, and K. R. Andrews' *Elizabethan Privateering* (1964) robs its subject of false glamour. On the history of ideas, scholarship and the arts the following will be found authoritative or suggestive: Joan Simon, *Education and Society in Tudor England* (1966); A. B. Ferguson, *The Articulate Citizen and the English Renaissance* (1965); H. S. Bennett, *English Books and Readers, 1475–1603* (2 vols., 1965, 1970); R. C. Strong, *Tudor and Jacobean Portraits* (1969); S. Anglo, *Spectacle, Pageantry and Early Tudor Policy* (1971); M. C. Boyd, *Elizabethan Music and Musical Criticism* (1962); A. McLean, *Humanism and the Rise of Science in Tudor England* (1972).

Finally there are the rows of biographies. Kings and queens: S. B. Chrimes, *Henry VII* (1972); J. J. Scarisbrick, *Henry VIII* (1968; Penguin Books, 1971); H. F. M. Prescott, *A Spanish Tudor: the Life of 'Bloody Mary'* (1953); J. E. Neale, *Queen Elizabeth I* (1952; also in Pelican Books); G. Donaldson, *Mary, Queen of Scots* (1974). Their great subjects: A. F. Pollard, *Wolsey* (1953); R. W. Chambers, *Thomas More* (1949); J. Ridley, *Thomas Cranmer* (1962); M. L. Bush, *The Government Policy of Protector Somerset* (1976); B. L. Beer, *Northumberland* (1973); Mary Dewar, *Sir Thomas Smith* (1964); F. G. Emmison, *Tudor Secretary: Sir William Petre at Court and Home* (1961); C. Read, *Mr Secretary Cecil* (1955) and *Lord Burghley* (1960); V. J. K. Brown, *A Life of Archbishop Parker* (1962); and A. L. Rowse, *Raleigh and the Throckmortons* (1962).

Index